BABY
A BAND
ON THE ROCKS

&Other Adventures with

AEROSMITH ☆ AC⚡DC ☆ VAN HALEN
PINK FLOYD ☆ YES ☆ JETHRO TULL
RITCHIE BLACKMORE ☆ KEITH RICHARDS

and many more!

G. D. Praetorius

sonicbondpublishing.com

BABYSITTING A BAND ON THE ROCKS

&Other Adventures with

AEROSMITH ☆ AC⚡DC ☆ VAN HALEN
PINK FLOYD ☆ YES ☆ JETHRO TULL
RITCHIE BLACKMORE ☆ KEITH RICHARDS

and many more!

G. D. Praetorius

SONIC**BOND**

sonicbondpublishing.com

Sonicbond Publishing Limited
www.sonicbondpublishing.co.uk
Email: info@sonicbondpublishing.co.uk

First Published in the United Kingdom 2021
This edition published in the USA 2021

British Library Cataloguing in Publication Data:
A Catalogue record for this book is available from the British Library

Copyright Gregg D. Praetorius 2021

ISBN 978-1-78952-106-1

Printed and bound in England

Design by Georgina Abella

DEDICATIONS

To my wife Pam
my partner in life, love and rock and roll.

To Tommy Uchlinger
my partner in crime and fellow seeker of truth through music.

To Michael Allen
a complete stranger that became my first big fan.

To Michael Benson
a professional writer who convinced me I was worth reading.

To Daniel "Dee" Snider
for friendship, inspiration, encouragement,
& for never calling me Clark.

To Steven Tyler
a passing acquaintance who barely knew my name
but provided a ton of great material.

To Keith Richards
whose instant kinship and generosity of wacked wisdom made me
realize that life's greatest success is just being whomever the hell you
are, and being proudly passionate about it.

Good things are sure to follow.

To my Dad
for urging me to write, and infinitely more.

CONTENTS

Back Row to Backstage

As I PULLED INTO the dusty gravel parking lot at Speaks, the crushed grey granite crunching under the tires of my third-hand Chevy Malibu, my mind raced with anticipation and trepidation. Every show that I produced was a new adventure, but an adventure as fraught with the possibility of calamity as success. When everything went right, the night could be magical. If somehow it all went horribly wrong…

In high school I had been a huge fan of Aerosmith as they ascended from bar band to one of the biggest rock acts in the world. But now they were off the radar, having blown a tire or two on the potholes of rock star indulgence. Word was that Steven Tyler had just been released from rehab for his most recent addiction. After what I'd been through with him just a few months earlier, I had no reason to believe that it wasn't true.

I got turned on to Aerosmith quite by accident, when they opened for Black Sabbath in December of 1975 at Madison Square Garden. My tenth-grade buddies and I boarded the Long Island Railroad with a few six-packs that we had cajoled a young woman into buying for us from a delicatessen at the station where we boarded. I always got elected to do the cajoling, everyone recognizing early on the value of my natural charm and winning smile.

Our party was well under way before the conductor even announced "Next stop, Jamaica!" and by the time we hit Penn Station we were amply excited and sufficiently primed to see Ozzy and his crew crank the decibels on their metal-laden dirges. A young band named Aerosmith (which most people still pronounce as Arrow-smith, like the title of the Sinclair Lewis novel of the 1920s, which always drives me crazy) was to be the opening act. Usually, openers were to be tolerated – a holding pattern where you found your seat, got settled, got high, fed your munchies with some overpriced concession junk and queued to take a pee before the real show began. On this occasion, though, we were thrilled to discover a true new talent, even better yet to be treated to a band that upstaged the act that we had paid our hard-borrowed money to see.

Despite the poor view from our typically cheap seats, my friends and I immediately knew Aerosmith were stars even though they were being compromised by the tight square footage and spare lighting that Sabbath had afforded them. Singer Steven Tyler let loose bone-chilling screams with a mouth as wide as your morning Cheerios bowl and he delivered lascivious syllables with lyrics that made you a partner in his phallic high school fantasies. He strutted across the stage like a peacock in heat, performing splits mid-air and tossing his scarf-draped microphone stand to and fro to punctuate the beat. Lanky lead guitarist Joe Perry and his jet-black hair with its hot white streak lurked about ominously while riffing and posing in a perfect shredder's stance for his solos. Joey Kramer pounded his drums with vigor while Tom Hamilton made his paycheck seem effortless, just as bassists like The Who's John Entwistle and The Rolling Stones' Bill Wyman did before him. And then there was Brad. Whitford was the under-appreciated rhythm guitarist who was every bit as good as Perry – possibly even better – but not considered as pretty and obviously not as pushy. These guys were fucking great, and they had all the elements of a band you could believe in as much as you could bang your head to. We, along with the critics of the day, were making our own comparisons to the Stones, which to me was a very good thing.

Just six months later, my friends and I were back at the Garden, this time to see Aerosmith headline in support of their highly anticipated fourth album, *Rocks*. In between then and December, they had broken wide open with *Toys in the Attic* and its unlikely album rock hit "Sweet Emotion" and the neo-rap sing-a-long "Walk This Way." They had simultaneously benefited from late-in-coming radio recognition of their debut album's power ballad, "Dream On," now re-released to Top 40 stations and catapulting their growing popularity even higher.

Aerosmith quickly became hugely successful and were soon officially christened as the American Stones by the tastemakers of the music media. They hit their peak the next year, fronting massive outdoor festivals, often playing to hundreds of thousands of fans. It wasn't long, though, before they began to spin out of control. Though *Rocks* had sported a quintet of exquisitely cut diamonds on its cover, it was becoming obvious that they were playing with the public through a clever double entendre that few outside of the band were in on.

Aerosmith's fifth album, *Draw The Line*, was a commercial dud whose title provided a much less subtle clue as to where the band's heads were at, or more specifically, their noses. The songs just weren't as catchy as before, and for a while, their sales half-lifed with each successive album release. 1979's *A Night in the Ruts* was almost devoid of melody except for a cover of The Shangri-Las' "Remember (Walkin' in the Sand)."

Tyler and guitarist Joe Perry – the Jagger/Richards of Aerosmith – became better known for their fights and addictions than for their music, and they were now instead being referred to as The Toxic Twins, a sardonic twist on Keith and Mick's producing alias as *The Glimmer Twins*. During the making of *Ruts* the two reportedly became so engulfed by their drug-fueled feuding that Perry walked off in a huff, and the album's guitar parts had to be completed by Whitford with the assistance of several stand-ins, including an un-credited Jimmy Crespo.

It was in December of 1979 that Pam and I began an intimate relationship with Aerosmith, a period that I think the band themselves would categorize as lost years. For us, it was an introduction to the instability of rock and roll life on the road, with brief returns to the college we were both attending in a poor attempt to keep up with our classes. I've read the band's authorized bio, *Walk This Way*, to which they contributed, as well as Steven's own autobiography, *Does the Noise in My Head Bother You?* Neither account deals in any detail with the goings-on that we were party to in the nadir of Aerosmith's career. Blackouts? A convenient lapse of memory? Perhaps both. But before I walk you into Speaks and the insanity ensues, I need to explain at least a little bit about how I ended up where I'm now leaving off.

I Know, It's Only Rock & Roll

BUT I LOVE IT, love it, yes I do.

And I love it as much now as I ever did, even though for a wide variety of reasons it is more difficult to obsess to the same extent that I did when I was a kid. But once upon a time, I was reckless and bold, and all I wanted was to rock and roll all day and party every night. As a young man, I got that opportunity, and for a too-short-a-time, I was in the thick of the heroics and hedonism of some of music's most fascinating and successful performers. Now in middle age, the pressure off because the kids have flown the coop and the wife has resigned to stick with me despite my excess pounds and lack of wealth, I've started rummaging my brain and tapping the keys to put it all down on paper (or at least in a Word doc).

Some years ago, following a chance encounter that morphed into an evening of carousing with Keith Richards, my brain began bringing me back to the '70s and '80s, a time when I was young enough to have the whole world in front of me and idealistic enough to believe that I could experience all of the possibilities that it held. I pursued my passion and became one of a lucky few able to work alongside some of rock's biggest stars, saddest has-beens and most talented never-wasses. I brought some of the era's hottest bands to clubs, theaters and arenas all over the East Coast, most notably an extended stint with a down-and-almost-out-forthe-count Aerosmith, who we all now know rose from the flames to enjoy a second coming followed by huge success on the Seniors Tour.

For a good six years, I lived a rock and roll life as one of the supporting cast for those Boston brats and many other stars, reveling in their talent, triumphs and tribulations as few people ever get the opportunity. I also learned that for all of their larger-than-life performances and press, they're ultimately flesh and blood, though not necessarily just like you and me. Sometimes they're nice, sometimes they're not, sometimes they're on, sometimes they're off, but no matter what, they're always guaranteed to be interesting and entertaining.

Though I was fixated on being in the music business, once inside, it quickly became work. Incredibly exciting work, but work nonetheless. As much as I was passionate about my music, a groupie or poser, I was not. And so I possess no mementos, no autographs, no selfies with stars, not even a stray drumstick or guitar pick. But what I did end up with was a hoard of experiences. Despite lacking the foresight to collect whatever artifacts I could forage, I chose to always be present in the moment.

Though my stint in the industry was relatively brief, it encompassed more than 150 concerts. Early on, I dragged Pam, my girlfriend and future wife, into the madness. We made a great team – she focusing on the more "business" side of the business while I managed the production – a back of house / front of house sort of symbiosis. Though I was exiting in '82, Pam's career outlasted mine by several decades, continuing on with the rock promoter/manager we worked for together before segueing into the publishing and recording side with one of the nineties' hottest producers of lighter, Top 40 sounds. Her love of the deals rivaled mine of the music, and so throughout her extended stay, I remained involved even while my day job put me on a more conventional path.

I started out by writing the introduction first, intending to give you a Who's Who and preview of where I was going to go. I imagined a pretty standard *"rubbing shoulders with..."* sort of thing. But along the way, I realized it was far more appropriate to write the Intro afterwards. The deeper I got into it, the more I realized that the story I was telling was as much mine as it was that of the stars.

A brief background check:

Dad was Don Draper minus the drama, a Manhattan ad man always flying elsewhere. Mom was a June Cleaver sort, but boy could she belt out a show tune. In the early '40s, Mom auditioned for Richard Rogers and Oscar Hammerstein, hoping to land the lead in the Broadway-bound *Oklahoma*. She didn't get the part. My older brother was Eddie Haskell and my straight-arrow older sister, Marilyn Munster. I attended 12 years of Catholic schools, which soured me on organized religion forever after. Despite my parochial education, I had a great childhood and adolescence. My high school and college experiences were full of the requisite blacked-out benders and embarrassing blunders with women. I developed a passionate love for loud rock and roll and a jones for surfing due to a six-year stint as a lifeguard in Montauk. Coming of age, I was more interested in hosting concerts and chasing swells, and along the way, I met a Greek diner man's daughter whom I've been tied to since she was seventeen. I followed rock full time for the few years recounted here before acquiescing to a more traditional life, following my dad's footsteps into advertising. My own almost-three-decades as a Mad Man were lucrative if non-eventful, allowing me to have a nice home, buy my wife some nice things, and raise two Ivy League sons who are now living out their own stories. I'm leading a happy life on my now fourth career as a marketing director for a major financial institution. Maybe if this book is a hit, writing will be my fifth.

On that note…thirty years on, I'm a corporate company guy who refuses to jettison his suits and ties. Folks are more often than not taken quite by surprise that my beginnings were so far from sublime, if not downright scandalous. But while in my mind I may have all too quickly bowed to the demands of The American Dream and *the man*, my rock and roll soul has never left me. Though weaned on classic rock, I continue to listen to new music as much as I can, still discovering fresh sounds from artists, both young and old, songs that somehow speak to me with new combinations of notes and words that make me think, smile, or cry. I watch concert DVDs while I try to burn off my midriff on the treadmill. (Besides inducing endorphins, I don't have to pay attention to dialogue – I already know all the words.) And I continue to attend at least a few live shows each year, buying a ticket for Slash every time he appears within fifty miles of home, dreaming that I'll witness some spontaneous Guns 'N Roses reunion, which hopefully by the time you read this may have actually happened. (It took so long to write that it has, though I didn't get to see it. I'll have to be satisfied with the eventual DVD release.)

I have no pretense that this work should in any way be considered an attempt at serious journalism or literature. (It may not qualify as "a work" in the literary sense, but it certainly was work.) Occasionally I will break from a traditional narrative arc – I thought that a strict adherence to chronology would prove quite boring, and besides: life just doesn't necessarily happen that way. I have done extensive research to supplement my memory… official websites, fan sites, music media, blogs and of course Wikipedia, to provide validation as well as to add context and color. I have rarely accepted one source as confirmation of my memories, though some have no public corroboration at all. Many of the moments recounted were quite private.

I have also made a conscientious effort to attempt to avoid rock and roll cliché, but clichés are clichés precisely because they are based upon at least a modicum of truth. So if at times a scene sounds like it came straight out of *This Is Spinal Tap*, well, chances are that *Spinal Tap* mirrored real events like those I was party to and not vice versa. There will also be times when events overwhelmed me, producing truly spiritual moments epitomizing the best of the rock experience, just as occurs for spectators of all performing arts and athletics, and the awe inspired in me was every bit as genuine.

Before you dive in, though, here are some necessary disclaimers and a few words of warning.

To all of the people mentioned: The characters portrayed are indeed meant to represent the individuals whose names are used. All scenes and dialog are presented to the best of my recollection, which is pretty damn good, and if any hearsay or opinion is involved, I will identify it as such. I've tried to recount events objectively and malice is intended towards no one. I actually liked all of these people, even the ones who drove me crazy. But if anyone has any complaints about me, I sincerely hope that they will include them in their own book. No press is bad press, I say. I think most of the stars mentioned and their PR flacks would agree.

A Side Note on "Opinion:" I'm not a big fan of critics. I certainly don't expect everyone to praise everything, but even the seemingly most embarrassing effort still took the effort, and there's a lot to be said for that. So I've done my own best to not judge people or their work, and I'll never question anyone else's tastes. We humans come in all shapes, sizes and proclivities, and mine may be as foreign to you as yours are to me. Let's live and let live.

To professional musicians and fellow fans: While I'm pleased to think that my own tastes have become quite broad, very little jazz or country has ever made my cut of favorites, so you'll find both poorly represented. I know, I know, jazz is the ultimate musical form – but I just never developed a palate for it, nor did I have the opportunity to work with very many jazz musicians. Jazz rarely fills arenas and doesn't sell much booze in bars. And while country certainly does, there wasn't much demand for it in New York in the early '80s. But hopefully, one or two of my rock stories will involve artists that you grew up with and will remind you of why you love(ed) them so much…or why you didn't, as the case may be.

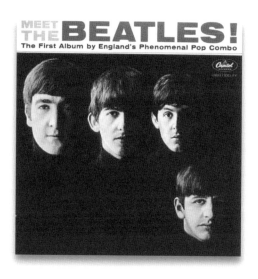

MEET THE **BEATLES!**
The First Album by England's Phenomenal Pop Combo

Learning to Listen

IT WAS JUST ABOUT two-and-a-half weeks before my sixth birthday, in February. Another frigid Sunday evening with the whole family crammed into my older sister Kath's bedroom. Little bigger than a walk-in closet of today's standard suburban McMansion, all five of us each week settled in to keep warm for the last three hours before bed, catching Ed Sullivan on CBS at eight, NBC's Bonanza at nine and wrapping things up with Candid Camera before our Mom and Dad could negotiate us to sleep at eleven.

As usual, Dad was stretched out on Kath's narrow, faux-French twin bed, antique white with gold-painted accents. Mom was squeezed in between him and the wall, her head cradled by the crook of Dad's left arm, his hand teasing her hair while her own left palm was comfortably placed on the center of his barreled chest. My brother Bill and I lay sprawled out on the floor, constantly beating each other with our hands, feet or the gold silk bolster we had borrowed from the bed to prop up our heads. And as usual, Kath sat in her faux French chair that came as a set with the bed and desk; her right leg tucked under her butt as the left dangled, her toes stroking the thick pile carpet beneath us.

For Kath, this was not just another Sunday; she was poised to lose all control as Ed was about to introduce The Beatles for the very first time. Like most young girls her age, Kath had heard that the Fab Four were all the rage, and she had worked herself up for this night since the day that Ed had announced it. The center panel of her desk that doubled as a vanity lay open to utilize its otherwise hidden mirror; Kath had been primping as if the lads performing tonight would actually be able to see her in her bedroom all the way from the theatre at Broadway and 54th.

When John, Paul, George and Ringo hit the stage, you'd think it was the Second Coming. No, I take that back; Jesus himself would not have received such a rapturous reception. (John later said so, himself, and caught a lot of shit for it.) The sea of screaming girls that packed Ed's studio rendered anything The Beatles played virtually inaudible, and Kath screamed along with them, as I imagine was the case all across America. They say that more than 70 million of us were watching. Bill and I covered our ears while our parents studied our sister with fear and disbelief.

"I really don't see what all the fuss is about," my Mom blurted with exasperation once The Beatles had finished "She Loves You," the final song of their opening set. "They're just a bunch of mop heads making loud music!"

"You call that music?" Dad chimed in with disgust. "Now Glenn Miller, Sinatra...*that's* music. And these guys look like a bunch of girls!"

My fourteen-year-old sister turned to scowl at their objections, briefly ungluing her attention from the TV but remaining speechless, unable to respond to my parents' disparaging comments about her newfound obsession.

My brother and I? We looked at each other with "What the hell was that?" in our eyes, but we not-so-secretly wished we could do it, too. Making noise and making girls scream was easy. But to make them *love* it? It couldn't get better than that!

From there on, my sister bought every Beatles 45 and LP immediately upon its release, then she played each one until the vinyl wore thin, ceaselessly spinning them on her portable phonograph with its powder blue pebble grain box and white plastic tote handle. She collected Beatles trading cards and carried a Beatles lunch box to school. And just six months after their Sullivan appearance The Beatles released *A Hard Day's Night* at the movies. My sister and I stood for three hours in the long, dense line of teenage girls in pastel cottons that encircled the massive Meadowbrook Theatre on an overly warm August afternoon, desperate to secure seats for the next possible showing. Finally inside and comfortably cool, The Beatles came to life in big-screen black and white, romping through London as they tried to escape both rabid fans and the stress of the star-making machinery that was already weighing on them. I thought the whole thing was one big, cool laugh, except for that melancholy moment where a lonely Ringo is strolling quayside.

Kath stuck with The Beatles for a couple of years but seemed to bow out as the band expanded its musical explorations. Thumbing through her record collection almost a decade later, it became evident that her flirtation with rock was fleeting. Her Beatles collection ended with *Rubber Soul*, where the psychedelic aesthetic was starting to become evident not just in the cover art but in the music itself. And aside from the inexplicable inclusion of Neil Young's eponymous 1968 solo debut and his second, *Everyone Knows This Is Nowhere*, featuring the fuzzed-out jams of "Down By the River" and "Cowgirl in the Sand," Kath's tastes soon after went into MOR mode, her collection filling with Barbara Streisand and The Carpenters.

As far as I know, Bill has never picked up an instrument of any sort, but being eighteen in '71, he absorbed the new sounds that had exploded at the end of the decade and my musical tutoring picked up where my sister's early introductions had left off.

During his high school years, Bill was a big man, literally. Upon graduation, he recognized his issue, closed the door to his room, ate nothing but oranges for six months, and just as he was about to ship out for his freshman year at a top-ranking Florida party school, he emerged at least eight stones lighter. To help motivate him adhere to his newfound Spartan diet and accelerate his metamorphosis, Bill ceaselessly spun Jethro Tull's "Fat Man," its lyrics inspiring him to leave behind his own excess baggage. On Bill's return home from school for breaks, and upon his academic retirement and return to the household after little more than a year, he brought with him Traffic, The Doors, It's A Beautiful Day, Country Joe & The Fish and a long, eclectic list that I found absolutely fascinating.

I began listening to the radio on my own – crackling AM on a little black transistor followed by a bedside clock combo before graduating to 8-tracks and FM played on my parents' more sophisticated equipment hidden in a cabinet in the dining room. Finally, after saving the necessary allowance and delivery income, I bought my very own first records and a cushy pair of Koss headphones just like the pair that Brother Bill had. For perfect stereo effect, I'd lay myself flat on the floor, legs under the table with my head dead centered between the speakers that my Dad had meticulously positioned to the left and right…even though I had my Kosses on.

My fourteenth birthday had brought me the gift of Jethro Tull's *Aqualung*, which I quickly followed with my own purchase of Tull's double-LP release, Living in the Past, and Cat Stevens' *Tea for the Tillerman*. *Living in the Past*'s leather-looking sleeve included a gallery of photos of the band that I studied for hours on end. But an annoying gouge in the grooves just seconds into the first track of the first record caused the needle to stick and endlessly repeat the opening bars of "Song for Jeffrey." Refusing to resign myself to forever beginning the record on its second song, I had the epiphany that simple physics were the answer. After considerable trial and error, I determined that placing precisely two pennies and a dime atop the turntable's arm added just enough pressure to force the needle through the gouge and to move on, an exercise of my budding ingenuity that would save me countless times later.

For a while, these three records constituted my entire collection and so, like my sister's compulsive spinning of the Beatles, they received hundreds of plays, ensuring that I knew every word and every note of every song. Before long, though, my meager collection grew exponentially as I discovered that the year before had provided a plethora of what I think are some of the finest discs ever recorded.

In 1971 *Led Zeppelin IV*, with "Stairway to Heaven," set the standard for the power ballad. *The Allman Brothers Band at Fillmore East* defined the meandering blues-based, twin-guitar jam forever after. Elton John's *Madman Across the Water* solidified his status as an intelligent hit-maker, he and lyricist Bernie Taupin ultimately earning their place alongside Lennon & McCartney. John Lennon dropped his solo outing, *Imagine*, its title cut becoming an anthem of compassion way before healing the world became all the rage. And Carole King would finally step into the limelight, *Tapestry* quickly becoming the world's biggest-selling album. There was *LA Woman* from The Doors, the swan song from a band whose refusal to conform made them ever more interesting in spite of and because of Jim Morrison's spiraling addictions. Heroin had put Janis Joplin to rest the previous year, but the posthumous Pearl brought her back for one last party. Two-hit wonder Don McLean's *American Pie* offered its eloquent tributes to the soul of rock and roll and the post-impressionist with the severed ear. Rod Stewart eventually aged into a crooner of Cole Porter covers, but on *Every Picture Tells A Story*, he was at the height of his rakish rock charm with a #1 album in both the U.S. and the U.K. at the same time.

T. Rex's *Electric Warrior* banged a gong to get it on and gave legitimacy to glam. Progressive rock became mainstream when Yes released not one but two classic creations, *The Yes Album*, followed by Fragile. *Who's Next*, the post-Tommy masterpiece of Pete Townsend, extolled the liberation of the teenage wasteland while in the same breath it presciently predicted that youth's newfound empowerment inevitably would yield a new boss that's every bit the old boss. Those and dozens of other works from '71 continue to inspire artists and fans almost fifty years later. Grammy voters today wish they had such tough decisions to make.

And of course, there was *Sticky Fingers*, introduced to me by my next-door-neighbor and best bud Louie, who sold me his used 8-track, he being savvy enough at just fifteen to realize that he should cash in his holdings before that format's impending doom. It is still my favorite Stones record, despite the critics' common choice of the band's follow-up, *Exile On Main Street*, as their defining classic. When my magnetic tape pinwheel-in-a-pastelcolored-plastic box got eaten by the player, I couldn't do without my Stones, so I bought a new vinyl version, lucky to be able to still land one with a working zipper not yet value-engineered from the Andy Warhol album cover. When vinyl eventually was deemed obsolete, I, of course, replaced my *Sticky Fingers* again, now with a compact disc – my third purchase of the same record. You know, now that I think about it, it would have been a nice gesture for Keith to at least buy me a round or two. But I'm getting ahead of myself...

At just sixteen, my junior high buddies and I were still too young to satisfy our primary desire, that of indulging our hormones, and we were also too late. We arrived at puberty just after the free-love gambit that was played so brilliantly by so many guys was shut down rather abruptly by the counterculture's climax; the chicks finally realized that deep-thinking guys weren't really messiahs – they were just horny intellectuals. But those same 1970s supplied us with this wealth of great music to distract us from our sexual Sahara, mostly the second-wave British invaders that we found to be superior to what we considered the passionate but sloppy American bands of the late '60s. Many were hitting their strides in popularity and audacity, and some exciting newcomers were just beginning to make their marks. The announcement of a new record release by one of our favorites – which then seemed to occur every twelve months instead of every twelve years – kept us in a constant state of anticipation, and we would be rewarded by the ecstasy of its first spin.

Invariably a concert tour would follow close behind, and each one that pulled into town seemed bigger, brighter, louder and more outrageous than the last. Madison Square Garden was little more than an hour's train ride and better still, Nassau Coliseum was just a mile walk from my front door. At first, tickets were exclusively paper tickets and sold only at the venue, so being at the head of the line or close to it when the box office opened for the first day of sales was essential. We met up in the dark of early morning to hike to the Coliseum, sleeping bags bed-rolled underneath our arms, ready to keep us warm on the cold concrete until the guards allowed us to camp within the halls surrounding the rotunda. We lost a lot of sleep and endured plenty of harsh weather, but our efforts sometimes earned us great seats.

Our high school hit list was full of future Hall of Famers, and in little more than four years, we were treated to visits from my beloved Jethro Tull, plus Yes, Black Sabbath, Deep Purple, Led Zeppelin, Rod Stewart, David Bowie and, finally, the headlining Aerosmith at The Garden.

I added balls to my resume while I was still a paying spectator. Just as with my virginal concert with Tull (later for that), I had endured another failed date for the first of Zeppelin's two *Physical Graffiti* performances at Nassau, on the day before Valentine's no less, with nosebleed seats just adding insult to the injury of my ego. She just wasn't that into me, I guess, but she sure was ecstatic to see Zeppelin, even if they were tiny, faceless toy soldiers a few football fields away. The next evening was when all of my friends had their tickets, much better than mine, theirs just one level up from the floor, on stage right. I hung around outside the arena trying to buy a scalped ticket in the February freeze to no avail. But I didn't go home. Instead, I lapped the Coliseum time and again and again to hear what I could when someone opened an interior door to hit the head or buy a hot dog. About 10 p.m., an older man (much younger than I am now) appeared with his toddler to pick up his teen, apparently thinking the show would soon be ending. I convinced the dad that if he simply asked, the guards would let him in. The dad was obviously not a fan, and even if he were, he wouldn't be showing up this late and with child in tow to crash the party.

"Oh, and while you're at it, please tell them that I'm your son so that they let me in, too."

He was game and it worked, no questions asked. I found my friends on the end of the row in Section 117 and sat on the stairs right next to them, arriving just in time for the closer, "Stairway to Heaven" plus a spectacular encore of "Whole Lotta Love," "Heartbreaker" and "Black Dog." Damn, did I feel clever, like the friggen' King of the World. (Three years later I would use the same ruse to see Eric Clapton perform a few songs.)

We caught some smaller acts at The Calderone Concert Hall in Hempstead and on some of the local college campuses. On occasion, there were shows at the biggest venues, too. We made a group outing to see Jethro Tull yet a fourth time in four years, this one at Shea Stadium, the band battling for attention with the jetliners overhead on their landing approach to La Guardia. And there was my solo adventure to Roosevelt Raceway, a decades-old harness track now the site of a mega mall, a Home Depot, and a seniors condo sitting smack dab where the Grandstand once rose. It was in September of '74, a full-on festival featuring Crosby Stills Nash & Young, Joni Mitchell and The Beach Boys on a brilliantly sunny Sunday following a particularly drizzly Saturday, making for a wondrously Woodstock-muddied scene. While my friends were using the "Monday's a school day" excuse or begged off because they were financially tapped, I had no fear of being on my own for 11 hours amongst almost 80,000 late-stage hippies holding on to the last vestiges of the '60s. I snuck out after church without telling my folks where I was going to be all day. It wasn't the sort of thing I thought that they would give me permission for, and probably rightfully so.

Arriving sometime after the whole affair had begun, I made my way down through the grand stand to the track's lawn and tiptoed my way through the patchwork quilt of edge-to-edge blankets, closer and closer to the stage. I finally squatted with a group, either gracious or stoned enough not to mind the addition of a young stranger to their family. Within no time, the college kids passed me a large loosely-packed joint and for the first time in my life, I got high. I had smoked pot once before, but my innocent ignorance of illegal substances precluded me from taking full advantage. Earlier that year, hitchhiking home in a fresh February snow from the midnight encore of Black Sabbath, I had scored a ride with a bunch of stoners passing a bong as they fishtailed their way along Hempstead Turnpike to Merrick Avenue before sliding to a stop a block from my home. Along the way, they passed me the plexi pot snifter, assuming that I knew how to operate it, which I didn't. I fumbled in the dark as the car slipped and swayed, inhaling what I could with undoubtedly bad form and little if any effect.

But at the Raceway I enjoyed the pleasure of being pleasantly high, hanging with my newfound friends and soaking in the sun along with the sounds of distinctly American music (though I am now fully aware that Neil Young and Joni Mitchel hail from Canada, and that Graham Nash's British accent is by way of Blackpool). The Beach Boys fittingly played midday, taking us away on the "Sloop John B" to ogle our own California girls here at the Raceway as they grooved braless and fancy-free, the sweat-soaked cotton clinging to reveal their young bumps and curves.

Late afternoon brought a mellower mood with Joni delivering her gentle, more feminine fare to a somewhat thinned audience as the sun began to slowly sink. Throughout her set, lots of the guys took the opportunity to make the long, difficult journey from the packed track to the grandstand restrooms in order to drain their bladders for Round Two. Then finally, CSNY took the stage, easing us in with "Love The One Your With," another first that I would have fulfilled with the blonde by my side had not her boyfriend already claimed that ground.

Me

The Stage

Roosevelt Raceway, September 8, 1974.
Crosby, Stills, Nash & Young, The Beach Boys, Joni Mitchell,
77,000 fans and me.

But again, the music was more than enough to keep me occupied, particularly Neil's wavering tenor and his oh-so-deep yet fathomable lyrics. I had become a huge fan not from my sister's odd ownership of his early recordings, but once again because of Bill. He brought home Neil along with his other finds, in the form of the singer's earlier incarnation with Buffalo Springfield and his own *After the Goldrush*, which led me in turn to Harvest and then the legendary *Time Fades Away*. The latter was an early experiment in fan loyalty: a live album exclusively featuring previously unrecorded work that left behind what had become Neil's signature sound and took an even darker turn. My tastes had already become more eclectic than most kids my age, and I was particularly smitten with "Don't Be Denied," a rebuke of his career thus far, chronicling an unlikely path from high school outcast to respected artist to pawn of the recording industry. I loved that song, and my grandest hope that day at Roosevelt was to hear Neil sing it.

Neil delivered, sitting solo center stage and squeezing in my favorite just before my curfew forced me to start out on the almost four-mile walk home while the music still played. If I hadn't already been hooked on rock I most certainly was now. Rock concerts became an addiction for me; I just couldn't get enough of the artistry and energy, the wattage and spectacle, the synchronicity of thousands of strangers sharing an exhilarating, one-of-a-kind experience. I quickly realized that I needed to be a bigger part of it, and I needed to be on the inside.

4

First Love

UPON MY BROTHER'S INTRODUCTION to the quirky creativity of Ian Anderson, Jethro Tull's St. Vitus-with-a-flute front man, I instantly had found my personal Jesus. My fandom quickly escalated to fanaticism, creating a lifelong follower who, like the most devout Deadheads, continues to proselytize about their fixation's genius even long after his or her best work is far behind them.

Stand Up's "Fat Man" had been fun, but *Benefit*'s "For Michael Collins, Jeffrey and Me" was literally stellar. While most of the world was churning out ditties about love lost, love found, love never reciprocated, etc., this crazy guy was writing about getting inside the head of the poor schmuck who got stuck circling the moon in the lunar excursion module while Armstrong and Aldrin made their small step/great leap to glory. And who the hell was this Jeffrey guy who's showing up again? (As any Tullafile worth his salt now knows, Jeffrey was Jeffrey Hammond-Hammond, who would be enlisted as the band's bass player for *Aqualung* and several more albums.)

No, like Neil Young, this maniac with the quintessentially British moniker was obviously a deeeeep thinker, and I loved it. A year later, Aqualung spawned the band's biggest hits, "Aqualung," the song, and the pulsating "Locomotive Breadth." But the first cut on Side Two, "My God," was the one that connected with my Catholic schoolboy soul, providing validation of my agnosticism with its seven-minute denunciation of organized religion. Most of the time, though, I actually had no idea what the hell Ian was talking about, and that made him seem only more erudite and intellectual. I was a sucker for what I considered to be smart rock.

I had to own everything that Jethro Tull recorded, including whatever basement bootlegs I could get my hands on. I knew every song, every lyric and I knew the name of every supporting musician and which obscure instruments they had played on each track. I became quite skilled at drawing freehand renditions of Ian in his uniquely distinct rock star pose – the one-legged Pan with the disheveled hair of a vagrant, swaddled in a thrift-store great coat, wild-eyed and worthy of every mother's child-napping nightmare – and it began to appear on desks and tabletops in every classroom and cafeteria at Maria Regina High School. Then I went so far as to take up the flute.

I had no talent, I had no rhythm, I had no soul, but oh, how I tried to play. There was a professional music instructor around the corner from my house; giving music lessons was a respected stay-at-home career that could earn enough to pay a family's full-time expenses. Mr. Shearer taught me how to read sheet music and its complex language of staves, clefs, long and short notes, dots and ties, etc., a skill that even many of my much more musically proficient friends were not able to master. He taught me how to purse my lips just so to create the perfect embouchure to moderate my pitch, volume and timbre. And he trained my fingers to find the right notes without looking and little or no hesitation. But regardless of how long and hard I practiced, I wasn't a musician, and I was never able to become more than even a mediocre technician.

Frustrated with the flute, I tried my hands at guitar. After all, Ian was just as clever and charismatic when he was perched at the mic strumming and singing. But I had decidedly no better results. This time my parents even sprung for private lessons with a guy that did house calls, but my tutor insisted that I master my études and arpeggios before I could even attempt to play any of my favorite songs. Seated in a straight-backed chair with a posture that suggested I had a stick up my ass, I was both sore and bored and quit in short order. The music just wasn't in me. No matter what instrument I was ever going to pick up, it was going to be an instrument of torture for me and for anyone within earshot. No, in spite of all the musical talent that my Mom was born with, apparently none ever made it into her eggs.

Tull was my first live rock concert experience. But that event was also my first romantic experience with a real live girl. I take that back: with a *woman*. As I entered ninth grade, Fran From Down the Block somehow took a liking to me. Fran was so cool – she was a dancer and musician, went to arts camps in the summers, ended up at Skidmore College. Even at fifteen, I was as much attracted to her sophistication as I was to her already well-developed chest, so I did my best to impress by taking her to see Ian and company at Nassau. Oh, and Fran played flute (but unlike me, she played it very well), and I figured that fact would give our date an extra level of interest and coolness despite my $3.50 seats being just three rows from the ceiling. I was a consummate gentleman, and that benign boyish behavior was possibly the cause of our courtship lasting all of that one date. I was scared to death to make a move, and she wasn't the kind of girl to make one first. We ended the evening with nothing more daring than a peck on the cheek, even that never to be repeated.

The show? In a word, awesome. Ian leaping around the biggest stage I'd ever seen doing his Pied Piper thing when it was still such a novelty, the music bursting from the loudest speakers I'd ever heard and the lights simply, spectacularly dazzling. The band opened the show with dramatic darkness and the heartbeat of the doomed album-length *Passion Play*, which they proceeded to play in its entirety, despite its critical drubbing as a weak attempt at recreating the groundbreaking "importance" of Tull's previous work, *Thick as a Brick*. The band then followed with Side One of Brick, with highlights from *Aqualung* rounding out the show.

1974 brought us Tull's *War Child* tour, Ian's capitulation to the bad press with a return to the more standard three-to-five-minute song format. But not without a swipe at those who gave him such grief for daring to follow his muse with *Passion Play*. "Only Solitaire," at little more than a minute and a half, speaks volumes to the world's naysayers, those who feel compelled to criticize even when they themselves are incapable of creating. The entire piece, until the final line, recites their derision of his showmanship and theatricality, whereupon Ian pointedly replies to one of the journalists who must have really gotten under his skin. *"But you're wrong, Steve, you see, it's only solitaire."*

The band played a two-night stand in our town on that *War Child* tour and I had to have tickets for both nights. Over the ensuing years, I've seen the band in its various configurations many more times, living each of Ian's set pieces with him: that codpiece-clad ringmaster of *War Child*; the medieval metalhead of *Minstrel in the Gallery*; the washed-up biker-beatnik of *Too Old to Rock and Roll*; the country squire of *Songs from the Wood* and *Heavy Horses*, the old salt of *Stormwatch*. As silly as that all sounds now, back then, each new character and costume change was highly anticipated and fully appreciated.

Along the way, I had indoctrinated my wife's young brothers and their tween friends, cultivating another platoon of Jethro Tull followers, new aficionados of Ian's intellectual exercises, wry humor and sarcasm. When Tull came to town in 1982 to push *Broadsword and the Beast*, I packed the kids in the car so they could finally see the band perform live themselves.

I was at this point all-but-officially out of the business, but I was still able to score complimentary tickets and backstage access post-show. As the arena cleared, I directed my boy scouts through the stage right vomitory and down the khaki-colored cinder block, cell-block hall towards the locker rooms normally populated by the New York Islanders hockey franchise. Hearing a more conversational version of the voice that was reaching for the rafters just minutes earlier, we trooped ourselves through Door #1 in the hopes of an intimate tete-a-tete. The room was moderately filled with what I imagine were local friends and media representatives, and the scene was quite sedate in comparison to many of those that I'd been in charge of over the years before.

At this point, the core band already consisted only of Ian and Martin Barre, lead guitarist since Tull's second album, supported by a revolving cast of bassists, drummers and keyboardists seeming to change with almost every record. Ian and Martin were at the center of the room, more casual than commanding. Ian was smaller than I, Martin shorter still. Ian had changed into what I heard had been his civilian uniform for years: black jeans, biker

My admission to the only Jethro Tull show
that I didn't have to pay for...
and of course Ian called me out on it.

boots and black leather vest over what may have been a stock Fruit of the Loom white tee. On stage, he had already taken to wearing bandannas to hide his receding hairline, but now he was letting whatever cropped locks remained, breathe. His wallet was stuffed into his right rear pocket, secured by a thick chrome chain anchored to the belt loop at his hip.

"Excuse me, Ian, but I've always been a huge fan of you and the band." I extended my hand, which he shook firmly before he graciously introduced Martin, who nodded and quickly retreated to his previous conversation.

"My brother turned me on to *Stand Up* and *Benefit* way back when, and now I've brought another generation to show them what they've been missing. I've actually seen you guys in concert at least a dozen times myself!" A small exaggeration, maybe, but not by much.

I had assumed he would be flattered and pleased by my pledge of devotion. Instead, without missing a beat, Ian looked at the All-Access Pass pasted on my chest before fixing his eyes on mine with the seriousness of a CPA and asked, "Oh, Really? And just how many of those shows did you pay for?"

Stunned and in disbelief at being dissed by my adolescent idol, before I could speak in my defense, Ian turned and walked away, abruptly ending the backstage visit I had fantasized about for almost ten years.

Despite the brushoff from the one I loved more than three decades ago, I have continued to follow Ian's work, but over time I lost fervor as his new recordings fell prey to misguided attempts to reclaim his musical relevance. As Ian's hair continued to go and his belly continued to grow, the songs became less and less memorable to me. Likewise, each new Jethro Tull tour proved more predictable and disappointing than the last. Even Martin eventually took his leave, I imagine having had enough in the bank and enough of playing second fiddle, or maybe he just became bored. Ian then began touring under his own name, at first with some fresh ideas but soon resorting once again to Tull's greatest hits, repackaging those same old songs into different combinations to create new records numerous times along the way. In 2012 Ian set out to celebrate the fortieth anniversary of the release of *Thick as a Brick*, only to use a youthful stand-in to mimic his classic moves and to hit the high notes he could no longer reach himself. At over $100 to rent my standard twenty-three-inch seat for less than three hours, I had no intention of attending the fortieth anniversary of *Passion Play*, if there was one (which there wasn't).

I'll never, though, part with my Jethro Tull collection, every original record in the band's official discography, plus Ian's solo records, though I keep those twenty-odd CDs hidden so that neither guests nor my wife scoff at my taste for something seemingly so gauche. But there was a time when Ian and I were good together, and I owe him for all of those great years he gave me. I'll still give a listen to whatever new music he puts out, no matter the state of his baldness or mine. There may be nothing more than a single song, or even a phrase, that works for me, but as small as the spark may be, at least for a moment, it rekindles the flame of my infatuation, even if our relationship has always been a one-way street. I now know that Ian is, indeed, only playing solitaire. And I'm OK with that.

5

Majoring in the Music Business

AFTER ATTEMPTING TO MASTER both flute and guitar, I rightfully realized that even if I practiced day and night for the rest of my life, I was never gonna make it to Madison Square Garden. I ultimately decided that the music business was the way to go in order to live the rock and roll life I so desperately wanted to be part of. I began my fledgling career with a brief dalliance in managing Delta T, a band of budding stars right in my own backyard.

My best friend, Tommy, had founded and christened the group. A chemical junkie, of the academic kind, Tom had co-opted the equation for change over time. The band's logo was actually a triangle – the Greek symbol for Delta – next to a capital T, but they took to spelling it out because everyone kept asking, "What the hell does *Triangle T* mean?"

Tom was the band's bassist, playing with a heavy hand and lots of personality, banging out rhythm and sometimes singing lead, his long, unkempt, hippy hair flying to complement his flannel and denim. Steve was a keyboard prodigy and the band's alternate singer. More classically oriented and prep school styled, Steve's ego and regard for his own talent made him Tom's natural nemesis, causing the two to incessantly bicker over the band's direction and choice of material. Steve was a fan of soft-core rock a la Chicago and The Doobie Brothers. Tom's tastes leaned towards the heavier side, preferring the more metallic riffing of Black Sabbath and Deep Purple.

Paul was a self-taught guitarist, illiterate to written arrangements but able to recreate whatever he heard almost effortlessly. His consuming passion was for his instrument itself; he just wanted to play, whatever the hell the song was. He caressed his guitar with the care one would give an infant, even though it was a bargain variety Carlo Robelli knockoff of the then-financially unattainable Fender Stratocaster. Eddie rounded out the group on drums, a serious German with a wicked streak who, like almost every drummer I've ever met, oozed the impression that he could be prone to periodic psychotic episodes. But Eddie kept great time and improvised tasteful fills wherever he saw the opportunity, all while rolling his eyes at his band mates' infighting.

After many months of moderate success playing school dances with their discordant repertoire of heavy metal segueing into sanguine pop, I was successful in convincing the owner of a local dive named Zolie's to allow Delta T to perform for a paying audience, even though three out of the four band members were not yet of legal drinking age. Their compensation was to be a cut of the cover charges, but with a following too young to make it through the door, the audience never grew past a few bikers and a handful of alcoholics there for the Tuesday twofers. Making matters worse, I managed to lose my meager first commission to a parking ticket while unloading their equipment from my mom's pea-green Ford Galaxy 500. Not a great start for a budding music mogul. I figured I needed a sound education combined with some bigger league experience to put me on the right track.

As with 99.99% of the dreams that are born in parents' basements and garages, Delta T eventually disbanded as my friends drifted off in different directions to attend college – Tom not surprisingly to study pharmacy. While most of them were still local, I have no doubt that they continued to play together periodically, though I never received an invitation to see them perform. I also don't doubt that each of them still plays today, likely again in a band but now with mates whose hair is gray or away, using their suburban garage for addressing their mid-life crisis through music instead of a convertible Corvette.

I chose nearby Hofstra University and enrolled as a Business major, but my real area of concentration was to be the Concert Committee. I knew that Hofstra had a pretty high-profile student organization that was quite competitive in booking appearances by a wide spectrum of both established and emerging artists. But when making my college application list, my awareness of the school's profile in rock didn't come from Peterson's, US News & World Report, or The Princeton Review, but from a momentary lapse of judgment.

During my junior year of high school, Tom and I had taken the municipal bus from our East Meadow to neighboring Hempstead to the box office of the Calderone Concert Hall, our purpose to buy tickets for a show starring the anything-goes garter-clad Fee Waybill and The Tubes. We arrived on Franklin Avenue to find the entry of thick glass doors wide open with the box office unattended. We waited awhile, popped out onto the sidewalk to see if maybe the ticket seller had gone on break to the

Tommy & Steve

Eddie & Paul

Delta T performs in a high school Battle of the Bands on
December 12, 1975, while Bruce Springsteen performs
just a few miles away at CW Post College, immortalizing his
rendition of "Santa Clause is Coming to Town."

deli or Sullivan's, the bar next door, but twenty minutes into it, no one showed. We began rooting around, opening drawers and cabinets out of nothing but curiosity. Upon discovering stacks of rubber-band-bound tickets and backstage passes for an upcoming concert at nearby Hofstra featuring Kingfish, a side project of Bob Weir of the Grateful Dead, we gave in to the devils on our shoulders and copped a few for ourselves, leaving before anyone returned and assuming that no one would ever notice.

Feeling quite smug, the evening of the show Tom and I set off for Hofstra, sufficiently-primed with a six of Schmidt's and a few tokes of cheap, stem-and-seed-popping Mexican. But the minute we arrived, about a hundred feet across the quad from the broad stone steps of the The John Cranford Adams Playhouse, we knew the jig was up. The pony-tailed Concert Committee chairman, megaphone in hand, was vehemently warning the arriving crowd that they may be holding stolen tickets, and if they were presented for admission, the bearers would be subject to arrest. Fear stricken, with visions of imprisonment and molestation at the hands of hardened inmates, we immediately did a one-eighty and went for a few more beers. Oh, the irony of what the near future held in addition to a valuable lesson in box office security! But I now knew that though Hofstra was a second-string college it had a Division One concert program and that maybe I could learn something from it.

Upon entering school in September, I immediately sought out the offices of Hofstra Concerts on the second floor of the Student Center. I offered up my volunteer services to become part of the organization which booked, promoted and produced rock shows in the University's venues of varying sizes: the self-proclaimed "acoustically perfect" Adams Playhouse; the awful, echoing warehouse that was the Physical Education Center and the more intimate Rathskellar Coffeehouse.

In the beginning, I identified more with the muscle than with the machinations of the business. I relished my role as a stagehand from the very beginning. As each artist was booked, a crew list was posted by the stage manager, an alphabetical manifest of who would be awarded the privilege of working twelve to eighteen hours for below-minimum wage. Everyone concerned was in a constant "Am I making the team?" anticipation until the list was taped to the Committee's office door. With boundless energy, bulging biceps and a Puritan work ethic, I quickly became a first-round pick. Humping riveted road cases from truck to stage, taping down cables and coiling the excess, stacking sound towers and winching trusses up towards the rafters, I found myself living my dream working alongside rock legends including The Kinks, Procol Harum, Jerry Garcia, Hot Tuna, Roger McGuinn of The Byrds, Dave Mason of Traffic and more. An eclectic array of stars-in-the-making passed through, too, college campuses providing a farm league for new-waver Elvis Costello, southern rockers The Outlaws and a young barroom blues devotee named George Thorogood who strutted atop our Coffeehouse tables, dodging pitchers of beer and plastic tumblers of white wine as he belted out his manic renditions of Chuck Berry and Elmore James.

On campus, we often booked doubleheaders – an 8 p.m. show followed by another at 11:30 that left us dragging back to our dorms at dawn's early light, with jammers like Tuna and Garcia stringing their late show out as long as 6 a.m. With sleep not an option, either during or between shows, regular pick-me-ups were supplied by our buddy Seth. Seth was one of the worst possible stagehands, not physically fit for even the least taxing tasks. But Seth always was generous with his wares, particularly some sort of concoction that he told us was speed, and so he always made the cut even if he wasn't otherwise needed. I really don't know what he was giving us; it may have been just baking soda for all I know. But whatever it was, it kept us going until the morning.

Along the way, I dragged in plenty of people for the ride. A host of friends were enlisted to hump stage shit along with me and later to accompany me on road trips to pick up or deliver gear for the likes of Aerosmith and the J. Geils Band. My roommate, Frank, became a crewmate, and following school, he went on to work the club scene before going on tour with Twisted Sister. And then there was Bruce.

Bruce walked through the Hofstra Concerts door not long after me, though for entirely different reasons. Newly anointed Chairman Ritchie wanted to take the organization's visibility up a notch. The effort began with a logo design chosen from submissions from the student body, the winner receiving two tickets to every show presented during the 1976-1977 season. Bruce created the winning design, but along with his creativity came his singular personality.

"Am I allowed to sell my tickets?"

"What if there's a show I don't like? Can I trade in those two tickets and have 4 for another show?"

"You know, I expected seats a little closer to the stage."

And on it went, Bruce driving everyone crazy all the time with his brilliant insanity. I developed a close friendship with him that continues after almost four decades of misadventures, luckily none ending with either of us in jail. Invariably people ask me, "How did you meet that guy?" and I'm compelled to reply, "I won him in a contest."

By my junior year, my formal schooling had decidedly taken a back seat. That's when I convinced Pam to join the committee in the role of Box Office Manager – a position that she was perfectly cut out for due to her experience minding the register and managing the money at her dad's Greek diner in Sheepshead Bay,

The Outlaws at Hofstra's John Cranford Adams Playhouse,
Spring 1977.

Jorma Kaukonen of Jefferson Airplane and Hot Tuna fame
with me (right), Bruce (left) and my roommate Frank (below left).

Brooklyn. Pam and I quickly achieved a certain celebrity status amongst our friends and classmates. While our fellow Bachelors and Bachelorettes of Arts, Science and Business were busy trying to figure out what they would do with their lives once their classes and the keg parties were over, we had already found our passion and were pursuing it as a profession. I guess we seemed somehow older and wiser, but I have little doubt that the free tickets and paying jobs we could dispense also had something to do with our popularity, particularly once we graduated from the Committee to go pro with Freefall Presentations, the organization of one of the for-profit Long Island concert promoters.

While it was indeed a diversion from my formal studies (I graduated with a not-to-brag-about 2.9 GPA), the Concert Committee taught me hard lessons regarding the real world, not the least of which I acquired at the feet of Chairman Richie, who ran it like a real-world business. Unlike your typical student-activity-fee-supported organization expected to empty its coffers by June, Richie took profit and loss very seriously, so seriously that by the end of his tenure, it was believed by some, myself included, that he was personally living large off of the Committee's finances. Before computers, selling tickets on the side for cash was easy, and it was just as easy to avoid getting caught. And by buying instead of renting items of recurring expense, subletting pianos and portable signage could bring ancillary revenue to the Committee's coffers while staying off the books.

I was incensed that any among us might be profiting from our wildly successful campaign to bring great rock and roll to the Hofstra campus, but as unethical as I suspected Chairman Richie of being, I was equally unrealistic in thinking that I could do anything about it. When I called Richie out on his extracurricular capitalism, I thought that I had hit upon at least a shard of truth – he virtually admitted as much when we sat face to face across an empty, echoing assembly room, and without denial, he asserted that simply no one would believe it. Chairman Richie had cultivated deep relationships within the university's administration, unnaturally so for a student, all the way up to the Dean, and I quickly realized that he was right. An exposé would only fall on deaf ears even it was shouted from atop one of Hofstra's 14-story Stonehenge-inspired dormitory towers.

That certainty, and my own desire to continue being a part of the live music scene, suppressed any inclination I had to go public with Richie's possible improprieties. If it all were true and somehow did become public, the school surely would have shut us down. So I kept my mouth shut and assumed the position of Stage Manager while a sophomore hanger-on was elevated to Chairman. The new King of Concerts seemed easily plied with freebies of all sorts, so ex-Chairman Richie held him in his hip pocket even after moving on to attend grad school. I rode out the first half of my senior year, now running the shows on campus before being recruited for the same responsibilities at The Calderone, the scene of my own crime.

First House

Hofstra concerts got increasingly ambitious and began aggressively booking more and more events, so when scheduling conflicts lost us some hot acts, we looked off campus to find alternative venues, which led us to the Calderone Concert Hall, just down the road from the university. In high school and after, I had actually seen a few shows at The Calderone in addition to The Tubes, including space-agey Be Bop Deluxe, the Irish electric blues of Rory Gallagher, and the punky, spunky hottie-rock of The Runaways featuring a teenage Lita Ford and future Rock & Roll Hall of Famer, Joan Jett.

The Calderone was an aging, nondescript movie theatre constructed in Hollywood's studio era of the late 1940s, a time when the cinema was still life's main entertainment. Sporting neither the gilded adornment of the vaudeville houses of the Victorian era, like Brooklyn's now-reborn King's Theatre, nor the colorful and chromed Deco splendor of landmarked Radio City Music Hall, The Calderone's chief attraction for us was that it could accommodate an audience of over two thousand, 2,432 to be exact, twice the size of the Adams Playhouse and a capacity eclipsed only by a few other venues in the region. The committee began to sublet the venue from Mark Puma and his Freefall Presentations, a professional concert promoter.

Six or seven years older than me, Mark had been a senior in Syracuse University's economics program when he ditched school only a few credits shy of graduating. I never heard the real story of why he bailed so close to them conferring his degree, but I imagine that he had become infatuated with rock just as I was, but he had either less sense or bigger balls, depending on how you choose to look at it. He constantly put his own money on the line.

Mark broke into the business as an apprentice to Phil Basile of Concerts East, "Philly" as he was more familiarly known. Philly was a founding father of the rock concert business, creating Concerts East in the '60s to compete on Long Island with the legendary San Francisco-based Bill Graham and his Fillmore East on 14th Street in Manhattan. Like Graham, Philly was early to recognize that there was a tremendous opportunity to cash in on rock's growing cultural importance while still being able to exploit the flower power naiveté of the artists.

Philly lost interest once the performers and their managers became savvy enough to begin calling the shots. He had learned, though, that alcohol was the real profit center of the equation, one with way less risk than guaranteeing bands increasingly ridiculous amounts of money with no assurance that he'd break even on their ticket sales. Philly pivoted to take advantage of the burgeoning suburban club culture of the late '70s and '80s, where he could pay a relative pittance to local no-name talent to play the hits of the stars note for note in exchange for collecting a cover charge – cash – and a few bucks for every bottle of beer – cash – which added up to a very large and liquid revenue stream with low overhead and minimal exposure. Mark, I guess, couldn't trade his lust for stardust for Phil's pragmatism, and so he struck out on his own to butt heads with the other promoters that swept in upon Basile's departure from the theatre and arena scene.

Upstart Freefall had to immediately go head-to-head with New York City concert kings Ron Delsener and Howard Stein, plus another of Philly's protégés, Larry Vaughn. In an effort to move beyond being the area's fourth-place promoter, Mark managed to land an exclusive lease of The Calderone from its eponymous owner and locked up one of Long Island's few potentially lucrative venues to form the basis of his ambitious new business.

When Chairman Richie discovered that the theatre offered the Committee a bright new pro forma, he began to book it as aggressively as he did the venues on Hofstra's campus, and we quickly presented a string of shows, including Jefferson Starship, comedian Bill Cosby and the MOR jazz of Chuck Mangione. Mark himself would have most likely booked those shows if he could have, but the artists had insisted on playing "colleges."

It was at this juncture that Pam and I turned professional ourselves. During our first Hofstra Concerts show at The Calderone, Pam kept a perfectly tight box office – reconciling ticket sales with actual revenue to the dollar. Mark was prompted to hire her for himself, and my management of the performance side won me a position as a permanent member of Freefall's own production staff. Not long after, I graduated to Production Manager and manager of the theatre itself.

I began my apprenticeship under a colorful cast of characters, some considerably older than I was, others having entered the business not so long before. With his lease, Mark had inherited a couple of grizzled veterans who, together with his own young recruits, created the perfect place to play for performers on their way up, some in the middle, and for a few already on their way down.

For a brief period, my mentor was Joey, Freefall's resident Production Manager. Stocky, with an Italian mustache and afro, Joey had been around the rock scene quite some time, road managing tours for a variety of marginally successful bands before settling down to work full-time for Mark. Joey was obsessive-compulsive, as I soon realized I was, too, which is a wonderful trait for show management. Though *close enough for rock and roll* has become a commonly accepted aphorism – false starts, wrong chords and missed notes can be found on a myriad of live records by even the biggest stars – a ton of planning and rehearsal goes on before the first gig does because ultimately it's still all about business. So many details go into the presentation of a rock show that if even one goes wrong, the audience may walk away disappointed, or worse.

Joey taught me to pay attention to all of those details and to bank on the fact that quite likely no one else would. Before each concert, he put it all down on paper, in what we called a Show Sheet – every necessary contact and their phone number, every requirement from power needs to whole wheat vs. rye vs. white bread in the dressing room, a schedule of events timed to the minute. In a college setting, it was fine for Hot Tuna to play a six-hour show, but in the real world, someone was going to have to pay for it.

Bob, The Calderone's facility manager, was a tough nut Korean Warrier who had been with the venue when it was still showing movies. With colorful, dragon-themed tattoos tracing his triceps, Bob insisted on wearing short sleeves to show off his Asian body art; his bright pastel-colored shirts tucked neatly into tight polyester pants that called attention to his swagger. Atop his head, he sported a really, really obvious blonde toupee. Bob fancied himself quite the ladies man and was rumored to be a bit of a Peeping Tom, too. Supposedly he had drilled a hole through the storeroom wall in order to surreptitiously survey the women's room, though try as I did, I never found it.

Despite his bad taste in attire and alleged restroom voyeurism, Bob knew the theatre business inside and out and he saw fit to teach it to me. Lesson No. 1 was the same one that Philly had learned: it wasn't so much about selling tickets for the sake of selling tickets. It was really about selling tickets so you could sell popcorn and soda – just like beer – at enormous markups. A captive audience needs to eat and drink, and since you've got a monopoly on where they can satisfy their needs and desires, you can make a lot of money if you run your concession business right. In time Bob left and Joey took over the concessions and he actually started selling beer; Schaefer at a buck apiece retail vs. thirty cents wholesale.

While Bob may have been the manager by title, the real keys to the kingdom rested with that loveable old soul, Carl, a lean, leathery Jamaican with an ever-present tweed flat cap who we assumed had been there since the laying of the cornerstone. A custodian Casanova, Carl had carved himself an apartment in the basement where he retreated to smoke ganja and entertain an ever-fresh string of buxom neighborhood mamas. Carl literally lived and breathed the place.

Being so intimately involved with the building, Carl knew every inch and every secret. His key ring was a thing of envy, seeming the size of a hubcap and sporting more metal than dinnerware for a dozen. A ball and chain to anyone else, Carl understood his keys to be the source of his power, and all deferred to his knowledge and judgment in regards to the facility's operation. An empty theatre is by nature cold and dank, and Pam would constantly lobby Carl to turn up the heat. But with his infinite Caribbean common sense, Carl always knew best. "Ms. Pam, once we get all 'dem bodies in here, you'll feel like you're on the beach in Montego Bay!" Invariably the man was right, and a half-filled house could become unbearably warm even before the opening act took the stage.

Carl taught me how the building worked and which locks were freed by each of his cornucopia of keys, front doors to back and everything in between. When I took over as manager, he gave me my own ring, a subset of his more comprehensive collection. He schooled me on the building's electric and lighting with its dozens of breakers and switches, each illuminating its own zone of the lobbies and halls, the offices, restrooms, storerooms and projector rooms, the auditorium and balcony, onstage, backstage, dressing rooms and more, a twenty-minute circuit that had to be run for every event's opening and closing. Carl taught me to operate and troubleshoot the theatre's air conditioning and heating equipment, explaining in detail the workings of the boilers in the bowels of the building, oil-guzzling giants that roared like locomotives as they toiled in their lonely, dimly-lit dungeon to keep the audience and Pam warm. We even held class up in the rafters, which one day would provide the support for transforming The Calderone into an A-list venue for acts carrying arena-scale sound and lighting systems.

A full-time produce manager in a Queens supermarket, Ira ran a side business managing the security staff for all of Freefall's productions. With bed-head black hair worthy of Larry Fine, a thick mustache and big toothy grin, Ira's everyman demeanor belied the seriousness of his responsibilities, as did his assembly of a ragtag group of moonlighting misfits and a few of Hempstead's off-duty finest to make sure our crowds stayed in line and that the artists remained safe and sound backstage. I think that because Ira's choices were not the hotheads and bodybuilders that tend to be employed as bouncers, because they were nice guys with small egos, guys like him that treated people with respect and addressed them with a smile, we rarely had incidents in the audience and the bands felt right at home.

Marion was the most colorful of Ira's bunch, his penchant for flashy clothes, his gold tooth and felt fedora leading to the common assumption that his only other source of income was from representing our sketchy neighborhood's ladies of the evening which the cops neither confirmed nor denied. What was certain was that Marion was perpetually high, and his hazy philosophizing made him something of a Rastafarian wiseman. Assuming that Marion didn't have any real commitments that would tie him down, we often called on him for odd jobs when we knew everyone else was otherwise working. One August afternoon, he accompanied Pam and I to Central Park for a Talking Heads performance to paper the crowd with flyers in promotion of our own upcoming show at The Calderone. Our flyers distributed, many now littering the park, we retreated to a boulder perched high above Wollman Rink to watch the show from the sidelines. Marion rooted through his fanny-pack and soon produced a cigar-sized spliff. With a wide grin that showed off his shiny-capped cuspid, Marion offered us a toke of some of his finest stash. We sat back and soaked in the last rays of the sun, spending what was left of the evening grooving to the Heads' hypnotic afrobeat-meetsnew-wave rhythms. Marion may have been questionable company, but that day he was the perfect captain, sailing us towards the dusk of a perfect summer's day.

Ira's wife, Gail, was our backstage nana who attended to all of the catering, conjuring home-cooked meals for the band and crews, which she served buffet-style at a communal table in The Calderone's basement. Pot roast was her specialty and it always went over big. She added a wonderful touch of comfort to break the road-weary monotony most of these folks forced themselves to get used to. Right next door to Gail's pop-up dining hall, we built and stocked a full-service bar for our own guests as well as for those of the bands, their crews and the media. Joe D. was the ever-open ear willing to listen to their boasts and bitches. I'd wander in during load out, boilermakers being my wind-down of choice.

Once Joey and Bob left, The Calderone was mine to manage, maintain and nurture; Mark eager to embrace almost any idea I had that would result in a profit and happy performers, pretty much in that order. Now that concessions became my domain, I upped the ante on our Schafer sales, first by doubling my bartenders and opening a new outpost in the balcony. 90% of sales took place before the show and during intermission, and I realized that we simply weren't selling fast enough downstairs to meet the huge demand. Next, after quizzing the crowd from an impromptu pulpit atop the lobby bar, a show of hands told me that they'd be happy to pay fifty cents more for a Budweiser... which only cost us another fifty cents a case. I was ending my evenings reconciling the take by peeling apart thousands of dollars worth of sopping singles and cautiously counting pounds of quarters, enabling Freefall to post a profit even when plenty of seats went unsold.

I also quickly understood the value of stepping up our game on the production side. When Cheap Trick rolled up with the most massive sound and lighting system The Calderone had ever seen and I showed the Production Manager our rickety, makeshift sound wings, he shook his head dismissively and said, "I don't think so. We fly everything."

"Flying" amounts to hanging tons of speakers and trusses that carry hundreds of lighting cans, and sometimes spotlights, from the ceiling. Arenas are engineered for such stress, but The Calderone had been a movie theatre, and back in the '40s, no thought had been put into the ability of its roof to carry the weight of that sort or amount of shit. But unwilling to say "No," I instead naively said, "Why not?" and without hesitation, I clambered into the crawl space that Carl had shown me, climbing through the small square access door and out onto the narrow eight-inch riveted steel that hovered a hundred feet or so above the orchestra. With the false security of nothing more than a half-inch of ceiling beneath, I confidently placed one foot in front of the other as if walking a sobriety line, no thought to the possibility of plunging to my death. Miraculously, no fall or cave-in ever ensued. We poked some holes through the thin asbestos, the toxic dust sparkling in the meager light as it floated like fine snowflakes down to the stage and seating. We lowered ropes with which to raise the cables, ultimately clamping them to the girders. The winches hoisted the gear above the orchestra quickly and quietly, no groaning of the steel from the stress of its unexpected new load. The show was the loudest and brightest that I had ever experienced up until then, and word went out that The Calderone had what it took to deliver top-tier productions. From then on, I became a fearless beam walker.

I had a hand in more than 50 events at The Calderone, and I spent a great deal of time there in between. Like Carl, the place became my home, my own knowledge of its nooks, crannies and idiosyncrasies becoming an important contribution to my success with both the bands and my boss. Though the practice of my craft amounted to well less than a Gladwellian 10,000 hours,

The Calderone Theatre under construction in 1948,
with the open steel beam work that I would be walking
thirty-odd years later when Cheap Trick rolled in.

BABYSITTING A BAND ON THE ROCKS

it was nonetheless an intense education that resulted in a high degree of expertise, one that prepared me for the management of events on the much larger scale of arenas.

I got sucked into the business of the music business, which I guess was my end game from the beginning, but in taking care of that business, my ability to actually enjoy the music began to take a back seat. Not that I was any less passionate, but there were simply more important things to pay attention to, not least of which was the audience's safety. But I still strained to keep my ears on the tunes and my eyes on the stage as I bounced around the theater, making sure that all was well all of the time, and despite the distraction of having real responsibilities, I still managed to enjoy some of the magic that had brought me there.

Classic Rock was the Theatre's bread and butter even before anyone called it "Classic," and its San Francisco subset was well represented. Appreciating the Grateful Dead but not being a Deadhead myself, I couldn't help but marvel at the trance that Jerry Garcia could weave over his followers. The tie-dyed and paisley never failed to swoon and sway with the shy shaman's sounds, even if he was only tuning his guitar. Always a bystander, never a true fan, I finally understood Jerry's extraordinary ability to evoke almost dervish devotion when I encountered two Jerryettes in the aisle losing themselves in the music. A young woman had settled into her groove dancing mid-aisle, her braless breasts swinging side to side while on the floor beside her, a lover-or-stranger unabashedly reached up through her skirt, whereupon the dancer gyrated to Garcia's "The Wheel" on the welcomed hand. Bobby Weir and the Midnights delivered their own more up-tempo trips, but the crowd was hardly as interesting. Ironically, I now ended up getting paid to present the same guy whose tickets I had stolen just a few years before. Funny how life works sometimes.

Jorma Kaukonen, of both Jefferson Airplane and Hot Tuna fame, is worth noting for plenty of reasons, mostly though for Jorma's marathon five- and six-hour performances. I don't know what fueled him – though maybe it was the 100-proof Smirnoff he quaffed from the bottle. I did the math one day and realized that if you added up the shows I produced at The Calderone along with those at Hofstra and other venues, Jorma easily cost me several days of my life just listening to him play live. Which, come to think of it, is nothing if you're a diehard Deadhead, and you paid for it.

I wish I could say that Santana blew me away, but I remember little about Carlos' performance other than the vision of his percussion players rapping out rhythms on every surface they passed on their way in and out. I was more enthralled by the presence of Santana's personal manager, Bill Graham. Graham's new conglomerate included artist management and merchandising (which is a glorified term for selling T-shirts and other items emblazoned with a band's name or logo) in addition to exclusive tour representation under the branding of Bill Graham Presents. Known to be a shark in business and the occasional bastard, Graham was nothing but charming that evening as he held court backstage despite his client's light sales leaving almost half the house empty. Bill was a legend, and to meet him was as exciting as guiding the guitar god himself onstage and off.

One of our best double bills was Tom Petty and the Heartbreakers opening for The J. Geils Band. Petty had just released *Damn the Torpedoes*, and three albums in their set was already chock full of hits. The Florida band turned the theatre into a smoky barroom blast that put Geils to the test. Pushing their tenth and newest studio release, *Sanctuary*, with its indelible palm print album cover, Geils put on a great show with Peter Wolf delivering his usual feverish footwork, but their songwriting

Jerry Garcia at The Calderone Concert Hall, February 14, 1981.
Since we both had to work I gave Pam my Valentine's Day sentiments
via the theatre's marquee.

paled in comparison to Petty's and you knew who'd likely be headlining if they ever toured together again. In July of 2016, that prediction came true. My boys treated me to a local stop on The Heartbreakers' 40th-anniversary tour. Peter Wolf was Tom's opening act. Sadly, that evening proved to be one of Petty's final performances.

Southern Rock was running rampant at the time, and we saw two relatives of Lynyrd Skynyrd roll through. The survivors of the fateful plane crash that had brought Skynyrd to such an abrupt end just as they were bursting to stardom constituted the even shorter-lived Rossington-Collins Band. Guitarists Gary Rossington and Allen Collins played a searing set from their post-trauma debut, capped by an instrumental version of the classic Skynyrd jam, "Free Bird," dedicated to the loss of their original frontman, Ronnie Van Zant. In contrast, little brother Donnie Van Zant and .38 Special spewed out their arena rock with little hint of their Confederate beginnings. The Macon, Georgia-based Allman Brothers Band graced The Calderone, too.

Then there was BritMetal. Ritchie Blackmore and his Rainbow were always amongst the loudest but didn't come close to the sonic onslaught of Judas Priest. Priest took the stage with singer Rob Halford astride a big ass bike whose roar shook the room with each twist of the throttle. The band's all black, leather and studded fashion statement wrote the rules still be being followed by headbangers today. Rainbow and Priest's opening acts, Scorpions and Def Leppard, were easily forgettable then but, like Petty, each soon became far bigger draws than either of the bands they preceded onstage.

The '80s began around 1977 with the rise of Punk and its more well-dressed cousins of New Wave and The New Romantics. The Calderone saw a diverse cross-section of the whole family. Elvis Costello's elevated lyricism made his show in support of his third album, *Armed Forces*, with its first single, "Oliver's Army," a greatest hits parade with many more to come. Pretenders (no "The") came through with *Pretenders II*, having worked their way up from their first American tour when we had presented them in clubs less than two years earlier. Graham Parker & The Rumor killed it with *Squeezing Out Sparks* and a wrenching rendition of "You Can't Be Too Strong," Parker's masterpiece of the angst of a young woman's dilemma with abortion. Joe Jackson brought his jazz-wave and Joan Jett returned with her Blackhearts and *Bad Reputation*, leaving the Runaways in her dust as her solo career took off. Talking Heads played their hypnotic funk while David Byrne convulsed in place under minimalist red and white lighting, and Devo, donning the same palette with their Lego-hats and hazmat suits, took everyone on a ninety-minute romp of kitschy sci-fi mixed with social commentary. Then there were The Plasmatics.

The Plasmatics were more of a performance piece than a real band. The troupe was created by Wendy O. Williams, a heavily mascaraed, surgically-enhanced blonde who took to wearing little above the waist but crisscrosses of electrical tape to black out her nipples. As hard as I tried, I couldn't muster the restraint to look Wendy directly in the eyes; the plastic strips never quite capable of doing their job. Soon after The Plasmatics took the stage, they proceeded to blow shit up, chainsaw guitars and bludgeon a television while playing indecipherable pseudo-songs. At the outset, their gimmick was in high demand, and they sold out our Calderone show after having set a new attendance record at one of the clubs where we had booked them less than two months earlier. Guitarist Wes Beech played with abandon like a mad dog with a Mohawk, and when he took a sledgehammer to the TV, he went down with the appliance, cutting himself on the shattered picture tube and bleeding all over the stage, the last bit I don't think meant to be part of the chaotic choreography. He resumed his footing and his thrashing as if nothing had happened, and the crowd went right back to ogling Wendy's beautiful bouncing boobs.

Then from the ridiculous to the sublime...

Though rock was our calling, we occasionally rented out The Calderone to third parties who produced performances by a variety of more mainstream talents, broadening our cultural exposure beyond three-chord riffs.

The legendary mime Marcel Marceau enthralled the room without a single word or note, engaging us in his one-act playlets, both comic and tragic, with nothing but his movement and expressions. I attempted to follow his pantomime with the white-hot Super Trooper I manned in the cobwebbed projectionist booth behind the balcony seats, only to always trail a second behind.

Country wasn't so far from rock, but on Long Island, it just wasn't the right time or the right place for Emmylou Harris. With her long straight hair flowing like a mare's tail almost to her rump, and still riding high on her Top 40 cover of the chestnut, "Mr. Sandman," Emmylou crooned to an audience of no more than a few dozen sitting in the first ten rows. We had the same pitiful turnout for disco queen Evelyn "Champagne" King. I imagine that since disco was meant to be danced to, it was better left in the clubs.

Dizzy Gillespie blew us away with his unique brand of big band bebop, bloated cheeks blaring his "sounds of surprise" from his bent brass trumpet. God, that man could sweat up a storm.

Sherman Helmsley, a.k.a. George Jefferson, led a review of has-been vaudevillians, and he was obviously not happy with the less than must-see status of his show; the room maybe just a fourth full. My asking him, "Hey George, where's 'Ouisi?" earned an angry glare to accompany his miserable mutterings throughout the entire evening.

Itzak Perlman showed off his extraordinary skills as a solo violinist, at 35, having earned numerous Grammy Awards following his being discovered as a childhood prodigy and multiple appearances on The Ed Sullivan Show. Today revered for his generosity of time and talent, that day must have been a bad day. Just like Mr. Jefferson, Itzak was not a happy camper.

In contrast, even Andre Segovia's fleet fingers and definitive classical guitar stylings were no match for the man's classy presence and modest demeanor. At the end of the evening, he and his equally charming wife, Emilia Magdalena, encouraged me to stop by their home in East Hampton next time I was en route to visit my parents, an invitation I regret that I never took up. Despite Segovia pushing ninety at the time, I foolishly thought that I would somehow, someday get around to it. Sadly, he passed away just a few years later.

And finally, I survived the scary evening that was the closed-circuit screening of Leonard vs. Duran II, the infamous fight night that left the theatre's almost 3,000 SRO fans of the Panamanian confused and angered that their favorite had walked out of the ring in just the 8th round with no more than a wave of his glove and "No mas." We sold a lot beer that night, though.

Today, The Calderone still stands at 145 North Franklin Street in Hempstead on Long Island, many years ago transformed into a revivalist church. The theatre's history as a temple of rock is long forgotten by all but those of us that worked there and by the fans that came over to our house to be thrilled by their favorite bands. There is constant talk of revitalizing the town and redeveloping the theatre, but I'll believe it when I see it. It'll more likely end up being condos.

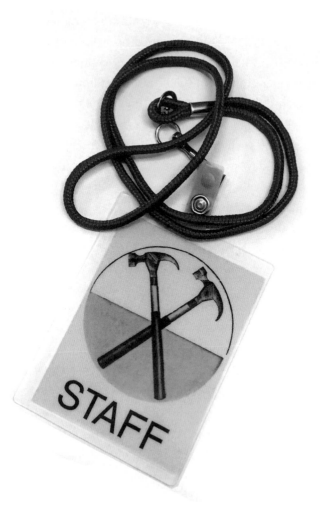

7

Driving Mr. Pink

BECAUSE FREEFALL HELD AN annual lease on The Calderone, it meant that we had to pay rent every day, not just on show days. Downtime for the venue was like an empty airplane seat – an opportunity for revenue that once the aircraft took off was lost forever. Therefore the theatre was open to sublet for virtually any other purpose on days when it was dark. Be it the local arts groups who presented Dizzy, Itzak and Andre, wannabe impresarios who lost their shirts on low-budget revues featuring washed-up sitcom stars, or filling the house with fight fans, we tried to keep the place occupied as often as possible. And when Pink Floyd chose our hometown Nassau Coliseum as one of only two U.S. venues to stage *The Wall* live, the biggest rock concert production up until that time, The Calderone was rented as one of just a handful of locations to sell the week's worth of seats. By then, the theatre had stepped into the automated age by having a Ticketron terminal installed in its box office, now offering security from errant teens as well as contemporary convenience.

It took a single day to sell out all five nights, and I made sure to pull 4th-row center seats for Pam and I on February 26th, the third show, and my twenty-second birthday. To this day, *The Wall* ranks as the most spectacular live event I've ever seen, not least of all for David Gilmore's death-defying solos atop the highest bricks during "Comfortably Numb." But this isn't my story. It belongs to them…and Brian.

Two years younger than I, Brian had worked for Freefall intermittently, at times covering the box office. When Pam came on the scene with her CPA-like precision, he was not long after displaced, but Freefall was a side job for him anyway. His main gig was working for Ron Delsener as a Production Assistant, a PA, or, as was more commonly referred to by those in the business, a *runner*. A runner's responsibilities are to basically do what the job title implies, to fetch things throughout the day and fulfill the impromptu requests of both the bands and the crews. Brian was apparently an excellent runner, and through determination and hutzpa, he had wrangled his full-time position with Delsener, able to earn and learn from one of the biggest names in the business. *The Wall* was being presented on February 24th through the 28th, the dead of the New York winter, always as cold as Holden Caulfield's Pency Prep.

"Floyd had been rehearsing for several days leading up to the first show. The night before the opening performance, the band's limo driver gets completely lost on the way out to Uniondale from Manhattan, where they're all staying. Floyd had arrived quite late and they were extremely frustrated. This snafu, combined with the fact that at the time, they weren't getting along amongst themselves at all, was not good. On the night of the first show, Ronnie tells me there's been a change of plans.

'The band will be coming out tonight, and the rest of the week, by helicopter,' Ronnie said, 'and I want you to pick them up over at the heliport in Mitchell Field. Take my car. Here's the keys.' Ronnie's car at the time was a pristine 1940's Packard, could have been in a museum. Big, long, beautiful curves…belonged in a gangster movie. The thought of driving it scared me to death…

"Because I wasn't the best of drivers. I'm still not. Two years before I had had an accident in my Dad's doody-brown Buick LeSabre when he lent it to me to commute to school. On a winter day, I was on the back roads of Old Westbury when the car took a bad skid, did a 360 and a rather large tree got intimate with the trunk. This incident is important because this very boring four-door family car was rendered even less sexy with the addition of two long strips of official rock and roll gray duct tape holding the trunk closed. Now because Pink Floyd was at each other's throats, they had demanded separate trailers to use as dressing rooms instead of the typical situation where the headlining band would set up camp together in the Islanders' locker room. I was asked to move one of the Winnebagos and while I was at it, I ripped off the rear bumper. Was I afraid to drive Ronnie's baby? You bet your ass I was.

"So I told Ronnie, 'Thanks, but no thanks, I'll use my car.' But he would have none of it and he pressed the keys into my hand. I politely but firmly put the keys back in his, but after a few rounds of Abbot and Costello, I came to the conclusion that I'd have to appease him. So I took the keys and headed toward his Packard, only to make a hard left to my beaten, doody-brown Buick LeSabre with the three-foot strips of now *dirty*-gray duct tape holding the trunk closed. Once I was out of Ronnie's sight, I pulled out and drove the half-mile to Mitchell Field to pick up that moment's four biggest rock stars in the world.

"Though I knew where I was going, the back and forth with Ronnie and the dodge to my own car had cost me a little bit of time, enough to make me a few minutes late in meeting monsieurs Waters, Gilmore, Mason and Wright. I found the four

Brits unescorted, huddled together at the curb, side by side seeking each other's warmth like hobos in an alley, their long, dull English topcoats flapping in the frigid February wind, their hands buried deep in their pockets, gloves apparently having not been on the top of their minds. As I pulled to the curb, I rolled down the window with the irresistible urge to ask, 'And which one's Pink?' but I wisely kept the thought inside my brain and away from my mouth.

"The band hustled into the car as I apologized for my tardiness, so happy to be in out of the cold that they didn't notice or didn't care about the LeSabre's lack of luxury. Roger Waters, however, sitting in the back passenger side seat, decided to make a point by admonishing me with the same snide English ire that his character would soon be spewing onstage. 'You know, mate, if you're to be the one picking us up each night, I suggest that you be on time.' Dave Gilmore, sitting next to me in the shotgun seat, just rolled his eyes and looked away out the window into the night. I figured that it was going to be one long week.

"The shows went on as they should, each night a bigger success than the night before, the press raving and the fans stupefied by what they'd just seen. Another of my runner duties was to man the Guest List at the Coliseum's West Gate. *Manning the List* is like being the guy that decided who was allowed past the velvet ropes into Studio 54. Literally, hundreds of people would jostle for position each night to get my attention in the hopes that I'd let them in, holding signs up to the glass from outside, trying to grease my palm, etc. The easy part was taking care of the legit guests of the band, their management, and the record company whose names were actually on the list. The not-so easy-part was when their names weren't, but should have been. A case in point was the quite British-looking gentleman in the long fur coat whom I recognized to be Peter Rudge, the manager of the Rolling Stones.

He certainly should have been on the list, but he wasn't. I welcomed Peter in (even though he was not on the list) and he thanked me, noting that Mick would be following along in a short while. Like Peter, Mick was also not on the list, but I let him in anyway, too.

"As the week progressed, the routine became established: each afternoon around 4:00 p.m. Ronnie would give me the keys to his Packard and I would move his car to hide it elsewhere in the garage. Then I would take the LeSabre to pick up the band, bring them to the venue, man the list, ensure that the catering was all in order, stock the Winnebagos with a supply of fresh towels, schmooze whomever needed schmoozing and help out with whatever needed to be done regardless of its importance or lack thereof.

"Every late afternoon in the car became just as routine, each band member taking the same assigned seat as they had the day before, just like the proper English schoolboys they likely all once were. Their conversations weren't about the music. Instead, they talked mundanely about matters of the rich, particularly about real estate. Roger was in the midst of purchasing a townhouse in Manhattan. Not be outdone, David had just bought his parents a home on the Caribbean Island of Mustique. Richard and Nick just seemed to put up with the wanking of their two higher-profile bandmates.

"On the day of the final show, I was on time, early even, but the band was late. They were very late.

"So I'm at the heliport waiting and waiting, keeping warm in the LeSabre as another freezing night's winds raged outside, and I'm actually getting worried about the boys. Back then, we had no cell phones, so I have no idea if they've called an audible and taken other transportation, whether there's been a problem with the helicopter or even an accident. There was no way of knowing what was going on with them, and soon I'd have to be back at the West Gate to again *Man the List*.

"Suddenly I hear the sound of rotors and the chopper comes into view. The helicopter touches down carefully; the band jumps out with their familiar wools and long hair flying. They run to the LeSabre knowing full well that there is a show to get started and that running overtime with the unions could cost them plenty of money – and I imagine that this extravaganza was already one hell of an expensive show. They settle into their familiar seats and brush off the cold. I decide that this time I'm going to speak my mind. All in fun, though, because by this point, I figured that our relationship, however brief, had nonetheless progressed to a point where a bit of good-natured ribbing would be acceptable. If not, well, hell, it's the last day. I'd never see them again anyway.

"Before I put the LeSabre into drive, I summoned the courage or stupidity to turn to Roger and scold him in quite the same snide tone with which he had dressed down me on the very first evening. I conjured up my best Brit accent and chided, 'You know, mate, I thought we had an understanding. If I'm supposed to be 'ere on time, I expect you would do the same.'

"For a few moments that felt like an eternity, silence hung in the air and I held my breath waiting for Roger's tirade. But instead, the four of them simultaneously burst out laughing. Roger reached forward to squeeze my shoulder and with a chuckle, he said, 'You're alright mate, you're alright. Fucking brilliant, in fact…'"

8

A Fallen Idol

MIDWAY THROUGH THE RECORDING of *A Night in the Ruts*, Joe Perry left Aerosmith and was replaced by Jimmy Crespo on lead guitar. A slight, quiet young man with a blond coif a la a mid-sixties mod band, Jimmy was the antithesis of the much more overt and larger-than-life persona of Perry and his thick black mane with its decadent streak of white. Jimmy shared a train ride to Long Island one evening with Mark and I following a meeting at the offices of Leber and Krebs. He was keenly aware of the shoes he had to fill and was more than a little intimidated. But he also realized that he had been given a career-making opportunity.

Steve Leber and David Krebs were arguably the first of the artist management teams to take what had been a very personal and seat-of-the-pants business to the next, much more serious level. Their company was a management *firm*, very seriously named Contemporary Communications Corporation. Both attorneys, Steve and David looked serious, and dressed seriously, too. Their hand-sewn couture suits announced their presence in the room and declared that rock and roll's low-brow art was now high finance. Their office was located on 55th Street, just down the block from Ralph Lauren's budding fashion empire and amidst midtown Manhattan's toniest power restaurants. They proved themselves to be star makers and wealth builders extraordinaire, the company's best days boasting an artist roster that, in addition to Aerosmith, included hard rock titans ACDC, Def Leppard, Scorpions, Joan Jett and…Michael Bolton and Beatlemania. David and Steve weren't purists; they were in it for the money.

One of CCC's strategies was to draft the sharpest young minds in the field, enabling the organization to attract the most promising talent by offering a combination of wise, seasoned and litigiously experienced business acumen with relevant handlers who connected with the artists and their music. Q Prime – managers of megastars Metallica, Muse and The Red Hot Chili Peppers – originated with the defection of protégé Peter Mensch partnering with friend Cliff Bernstein to start their own competing organization. Another alumnus, Paul O'Neill, went on to create The Trans Siberian Orchestra, a rock-theatrical outfit that he trotted out each Christmas season to deliver metal renditions of classic holiday fare to thunderous applause and huge ticket sales.

Leber and Krebs had managed Aerosmith from their early days, reaping the rewards of the young band's huge success. But they now grew weary and wary of Aerosmith's increasing dysfunction and diminishing sales. Having developed a relationship with Mark over his past several years as a regional promoter of the band and being impressed with his attention to detail and control, I think that Steve and David were hoping that Mark could prove to be yet another of the youthful business talents that they could enlist to manage the artistic ones. So they began an experiment in entrusting Mark with trying to salvage their investment, or at least in keeping Aerosmith from self-destructing. The reconstituted band was about to hit the road, and Freefall was awarded the first two dates on the nationwide tour in support of *Ruts*, perhaps a way to ensure that Aerosmith got off on the right foot. It didn't quite turn out that way.

On December 5, 1979, we kicked off the tour in Binghamton, New York, at the Broome County Arena, a hockey rink in a third-tier market with a capacity of about 7,000. Not sure what degree of fan fallout the departure of Joe Perry would have, Leber, Krebs and the booking agent's strategy appeared to be to work the band in some more modest-sized arenas to ensure that the shows would sell out, avoiding the embarrassing possibility of Aerosmith having to play to half-full halls.

Binghamton was indeed a sellout, but with general admission festival-style seating, no chairs were set up on the arena's floor. *Festival seating* is a euphemism for a first-come-first-served free-for-all. All tickets are the same price and when the venue opens the doors, it's a mad dash by the fans to get as close to the stage as possible – essentially a huge rock club with far less control than the beefed-up bouncers supply even in those more alcohol-centric settings. Just two days earlier, on December 3, eleven people had been trampled to death at the now-infamous tragedy in Cincinnati, Ohio, at a festival-seating concert by The Who, where anxious fans had stormed the doors in their fervor to stake out front row standing room. Everyone in Binghamton was on edge – the venue staff, crews, the band, and I imagine even the fans.

I had arrived on that fateful evening of the 3rd, keyed up to produce my first arena-level show all on my own. The next morning I met the sound and lighting crews and began the set up for the band rehearsal to take place later in the day. A budget-conscious tour had been planned, free of expensive staging gimmicks except for some smoke and a few over-sized power fans to clear the air and dramatize the hair. A relatively simple production, the show required only a few semis – the 40-foot eighteen-wheeler cargo trucks that roll from town to town stacked deck to ceiling with sound, lighting and stage gear.

By mid-morning, the band's chronically hung-over sound engineer, George, trudged in with Neil the Guitar Tech in tow. At that point, most of the other band crew had either quit or been let go, Aerosmith's finances having gone down the toilet with their creativity. A Mutt and Jeff team that I don't think were much older than me; both already had the aura of dissipated old-timers, their downtrodden demeanor broadcasting "Here we go again" defeat mixed with "it's just another day on the job" boredom.

We got about setting up Aerosmith's personal band equipment – backline, drums and vocal mics, including Steven's, with the taping of a setlist along with the lyrics to several select songs on the floor at his footing, hand-written with a black Sharpie on white vinyl in an easy-on-the-eyes size, stretching a good six-to-eight feet across the stage. I thought it odd; more than ten years into it you'd think Tyler would easily remember the words to the classics, and the new tunes should have been fresh in his head. We'd make good use of these low-tech prompts in the months to come.

Next to arrive was Joe Baptista, Aerosmith's tour manager and father figure. Joe could have been Jerry Garcia's long lost twin, a disheveled head of graying hair, a bulging midriff and man-boobs draped in a too-small black tee that clearly exposed a life of overindulgence. Joe's gravelly voice implied "I'm one mean son-of-a-bitch!" but he was actually a softie at heart, and over the next few months while babysitting Tyler and company, he also became a mentor to me, guiding my education in the delicate art of dealing with the prickly personalities of rock stars and their entourages.

The rehearsal went well enough, with the band running through "Remember" several times as well as a few other new cuts on *Ruts*. I was in awe. Here I was, basically alone with a private performance by one of the biggest bands in the world – albeit missing their star guitar – and even now, I am at a loss for words to describe the high that that twenty-one-year-old was feeling then and there. For all I know, they could have completely sucked, but it wouldn't have mattered. This was as inside as anyone could ever get. Or so I thought.

The next night the paid performance was indeed a bit sloppy, even to my charitable ears. Despite the rehearsal, the guys were still out of practice and Crespo had yet to get into the groove and develop his chemistry with Brad. It must be extremely difficult to be the new guy in a band where the two founding guitarists had developed a sixth sense of each other. For Brad, I imagine taking on Jimmy was like breaking in a second wife. While there certainly may have been a novelty and excitement to trading licks with his new spouse, he must have missed the comfort of the old one always being able to finish his sentences. For Jimmy, everything was new, and I imagine that he was not only nervous but also a bit starstruck himself. Steven, for his part, seemed in good voice, able to hit his high notes and wring every bit of syrup out of his vocal cords. The show went well enough despite the band's rust, the fans behaved themselves, and the show concluded without any Cincinnati-sized problems. My first big show now behind me, up and down without a hitch. The next day, though, I wouldn't be so lucky.

We finished the breakdown and loadout in Binghamton at about 1 a.m. and we immediately began the more than 400-

mile trek to Portland, Maine, to the Cumberland County Civic Center. We had brought along Ira and a few select members of his security team to keep an eye on things and to drive, so I curled up, contorted and fetal in the back seat of Ira's car, snatching whatever sleep I could along the way, which was hardly any at all. We arrived alongside the sound and lighting equipment a little after 9 a.m. and got to work putting it all back together again. Although everyone was dragging ass, exhausted like me from the overnight haul, load-in and set-up went smoothly and the Maine lobster dinner was, as I would learn it always is, one of the highlights of being in Portland. There was no sound-check that evening, so the band didn't appear until shortly before they were to go on stage.

Innocent bystanders to the impending debacle were the show's opening act, Scorpions. With already half a dozen album releases on their resume, Scorpions were stars in their native Germany and pretty much throughout all of Europe. In the States, though, they were still relative unknowns, their breakout hits "No One Like You" and "Rock You Like A Hurricane" still a few years off. They landed the lead spot because they were yet another client of Leber Krebs, so it made sense to package them with Aerosmith and assure that Scorpions would introduce themselves to America via already-welcoming hard rock audiences.

Opening acts can be in a tough spot, generally treated as inferiors by the headliner and an afterthought by the audience. Their sets are limited to about forty-five minutes or less, their catering is minimal and their dressing rooms are whatever is left over once the star act has been satisfied. That evening they were being relegated to an ER-style space that I was forced to improvise in the middle of the garage, scrounging four of the arena's portable blue draperies normally used for separating the booths at trade shows. The arena had only three small dressing rooms available that day and Aerosmith was using all of them, Steven insisting on his own. I took full advantage of the fact that I had gained Scorpions' trust and goodwill just a week before when they had opened for Ritchie Blackmore and his Rainbow at The Calderone. That and the German band's limited understanding of English allowed me to double-talk my way to their agreeing that this makeshift suite was better than having to drop their trousers, ditch their skivvies and peel on their leathers in one of the public men's rooms. But I digress…

Another festival-seating event, I had no desire to roam the densely-packed floor, no intention of squeezing myself through the tightly packed bodies, so I decided to position myself in the pit, the three to four feet of demilitarized zone behind the plywood barricade that separated the stage from the audience and stay there. I parked directly in front of Tyler, making sure that his cheat sheets were all in order at his feet.

As they had done the night before, Aerosmith began their set with "Back in the Saddle," priming the audience with a preamble of the shrieks of orchestra strings that scored the bathtub stabbing of Janet Leigh in Alfred Hitchcock's *Psycho*, followed by the clopping of Clydesdales and the slow build of the ominous notes and chords that lead to the song's opening thunder, all under cover of complete darkness.

"I'm baaaaaaack…." Steven wailed as the stage lights exploded and Tom began banging out the melodic bass line that drives through the song…and Aerosmith began what was to become a legendary show for all the wrong reasons. A good start, I thought, as Jimmy was now beginning to make me forget about Joe Perry, and the audience was pumped despite the stand-in. Steven, though, seemed lethargic and lacking the energy to perform his branded moves; his studder-steps, leaps and dips few and far between. As the set progressed, he began to appear more and more disoriented, becoming wobbly and increasingly leaning on his mic stand to retain his balance.

Soon after the band launched into "Reefer Headed Woman," Steven swooned for a moment and collapsed, falling limp like a marionette whose strings have been snipped. "Oh shit!" I yelled to myself above the roar as the rest of the band kept riffing, looking from one to the other, bewildered and in search of some clue as to what Steven was up to. What spontaneous performance piece had he concocted now? Or has he indeed passed out?

After several frozen moments of Steven on the floor with no movement, Brad bent over him but received no response. Big Joe B. suddenly rushed from the wings like a medic to attend to a fallen soldier, scooping up Tyler in his arms and hauling him offstage, Joe's panic evident to everyone in the arena. The rest of the band finally stopped playing. One by one, they simply petered out their parts and walked off, so I scrambled out of the pit and bolted backstage. All were attending to Tyler, but Steven was out cold. He was still breathing, but despite his opening declaration of being back, he wasn't going anywhere now or anytime soon, and the show wasn't going to go on.

Mark and I took to the stage as the house lights came up and the crowd was hushed; they, too, now wondering what was going on. Mark bravely stepped up to Steven's microphone as I stood by, awaiting the next development in this unforeseen crisis, envisioning a riot that could quickly become our very own rock debacle. Lowering the mic to adjust it to his shorter stature, Mark announced to the audience that tonight's show had to be canceled and that everyone's ticket would be honored for a replay in the near future, even though none of us had any idea what Tyler's status would be tomorrow, next week or next year. The crowd returned boos and jeers, and a few bottles that had been snuck in past the frisk at the gate rained down out of the darkness, smashing on

December 6, 1979

Steven goes down for the count and Joe B. comes to the rescue.
The fun is just getting started, and Jimmy Crespo likely wonders what
the hell he's gotten himself into.

the stage. I ducked behind a speaker stack for cover, but to Mark's credit, he toughed it out, a Napoleon-sized promoter facing the roiling mob. Eventually, the audience calmed, accepted the reality of having to call it an early night and headed for the exits. We broke down the set an hour sooner than usual and turned in for a well-deserved sleep.

For us, the tour would have gone on hiatus for the holidays even if the show had gone well, other promoters assigned to the tour's subsequent cities. But after a week of R&R – rest, and either relaxation or rehab, take your pick – Aerosmith went back out on the road to fulfill another half dozen or so commitments before Christmas and returned shortly after New Year's to complete what was to be the first and only leg of the *Ruts* tour. The band played a third show for us, this one at Nassau Coliseum, a fourth in Syracuse and they made peace in Portland by replaying the gig that had been aborted. The band continued to tour for a few more weeks but closed down shop in early February, never getting past the Mississippi. Then Aerosmith simply disappeared for a few months, dropping off of everyone's radar, including ours.

All seem to agree that Tyler's Cumberland County Civic Center crash was a result of his intensifying addictions, but Steven attempts to soften the fiasco in his autobiography, claiming to be simply too drunk to perform and having feigned his collapse in order to purposefully put an early end to the evening. Regardless of nuance, the fact of the matter was that he was living so close to the edge that he had fallen down and he couldn't get up.

9

Up-and-Comers, Has-Beens & Almost-but-Not-Quites

IN THE LATE '70S and early '80s the rock concert business was like no other business, but in certain respects, it was like every other business. Because no matter how glamorized or romanticized some have made it, ultimately, it still was a business, and it worked like this:

The artists were their own *Corporation,* producing their product and developing and maintaining their *brand.* The corporation was usually in the form of a band – Aerosmith, The Allman Brothers, Deep Purple, Journey, Yes, etc. – who pretty much split the pot evenly amongst the partners, at least until someone realized that they were the *Star* and quickly assumed the role of *CEO* and rendered their bandmates subordinate. Otherwise, the artist was already a solo performer (Eric Clapton, Elton John, Peter Frampton, etc.) who by then had already realized that they were the Star, and these talented and lucky individuals paid salaries to the players who accompanied them, sometimes generously, sometimes not. Successful artists' revenue streams included record sales, publishing/copyright royalties, concert ticket sales and merchandising (T-shirts, hats, etc.).

The artists' Managers were devoted *Chief Operating Officers*, guiding the business aspects of their corporation, acting as their representative with the outside world and getting paid a cut of revenues to do it. Notable of the early class were Brian Epstein (The Beatles), Andrew Loog Oldham (The Rolling Stones), Kit Lambert and Terence Stamp (The Who) and Peter Grant (Led Zeppelin). If you want to witness a classic rock manager in action, see Peter Grant's brief scene-stealing appearance in Zeppelin's tour movie *The Song Remains the Same*. Grant chews out Concerts East promoter Larry Vaughn at Madison Square Garden over bootleggers selling T-shirts on 7th Avenue. Right there, a cliché was born.

Booking agencies were the *distribution* arm of the concert revenue stream, with Premier Talent and American Talent International (ATI) dominating the field, both formed during the first dozen or so years of classic rock concert evolution by entrepreneurs little older than the artists themselves. These gatekeepers quickly grew more sophisticated and began to wield tremendous power, determining where their clients would perform and who was going to pay them for it while collecting a commission on every performance.

At the end of the supply chain were the *retailers*, the ego-driven concert promoters who took all the risk in purchasing the product and reselling it as tickets, hopefully for a profit. If a show sold out, everyone made money, leaving even the promoter smiling. If a lot of seats sat on the shelf past their expiration date, the Promoter was shit out of luck.

Among promoters in the New York area, there was a defined hierarchy, based mostly upon personal relationships but also divided by geography. Once Basile got out of the business, Brian's boss, Ron Delsener, became the top dog in New York City. Ron had been early on the scene promoting events in Central Park and moving on to Madison Square Garden and the even larger venues of Yankee and Shea Stadiums. In New Jersey, it was John Scher with his Metropolitan Entertainment. On Long Island, there was by now ex-Concerts East staffer Larry with his own new organization, despite his public humiliation by Grant. And then there was Freefall.

In almost any other market across America, one promoter was enough, and in some markets, even that monopoly struggled to succeed. But on Long Island, coupled with New York City constituting the largest Statistical Market Area in the world, Mark could make a living if not become wealthy by eking out whatever shows he could, helped by Freefall's one competitive advantage, its hold on The Calderone.

But another way Freefall could make inroads with the managers and the agencies while generating revenue to pay its overhead (i.e., me) was to stretch the supply chain even further. We became the middle-agent between national talent and the club scene – acting as a sub-distributor for Premier, ATI and their handful of smaller competitors. Agencies usually found it beneath themselves to work directly with the barroom brawlers that they perceived the club owners to be. In most cases, they weren't wrong to think that way. Club owners cared about nothing but the bottom line, least of all about the self-respect of the talent.

Filling their rooms as many nights as possible was paramount. Providing a pleasant experience for fans and a fair paycheck for performers was not. Mark and Pam quickly learned how to deliver big names that drew large crowds who drank a lot of beer. And Freefall was paid a worthwhile commission for doing so. If the act was promising enough, Freefall took the chance on the ticket sales themselves with the hope for a larger payday while the club would forgo asking for rent in exchange for the prospect of packing the place.

Besides its direct financial benefits, booking clubs also supplied opportunities to perform big favors for the agencies, enabling Freefall to build what is now commonly referred to as personal capital. In addition to the superstars, the agencies also represented new bands and singer-songwriters who would hopefully be future cash cows. Those artists needed to be heard, and to be heard, they needed places to play, places even smaller than The Calderone. In addition to these up-and-comers, the agencies each had their roster of has-beens, the clients who were on their way down and sometimes on their last gasp due to either a drought of creativity or an abundance of bad habits. And then there were the eccentric artists who were critical favorites and consistent draws with devout but only cult-sized followings that could be counted on to turn out every six months or so.

This lower-strata of touring talent helped the agencies pay their own overhead between the mega-tours which bought them their brownstones. Many managers of the star attractions, like the agencies, often had more than one artist as a client. To preserve their relationship with their arena-sized acts and to perform their own favors, the agencies had to find work for their managers' less-than-stellar artists. The more entrenched promoters were disinterested; none seemed to have the stomach to deal with the club owners either. Freefall did, and we did it well.

The clubs in which we did most of our business were Detroit, in Port Chester, New York, at the northern boundary of Westchester County; *Hammerheads* in Islip, and later *Malibu* in Long Beach, both on Long Island. These were the three biggest suburban rooms outside of a few in Jersey. (FYI: Clubs are almost universally referred to as *rooms*. Theatres are *houses*. Arenas are *halls*.)

When you first walk through the door of a typical rock club – especially as they stood in the late '70s and early '80s – the aroma is a heady blend of stale beer and diluted Pine Sol. Your feet stick to the floor then make that ripping sound when you walk; those floors never quite get clean, receiving little more attention than a quick pass with a dirty mop that's been dipped in even dirtier water. The walls are painted black or an almost equally dark hue, with no art for the drunks to break or deface (though they discover every exposed patch of broken drywall and decorate it with crass graffiti inspired by the limited imaginations of their ever-adolescent minds). Duct tape is ubiquitous, the cure-all for every maintenance ailment, offering first-aid for the vandalized vinyl of what little seating the club provides; patching the holes that rowdy patrons have punched through the cheap hollow-core restroom doors; securing bits of threadbare carpet remnants in the closet-sized dressing rooms; and binding together all sorts of piping and PVC whose joints are straining to separate from the rumbling of hard rock rhythm sections. Throughout the room, the lighting is almost nonexistent, perpetually dimmed if not entirely snuffed so that the audience won't notice what a shit hole the place really is.

But the clubs ran a lot of cash, and so they were attractive properties for the guys with bent noses, as it was assumed that most of the clubs were in some way connected to the Mob. I ran the productions at Hammerheads. Frank, my ex-roommate and crewmate at Hofstra Concerts, was the Production Manager at Detroit. Malibu, a more upscale venue, had their own staff that was competent enough and could be trusted to carry off the events with an acceptable level of professionalism. At Malibu, we could simply show up at showtime to schmooze the artists and pick up our check. It was great work when you could get it.

In the early '80s, the clubs saw plenty of punk and new wave acts come through as those rookies were all hard at work playing anywhere that would have them, building their fan base in the hopes of someday making the leap to theatres, and ultimately arenas. The Ramones were one of them. Though they eventually came to be extremely well-respected as the progenitors of American punk – their deaths securing their legendary status before they had a chance to metastasize into a self-parody – they could never really break wide while they were all alive and playing live. They were a fixture on the club circuit year after year, bumped themselves up to theatres now and again, but then they'd be right back in the clubs.

In June of 1976, Delta T's Tom introduced me to The Ramones' debut album; his straight-laced brother-in-law, Don, had given it to him for his 18th birthday. I dropped by that afternoon to take Tom out for a few beers, raced up the two flights to his attic bedroom and when I entered, he couldn't contain himself. "Man, you gotta hear this shit!" He handed me the record and I looked at the cover: no intricate and colorful conceptual scene, no abstract splashes, no color at all – just a stark black and white group photo of four dorks with attitude against a crumbling brick wall. Then Tom put the needle to the grooves. "Blitzkrieg Bop" was strange enough, but one listen to "Beat the Brat" *on the head with a baseball bat* and I thought Don was playing a wicked joke on him. Little did I know that "Hey ho! Let's go!" would be heard around the world.

Despite their now being held in high esteem as influential *artistes*, back then, The Ramones just couldn't cross over. Never seeming to grow in artistry or audience, they came across as a bunch of bumbling, stumbling misfits with a silly sibling shtick and a roaring repertoire that ran together like one long punk power chord. Despite enduring numerous sets, I could still never tell the difference between "Rockaway Beach," "Rock and Roll High School" or "Do You Remember Rock and Roll Radio?"

Joey Ramone (God rest his soul) was one truly unique dude. His sunglasses seemed glued to his face; I can't recall ever actually seeing Joey's eyes. Whether he was almost blind or just burnt out, I don't know, but I'd have to lead him by the hand like a toddler so that he wouldn't end up in the audience instead of onstage. Ever unsteady, he would clutch the mic stand as if his life depended upon it and flail while finding his balance with splayed legs, a Big-Bird in ripped denim and black biker's leather. The rest of the band? All they did was argue and yell at each other, onstage and off while poor Joey would shrink to avoid the constant conflict.

I didn't appreciate their talent then, but I do now; they were fucking amazing songwriters! When you strip away the machine gun guitar attack and re-cut Joey's almost unintelligible vocals, you're left with a slew of memorable melodies and indelible hooks. Give a listen to *We're A Happy Family*, a tribute album where second-generation punks-at-heart like Green Day, The Red Hot Chili Peppers, Eddie Vedder, U2 and others re-imagine the originals, offering up their own interpretations which paint a whole new picture of where the Forest Hills band was coming from. It's evident to me now that The Ramones were their own worst enemies in their quest for success. But hey, ho, maybe that was exactly their point.

Just one of many evenings in the clubs with The Ramones.

Before presenting Pretenders at The Calderone, we introduced them to America during the spring of 1980 with one of their first shows on our shores, selling Detroit to triple the legal limit despite incessant rain and just a night before we would set a new club record with those provocateurs of musical mayhem, The Plasmatics. This night – one of the band's only performances in the New York area – even drew a few semi-stars to see what all the fuss was about, including Mick Ronson, David Bowie's go-to guitarist on *Hunky Dory*, *Ziggy Stardust* and *Aladdin Sane*, and Lenny Kaye, just making a name for himself with Patti Smith. Even Larry T., the rough and tumble owner of Detroit, thought the evening to be special; he personally presented Chrissy with a dozen red roses before she went on stage.

The band got primed on scotch and tequila, spilling into the narrow hallway outside their closet-sized dressing room. Chrissy donned a coonskin cap a la Disney's Davy Crockett before taking the stage with her bright white Fender Telecaster to bang out the hits that had already taken hold from their debut album released shortly after New Year's. Their chart-climbing take on the obscure Kinks tune, "Stop Your Sobbing," Chrissy's own "Kid," "Brass in Pocket" and "Precious" all pumped the sardine-packed, sweat-soaked audience, the set peppered with lesser-known songs that shined a light on charismatic but doomed guitarist James Honeyman-Scott's skills and showmanship. Enjoying her newfound adulation after several years of failing to achieve fame in London, Chrissy bowed to the crowd's wishes and gave them an encore of a second "Sobbing."

Some weeks later at Hammerheads, I found myself on the receiving end of a Chrissy-fit deriving from something about the sauce on her spaghetti, ravioli, gnocchi, or whatever the hell it was she had ordered for dinner. This after I had gotten the pasta joint next door to open early, expressly for her, the whole place serving as her private dining room. Gentleman that I am, I had hoped to give her an opportunity to dine like a human being instead of grabbing a slice on the run or settling for the salt-saturated cold cuts that the club was providing. But there must have been a pea that bothered the punk princess, and she wasn't shy in showing her displeasure. "No one can be meaner, and no one can be more of a cunt than I am," Chrissy was quoted by Rolling Stone in a feature covering that first US tour. No understatement there. Nonetheless, Chrissy got past it and that evening, the band delivered another blistering show to another oversold audience.

In addition to Hammerheads and Detroit, Freefall also began booking talent for the Malibu Beach Club, an out-of-the-way outpost on Long Island's Lido oceanfront. Considerably glitzier than Hammerheads, the club became the gateway to America for the careers of many more new wavers, particularly of the British Isle variety, including Boy George and Culture Club, Billy Idol, and a boyish Bono and U2.

For U2, the club was little more than half full; the Gaelic band's first fans had been kept at bay by the blustery, snowy, single-digit December evening outside. But in spite of a small audience and a still shallow catalog of original material, U2 was there to please, just as Chrissy had been at Detroit, and so they opted to perform for their encore their only hit thus far, "I Will Follow," a second time, instead of covering a Merseybeat or Motown classic as they so often would later. U2 would one day become one of the biggest rock bands in the world, arguably as popular as the Rolling Stones. But at the time, we thought that they were merely a more intelligent and intelligible Ramones.

A young, mulleted U2 working the room at
Malibu Beach Club on a snowy December 13, 1982.

The clubs were also home to plenty of stalwarts of the '60s and '70s whose best days had passed. Here they were trying to make ends meet by cranking out their classics.

I spent the better part of a freezing February evening in the cold of the garbage-strewn back alley of Hammerheads nursing a strung-out Leslie West of Mountain. Then obtusely obese, sweating profusely and barely able to walk, Leslie could find neither his confidence nor concentration to perform. I tried to straighten him up with water and coffee, but it took me until well after midnight to convince him to plop himself down on an equipment case in front of the increasingly impatient crowd, only for Leslie to spend the next forty-five minutes mindlessly noodling his Les Paul. The audience almost at its limit; he was finally able to summon up the riff to "Mississippi Queen," but he then lost it almost immediately, again wandering off into unrecognizable musical side trips.

Johnny Winter, Edgar Winter and Rick Derringer all were part of the circuit, sharing a common manager that kept them working individually and sometimes pairing them up. John Kaye and Steppenwolf kept afloat with endless repeats of "Born to Be Wild" and "Magic Carpet Ride." The ever-present Jorma Kaukonen would bounce between Hot Tuna and solo acoustic outings, playing any size room that would take him as long as the price was right. Before reinventing himself as wedding and bar mitzvah lizard Buster Poindexter, a post-New York Dolls David Johansen, took off his makeup and drag to set out solo, but glam was still what the fans were clamoring for. And when Blue Oyster Cult's popularity took a dive, 1977's "Godzilla" being their last bona fide hit, they toured the clubs under the band's earlier name of Soft White Underbelly in order to drum up some money while attempting to not tarnish their brand.

Perhaps though the biggest surprise to hit the clubs was that band from Boston with the Jagger-lipped lead singer who just a few years earlier had headlined stadiums. And so it was that we set out on the long strange trip that Mark not-so-mysteriously promoted as *The Aerosmith Mystery Club Tour.*

10

On the Road with a Band on the Rocks

TYLER'S COLLAPSE IN MAINE had made its fair share of headlines, and though Steven recovered enough to perform the band's handful of gigs left before a Christmas break and to set back out on the road in January, by the first week of February, the tour again came to an abrupt halt. The talk was that Steven had entered rehab, and Aerosmith went into hibernation.

Having little patience left to tolerate Aerosmith's unpredictability, Leber and Krebs now enlisted Mark to babysit full-time, hoping that maybe he could salvage something out of what had such a short time ago been considered America's hottest rock and roll band. The *Ruts* album sold relatively poorly, and the band seemed to be hitting a new financial bottom, as much due to their bad business decisions and continued bad behavior as to their lack of quality product.

As spring approached, Aerosmith seemed desperately in need of money but not able to commit to a full-fledged production or tour. Mark convinced Leber and Krebs to allow him to book Aerosmith on a short string of gigs in a few close-to-home suburban rock clubs in order to generate enough cash for the band's members to pay their most immediate bills. *Cash* was a critical attribute to whatever income they could generate because taxes were probably the last thing the band could afford. Mark dubbed these dates *The Mystery Club Tour*, never publicly advertising that Aerosmith was to be performing but allowing rumor to spread with little effort to prevent it, if not outright abetting it. The first three shows of this off-Broadway experiment sold out instantly as Pam opened a pop-up box office at each of the venues in order to bring back the proceeds of the advance sales, enabling the band to stay afloat at least as long as the money would last, money that had likely already been spent before the performances were delivered. Again, in the revisionist history recounted in Aerosmith's biographies and memoirs, these-under-the-radar performances have been virtually ignored. Hell, if I were any of them it wouldn't be a time I'd have fond memories of either. That is, if they actually remember much of it at all.

So, finally, we get back to Speaks, or The Action House as it was known in its previous incarnation before Phil Basile put money into its makeover instead of continuing to pay for top-shelf talent. This was the same stage that a dozen years before had presented an A-list of rising rock and roll legends, including Cream, The Doors, The Grateful Dead, Chicago, Fleetwood Mac and many others. Today it was to host yet another superstar act, but this one was precipitously on its way down.

The load-in of sound and lighting equipment began around 11 a.m. because Aerosmith wasn't to take the stage until after midnight. The band's performance time was yet another compromise caused by their demotion. As almost all of the ticket revenue was going to Aerosmith, the club owners insisted on a very late start in order to maximize their bar take. In fact, club owners could be quite creative in attempting to push it back even further.

Late that afternoon, the band arrived for soundcheck, Steven strolling in with his wife, Cyrinda, on his arm, the two of them looking gaunt and strung-out, Tyler barely filling out his typically formfitting bellbottom jeans. Cyrinda, a tall thin blonde with a wide party-girl smile, was the classic rock and roll chick. By that point Cyrinda was the ex of David Johansen, lead singer of groundbreaking glam band The New York Dolls, before that a fixture of David Bowie's entourage, and even before that one of the many muses of pop artist Andy Warhol. She was thought of as a serial starfucker, and probably not a good influence. She was also mother to Steven's year-and-a-half-old second daughter, Mia.

The rumors were still fresh that after the cancellation of the formal *Night in the Ruts* tour that Steven had entered rehab for heroin addiction. That being true or not, I don't know, but in any event, his drug of choice had become cocaine. Throughout that first *Mystery Club Tour* performance, Steven would intermittently reach to the drum riser for a coffee cup with a straw. "What the hell is he drinking?" I questioned George while sitting by the engineer's side as he mixed the performance from our barricaded oasis in the midst of the maximum-capacity crowd.

George scowled at my naiveté and drolly stated, "He's suckin' blow." Even though I hadn't been living in a cave, it took me a few moments to fully comprehend that what Steven was doing was slurping cocaine like it was a milkshake instead of snorting it. (I guess that getting out of rehab doesn't mean you're clean. Sometimes it just means that you've replaced your old vice with a new one.) Nonetheless, that evening at Speaks was a relatively normal one, assuming anything could be classified as normal in regard to this traveling circus that was just getting on the road.

A few days later, our next stop was Detroit, a friendly club since Mark and Pam routinely booked talent there, and due to my college roommate Frank being the show coordinator as well as the floor manager for the bars. It was great to see Frank, his wide bright eyes sparkling behind his wire-frame granny glasses, the dim club lighting shining off his prematurely bald head, his hyper dashing about to cover all the corners of his room making me dizzy. Frank and I had both started in the business when we met at Hofstra, and we had worked on plenty of shows at The Calderone together, in addition to those across campus. Frank knew what he was doing, which was always reassuring. Unfortunately, though, he had become accustomed to the club mentality of pinching pennies, and he would cut whatever corners he thought the club could get away with.

As Aerosmith took the stage around 11 p.m., the room was full, wall-to-wall fans so densely packed that you could almost lift your legs and tread air, held aloft by nothing but the pressure of the sweat-soaked bodies around you. Detroit was again a sold-out performance, and just as we'd done the month before for Pretenders and then The Plasmatics, we squeezed over 1,500 bodies into a space with a legal occupancy of 505.

The band was still opening with the sound effects from Alfred Hitchcock's *Psycho*, so as the room went black and the film's soundtrack began I turned to Frank in the dark and asked him for the dozen brown towels that the band's contract rider required for Steven. Frank said, "No problem, be right back," and he about-faced into the club's rear. He returned just moments later, producing a dozen *white* hand towels, stacked in his arms from his belly to his chin.

"Frank, what's the deal? Where are the fucking brown towels? The rider says brown towels!" I had to shout in Frank's face to be heard above the band's roar as they once again launched into "Back in the Saddle." He flinched. "What's the difference, man? A towel's a towel."

"Not to Steven, man! A *white* towel leaves *white* fuzz in his *brown* hair! The lights pick it up and it looks like he's been rolling around in a fucking terrycloth mill. The guy'll fuckin' freak on me, Frank, do you understand? I gotta give him brown towels!" Unfazed, Frank flatly stated, "Forget it. I don't have any, and every store in town is closed now."

In a panic but with no time for indecision, I ordered Frank to follow me. Realizing that what Frank said was true, there was just nowhere to turn at that hour, I instantly improvised in order to avoid the tantrum of a cosmetically compromised diva. I led Frank out the front door and across the strip center parking lot, angrily kicking the empty beer cans that littered my path from the fans' earlier tailgating. We quickly located my car and I unlocked the trunk. Inside was a large green lawn and leaf bag where I had heaped the brown towels that Steven had used the other evening at Speaks. I had taken them from the club, foreseeing precisely this type of emergency. I also had intended to wash them at home in-between gigs, but I hadn't had the chance.

"Start folding, man, and fast. Hopefully, Steven's fucked up enough tonight to not realize they're dirty."

As it turned out, Steven was, in fact, fucked up more than enough for me to pull it off, and I may have even gotten away with giving him white ones had push come to shove. In fact, Tyler collapsed on us once again that evening. But by now, we all were ready for just about anything, so Steven was instantly whisked from the stage, got his shit together after just a few minutes of the fans' confusion, and he was able to return to make it through the set. A close call with déjà vu was narrowly averted.

I was greeted with a fresh form of excitement the next week at Hammerheads, back on Long Island. Hammerheads was one of the bigger clubs we played – big enough to fit two absurdly large boat-shaped bars just in case you didn't catch the club's theme from its name. The power supply turned out not to be adequate to sustain Aerosmith's sound and lighting, and the stage went dark in the middle of the show, the result of a blown fuse or two. The band played for several more minutes in the dark before they realized that the lights were gone for good.

A far bigger problem than the potential fiasco presented by white towels, this time, I had no Plan B to fall back on, and Steven's wrath was immediate. When I saw him bound off of stage right, I dashed to meet him in the bite-size dressing room, knowing that I'd have to talk him off the ledge before I could get to the root of the power problem.

"What the fuck just happened and who's responsible?" he screamed at me.

"Steven, man, I don't know, but I'll get it fixed, I promise!"

"Yeah? When? And where the fuck are those guys that own this shithole?" Tyler insisted on drubbing the club's owners on their obvious lack of respect for his superstar band's most basic production needs, demanding to confront them personally. Resigned to it being unavoidable, "This way!" I said with a tilt of my head and I chaperoned him on a mad dash through the audience to the maze of bare, battered, unpainted sheetrock hallways that led to the club's basement business office.

Bobby A. was a beefy ex-cop, toughened by the streets of his beat, now part-owner of this seedy rock palace that pumped out bottled beer and watered-down booze for a big profit. Bobby was a dapper Don, jet-black hair, slicked back to accentuate his sharp widow's peak, and as always sporting a crisp white shirt unbuttoned two down to display his healthy chest hair. His sleeves were rolled just enough to give you a glimpse of his powerful forearms that portended even more powerful biceps. As menacing as he looked, Bobby was actually a pretty even-tempered guy, for the most part. But on occasion, I had seen Bobby's temper flare and it wasn't pretty. So I knocked gingerly on his door with Steven by my side, angered and antsy. The door swung open to reveal Bobby behind his desk, hands calmly folded. His partner Matty, the contrastingly slight elder major-domo of the club, toupee precariously in place, retreated to his side, arms crossed and legs now rigidly rooted.

Standing in full stage regalia of red and white striped satin, in this dingy, shitty basement backroom, Tyler instantly began ripping Bobby a new asshole, and if you've ever heard Steven rap or scat, you know that he can get a lot out of his mouth in very short order. I stood by his side with anticipation and dread of what would come next. As I said, I knew that despite Bobby's outwardly placid manner, he was not one to take any shit. And though decidedly smaller than Bobby, Matty was an old-school tough guy who you just knew you shouldn't mess with. In the middle of Tyler's rant, Matty uncorked his indignation at the affront.

"Who the fuck does this guy think he is?"

Steven was about to pounce and I sincerely feared that Bobby was going to pull out an NYPD-issue .38 Special. But he didn't. He waived off Matty and he remained calm and quietly seated, patiently keeping his temper in check as Steven continued his rant and threats of canceling the show.

"Are you finished?' Bobby calmly responded to Steven.

Pumped for battle, Steven was perplexed by Bobby's courtesy and lack of a counterattack. It took an uncharacteristic moment for him to find his words, and though still outraged, he toned down his delivery as he leaned on the desk and stared down Bobby.

"So what're you going to do to fix it?" he demanded.

Bobby simply promised that he would solve the problem, that the power would resume and that the show would go on.

Then, with just the right amount of menace, he told Tyler to let it go. "Now you go back upstairs, get back on stage and…don't ever fucking talk to me like that again. Do you understand me?"

Even the singer suddenly understood that Bobby didn't give a shit *who* Steven Tyler was. I gripped his arm and pled with him. "Steven, please, please let's go, let's get out of here!" Satisfied that he had won the battle despite his loss of face, he agreed and we left to join the rest of Aerosmith upstairs. The club got the power back up and running and the band finished the show, but not without whatever additional delay Bobby and Matty could eke out to boost their take at the bars.

Next up was The Fountain Casino in Aberdeen, New Jersey. The Fountain Casino wasn't a casino at all, though I imagine the owners thought that invoking the word lent some boardwalk cache to their catering hall astride the strip malls of Route 9, a good 75 miles from the action in Atlantic City. The room was cavernous, cheap and glitzy, complete with over-ornamented crystal chandeliers, faux Persian carpet and ripped vinyl dining chairs now stacked on the perimeters to avoid being used as projectiles should the crowd get out of hand. For Aerosmith, it was just another show in another shitty venue that ten years ago they had hoped they'd never have to see again, but from which tonight they'd take home some much-needed cash on the way out. Little did they know it almost became a pro bono gig if not for young Pam's tenacity and naiveté.

The owners of The Fountain Casino were again the de rigueur club wiseguys. This family, though, all sported bespoke black pinstripes, universally size XXL. Despite their stab at style they were far from classy in their intention to shortchange the band.

They first tried Soprano math, but Pam wasn't buying it. She had run the register in her dad's Sheepshead Bay Diner and the girl knew her numbers. Soon came threat through innuendo, which went right past Pam; being raised in a home where English was still a second language, she had a poor grasp of even fairly common American idioms, let alone double entendre. No, young Pam stood her ground to wring out every buck the band deserved, and the four goombahs locked up and went home having been bested by a spunky Greek girl in Jordache jeans.

After a brief rest, in late May, we got Aerosmith back on the club circuit, this time setting out for more of suburban New Jersey. The first gig on the route was The Soap Factory, in Fort Lee, a vintage manufacturing building-turned-seventies-disco, which on occasion was pressed into service as an ill-fitting rock club. Designed for dance, The Soap Factory was a bad room for rock in that the stage was astride the long wall, so bands fronted a shallow expanse of fans with the audience streaming off in the distance to the left and right. Musicians played to the brick directly opposite and not more than a first down from the stage. The club's less than desirable setup was enough to put Steven in a foul mood from the start, feeling that his fans were getting screwed by bad site lines as well as by the acoustical nightmare created by the building's bare masonry. With the room empty during soundcheck, the mix was hellish and Steven's vocals were mud.

To make matters worse, the crowd that evening was an exceptionally rowdy crew of Jersey boys and girls, some quickly becoming annoyed by the sonic soup. Boos soon ensued and before long, a few of the more toasted audience members began to taunt Steven outright.

"You can't fucking sing, Tyler!"

"Where the fuck is Joe?"

"You guys fuckin' suck!"

"Fucking Aerodicks!"

It didn't take long for the jeers to become too much for him to take, and Steven lost it mid-song. Having focused on one of the offenders, Tyler took a few steps back into the shallow stage, almost bumping into Joey's bass drum, and sprinted to the edge before leaping headfirst into the throng. He landed atop his target as well as a few neighboring fans and began punching indiscriminately, quite possibly as much out frustration at his current situation as to silence his hecklers. But it didn't take long before Ira and his security team were able to wrest Tyler from amidst the melee and push him back up on the stage. Thankfully, Steven once again had the good sense to let it go and get on with the show.

"Sweet Emotion" came about halfway into Aerosmith's set, and mid-song is a moment when Tyler's verses end and the guitars bleed out. Joey Kramer steps up with an angry attack of the snare drum and the band explodes into a raucous extended jam, the cut closing with Tyler bouncing up and down to the crescendo, tossing his scarf-draped mic stand hand to hand while doing splits in midair. Joe handed me the ignition switch that would light all of the room's neon, and I was to flick it just as the guitars would kick in following Joey's final snare beat. But...

I got into the tune too much myself and I missed my cue. Joe instantly shot me a panicked glance, which woke me from my reverie, though not in time. I lit the room a few seconds in, missing the moment that would have created a truly exquisite experience for the crowd, the kind I had burnt into my own memory at more than a few of the many events I had attended as a civilian. Afterwards, Joe D. thanked me for my help but also advised that I should stick to my regular duties. As far as I could tell, though, no one else had seemed to notice my faux pas – the audience thought it was all quite spectacular.

The band remaining relatively healthy and interested; in June, the train kept rolling for a third swing, this time up into

New England, starting in Massachusetts, Aerosmith's home turf. First stop, Mr. C's in Lowell, a depressed, drug-addled working-class town that I don't think has improved much with the intervening years. Unlike the battered Long Island rock clubs that somehow managed to put on a good face, and far from the discos and catering establishments that did double duty in Jersey, Mr. C's was unabashedly as low as it goes. There was no pretense here; the toilets probably hadn't worked in years, if ever at all.

The club was owned by an uptight, older husband and wife that were off the wall and at odds with us the entire day and evening.

"What time do they want to go on? Oh no, that's too early."

"Why do you want to count the door? Everyone trusts us."

"Oh, we don't usually feed the bands…"

Despite their constant questions, objections and contradictions, the show went fine until it was over.

While we were in the middle of the breakdown and Aerosmith prepared to leave to drive back to their homes or hotels in and around Boston, the couple corralled Steven and I in the middle of the now-vacated floor, slimy from spilled beer and littered with clear plastic cups. They proceeded to double-team us with their accusations.

"We just checked your dressing room and the mirror is gone!

Where the hell is our mirror? You stole our goddamn mirror!" Stunned by such a strange, left-field accusation, I think Steven was too bewildered to react until they invoked his estranged songwriting sibling. "You know, Joe Perry played here last week and he's a good guy. Joe never would've done something so low…"

Once again, ever-present when shit like this happened, Ira and his boys gathered around and escorted Steven out before the incident escalated into another instance of Tyler versus the

HAMMERHEADS

SPEAKS

Detroit

THE ROCK NITECLUB

Emerald City

THE
FOUNTAIN
CASINO

Soap Factory

mr. C's
rock palace

UNCLE
SAM's

STAGE WEST

world. The fact that Steven was ready to actually engage the crazy couple in the argument was indicative of how pathetic our carnival could get. The fact that they accused the star of stealing a mirror of all things was particularly ironic, leading me to reconsider their own erratic behavior and conclude that they were slaves to the powder themselves.

From Lowell, we headed to the Cape, skirting Boston itself. Boston was just too close to home right now; playing to club-sized audiences in their front yard, no matter how much fast money could be made, would have been too embarrassing to stomach. When bands of Aerosmith's stature did small shows like *The Mystery Club Tour* was doing, they were usually impromptu, unannounced, and the band often didn't get paid at all. They did it for the press or just to reconnect with the live audiences that move further and further away as the venues they play become bigger and bigger. Besides, with the wildcard quality of Aerosmith's performances each night, having close friends and family possibly witness a meltdown was not a chance anyone wanted to take.

So next up, and possibly the real low of this whole exercise in cheap prostitution, was Uncle Sam's, a Nantasket Beach bar perched on the third floor of a commercial strip in Hull on Cape Cod. Though the touring gear we were lugging around to the clubs was a small load compared to the massive rigs needed for arenas, every case had to be humped up three flights of un-air-conditioned stairs in ninety-degree heat and one hundred percent humidity. It was going to be a bad day for sure.

With no backstage at all, the band's RV had to double as a dressing room, the same three flights down that we had climbed to get all of the band's shit up to the stage. But where we had loaded all of the gear in the front door, the RV was parked out back, and a steep, zigzagging deck-wood stair was the only way to get down there.

When show time rolled around, one by one, the band appeared; Crespo and Whitford, then Hamilton and Kramer, and they all began loosening up before going onstage, Joey vigorously shaking his appendages to work out any kinks. Joe B. and I waited a few moments with our eyes still on the door, but with no undue concern. After all, even in the worst of times, we would expect Steven to be the last up, always angling to make a grand entrance no matter how small the event. But as the opening drew close, there was still no Tyler. Joe and I exchanged confused looks and he turned to one of the guys in a percolating panic.

"Where's Steven?"

"He said he's not coming."

"What? Why not?"

"I don't know; we didn't ask," one of them replied with nonchalance, weary of Steven's continuing irrationality. "We just figured he was fucking with us and that he'd be right behind. Guess not."

And with that, the recorded violins began their Psycho screech signaling the show's start. Out in the house at the soundboard, George had no idea that there was bound to be a delay.

Before the horse hooves could begin their gallop, Joe about-faced, flew out the back door and down the three flights to the RV, huffing and puffing while waddling all the way as overexerted big men do, the rickety staircase swaying with his weight. I trailed behind, fearful that my mentor would go tumbling to the bottom, killing himself and leaving me to deal with an uncooperative Tyler on my own.

We barged open the door to the RV; normally, we'd have manners and knock, but Steven's tardiness now fueled our worst fears, leaving no time for formalities. There, at the back of the camper, sat the lead singer on the cream-colored vinyl banquette with a huge pile of powder in front of him on the Formica fold-down dining table, a real-life rock and roll Tony Montana. The mound sat in the center like a mini Matterhorn, screaming to be knocked down a peg or two. I don't know how much he'd done–at least at that moment, no lines were drawn on the table – but he was just looking at it intently, savoring his wealth like Scrooge McDuck.

Wide-eyed and wired, he was overflowing with paranoia. "I'm not doing it. I'm not going out there. This is bullshit!"

Knowing a cancellation of the show was impossible – hundreds of kids were packed upstairs, sweating their nuts off in the June evening's heat – Joe and I calmly sat down and cajoled Tyler, offering encouragement and flattery as if he were a spoiled little boy, but with no success.

Joe quickly got fed up with going nowhere tossing softballs, and suddenly he realized that the answer was right in front of our own noses. "Steven, the simple fact is that if you don't perform, you won't get paid."

And so the show went on. We rushed Tyler up the long steep stairs and he leaped on stage with his bandmates, the four of them having spent the last several long minutes opening the show with an unscripted jam until he joined them. Needless to say, it was not one of Aerosmith's finest performances.

Despite our common attraction to the thrill of the action, at this point, Joe and I were all but spent, and the prospect of returning to our respective homes was more than enticing. But we had one more commitment, for two days, at Stage West in Hartford, so we sucked it up and prepared for whatever could be even worse than our close call on the Cape. We were staying overnight in between shows – a luxury even when you were on the far richer arena circuit – so worse came to worst at least we knew that we could crash in a hotel instead of cat napping in a car or bus from two a.m. to whenever.

But at Stage West, nothing bad happened. In fact, the whole thing was quite enjoyable. The club was professional, had adequate power and a nice-sized stage, the owners were actually accommodating and polite, and as a bonus, the place was reasonably clean.

On the first evening, the band was sober and tight, the crowd was psyched, and everything just went the way it's supposed to. No incidents on any front and everyone went to bed happy. Then, better yet, on the second night, the stars aligned and it all came together to create magic, the kind of concert experience that I had remembered Aerosmith capable of when I was only a teenage fan, at times giving me the same goosebumps that popped from my pores way back when I had first seen the band as Black Sabbath's opener at The Garden.

At every show that I've ever worked, I've found my spot, a place where at least for a little while, I would be able to appreciate the performance. This night I posted myself towards the rear of the stage, not far from where Cyrinda, Brad's wife April, and Tom's Terry were watching the show together, three grown groupies grooving to their rock star studs. The band was in the zone, the energy was infectious, and the entire room was dancing and singing along with every song.

Mid-set, Aerosmith launched into "Train Kept A Rollin'," the blues-era classic that the band had adopted as their own on their second record, Get Your Wings, and it had become a big fan favorite. When the chorus came up, Steven spontaneously slid over towards the girls, and after belting out his own "Train kept a rollin..." he tipped his mic to the trio. Without missing a beat, the girls finished the phrase in unison with a rousing "All night long!" delivered with all the gusto of the kids who had slept at the doors in order to stake claim to their coveted front-row real estate. Throughout the song, Tyler repeated the gesture, each time with the same magical results. After all the shit we'd been through, it took only this moment to make it all worthwhile, and it was a welcome reminder of what had jazzed me about this whole crazy rock business in the first place.

A Day in the Life

AT A TYPICAL ROCK concert, the Production Manager does weeks of advance preparation and then manages the show on-site from start to finish, fulfilling not only critical technical requirements but also catering to the most outlandish of whims. It's a job that's flush with details, ripe with surprises and it requires the diplomacy to persuade band crews, venue personnel, stagehands, caterers and the performers themselves to play nice and work together as one big happy family. It rarely comes off without a hitch, but if you do your job well, the audience never knows what problems may have been overcome before the band ever hit the stage. That's an extremely difficult position to be in, particularly for a guy who can't yet grow a beard.

To set the scene for the several chapters involving big productions that follow, I should give you more color than Tyler's catastrophe in Maine or Brian's Pink Floyd recollection allowed. While the basics for running shows in arenas may be pretty much the same as in clubs and theatres, the big difference is that as a promoter, you take great economic risk while having control over very little. That, and the fact that everything is on a much grander scale, leaves little margin for error.

There is possibly nothing like standing alone in the center of an empty sports arena. The vastness of the coliseum's space envelops you, a solitary ant at the bottom of a massive concrete sinkhole. Rows upon rows of empty seats, their steel or plastic bottoms aligned like the shields of a Roman phalanx, rise precipitously from floor to ceiling. It's cold. And the absolute silence is antithetical to the chattering white noise of 15,000 or so fans that will be followed by the 120-plus decibels of three-chord rock that will be bouncing around the room twelve to fourteen hours later.

It's just 6 a.m. or so and you're the first to arrive, other than the people who work for the venue itself. You have to get there before the band buses and trucks do to make sure that everything is in order when they all roll in. Show-Sheets in hand to distribute to all important parties, you quickly make your rounds to say hellos to the stewards and chiefs in charge of the trades – the Teamsters, the stagehands, the electricians, the carpenters, the riggers and security, in addition to the folks who manage the venue – stopping long enough with each to be friendly but not so long as to be waylaid. You work with these people often enough to know their names, but not so frequently that you can chat them up on family matters. Just as well, because one of them just may screw with you tonight and you have to keep a professional distance.

The Show-Sheet is your bible for the day, a comprehensive who's who and what's what, a schedule, a guide to the venue, a synthesis of the artist contract that the promoter has signed his name to, all aggregated into a single document that spends its day rolled up in your back pocket, ever ready for reference or vindication that you've done it all correctly.

You make sure that the breakfast catering is set up and hot; a well-fed crew always gets the day off on the right foot and shows that you give a shit about everyone, not just the rock stars. They straggle in half-awake, many if not most sporting bedhead resembling abstract art, hungover from either late-night partying or more unintended sleep deprivation, having tossed and turned in their bunks with the bounce of the bus which drove several hundred miles overnight from the gig the day before. You make sure that catering has enough of a spread to feed the union crews, too. You're not obligated to, but it's in your best interests.

As soon as caffeine has been quaffed, the semi-drivers lumber in with the first of the tractor-trailer trucks and the show set-up begins. Depending upon the size of the production, four, six, eight, or even more 45-foot trucks of gear can be involved. They enter through the garage, maybe via a ramp, descending into the bowls of the building, as was the case at Nassau Coliseum. Or, maybe it's just a huge roll-up door facing a side street, where the white whales are forced to jockey to and fro in order to park their ass up to the opening and start spewing their diarrhea of equipment, as it was at Cumberland County Civic Center in Maine. As soon as the equipment comes off the truck, it is whisked towards the stage through the vomitory, another paean to the Cesarean empire's own entertainment facilities, a modern manifestation of the entrance through which gladiators and lions marched into the bay of their battles.

The first gear to be unloaded is always the lighting unless the band happens to be traveling with its own stage. Additional risers for drums, keyboards, backup singers, or other supporting players occasionally accompany the band gear, but typically the house stage sufficed and could be configured to almost any artist's touring plan, which is often meticulously laid out within the artist's performance contract.

As a subset of lighting, rigging is the first of the first to come off, ridiculously heavy cases of winches and chains that will ultimately hoist the PA sound and the lighting trusses halfway to the venue's ceiling. House riggers walk the beams as I did at the Calderone, though at twice the altitude, and carry with them ropes to lower to the floor for the winches' cable cinches and chains to be attached, which the riggers will then reel in to clamp around the steel under their feet. The winches are leaden, lozenge-shaped UFOs that suck in the thick chain on one end and shit it out the other into a catch bag as the steelwork is hoisted from the floor.

Next removed are the lighting trusses themselves. These lengthy horizontal honeycombs are extricated from their berths underneath the roof of the trailer by multiple sets of human arms raised overhead, guiding them hand over hand out of the trucks to the deck of the stage where they're assembled, usually into a rectangular cage to rise above and frame the band's playing area. Individual lamps are clamped to the trusses and thick snake cables are run, uncoiling foot after foot from their road case lairs. The headliner's backdrop – maybe just a huge logo, sometimes a screen for more sophisticated productions that involve a short film or projection synchronized with specific songs – is laced to the rear truss to be unfurled once the steel has been flown. Back in the day, no one carried the video screens that now bring even the most remote ticket-holders right onstage. The fans came to see the band live and in the flesh.

The PA System follows. Archaically still referred to by the acronym for *public address*, which was coined almost a century ago, this massive and explosive audio equipment bears little if any resemblance to its namesake. Tens, sometimes hundreds of black cabinets, are joined together to create walls of sound that arch top to bottom like a gymnast bending backwards and splay side to side in an effort to spray the arena with roaring riffs and decipherable vocals. Usually, everything is painted black, so it melts into the darkness at showtime and doesn't detract from what's happening onstage below.

The sound and lighting boards get set up about 200 feet out front on the floor behind a stockade of steel barricades that keeps the invading hoards out. Tweaking the knobs and faders of the massive consoles before them, the sound and lighting engineers are a bit like puppet masters, controlling much of the action onstage based upon complex cues and often extensively rehearsed choreography. Unfortunately, as virtually any music fan can attest, while the sound guy will try to optimize the acoustics everywhere in the arena from this singularly perfect position, he or she usually meets with little success.

As the PA is raised, the headliner's band gear comes out of the trucks and the actual stage set begins to take shape. Stacks of amps and speaker cabinets flank the centered drum kit two, sometimes three high to impress the crowd with a visual representation of earsplitting audio, but on occasion, the top row is lightened and neutered by the removal of their innards. Pianos are tuned and guitar pedals wired to allow a myriad of effects with the touch of a toe. The stage is set with monitors – traditionally wedge-shaped speaker cabinets aimed at the band so they can have some idea of what the audience is supposed to be hearing. Today's performers often opt to wear an earpiece, particularly singers.

Instead of music, the bangs and cranks of steel on steel and the thud of wooden road cases hitting the deck of the truck, the floor, or the stage and being unlatched is the soundtrack of the workday. No one even thinks to play tunes or whistle while they work. There is even little talk, though the occasional outburst echoes through the hall when someone has done something careless. With such a complicated erector set to assemble, anything is always liable to malfunction. But carelessness by a crewmember or stagehand can easily cost themselves or someone else a finger or worse.

For all except the unions – who have 30 minutes or a full hour off written into their contracts – lunch is less of a break than a drive-thru, no time to relax until the surety that everything is in its place and works the way it is supposed to. But with this second mention of unions, please allow me to sidetrack for a moment to indulge in a little tirade about *the trades*.

Labor unions were, and I imagine still are, a never-ending source of anxiety to everyone creatively involved in live entertainment, driving costs to the point of effectively restricting how long an act can perform. Ironically, the performers have their own unions, in the AFofM (American Federation of Musicians) and SAG-AFTRA (Screen Actors Guild-American Federation of Television and Radio Artists).

The Calderone was technically a non-union venue. Nonetheless, we hired the IATSE local instead of staffing the stage with far less costly student hands. We did so as much for insurance as for their production skills, which paid dividends when we worked the Coliseum. The fact that we were willing to pay their steward, who never once actually showed up for work at the theatre, no doubt solidified their friendship as well. Nassau was a union building, and the brotherhoods essentially controlled every movement. So it paid to have friends.

IATSE, The International Alliance of Theatrical Stage Employees, represents "technicians, artisans and craftspersons," though in my world, they mostly humped shit. The more talented among them also worked spotlights. IATSE's Teamster brethren were even less ambitious, generally responsible for nothing more than unloading trucks, and then only to the point of the rear bumper, unrelenting in their strict adherence to their contract's stipulations. I once had to pay an additional four men for eight hours, each, simply because one piece of band equipment couldn't be lifted eighteen inches to the truck's deck by the four teamsters already on call. Though we were compelled to pay for the four extra bodies, they, too, never appeared to work. The man in charge deigned to allow me, and one of the band's crew, to tread within the hallowed trailer to assist him and his guys. The entire endeavor took all of ten seconds.

Journey were one of few acts at the time to go on the road carrying their own custom-built stage, and each time they came to Providence, Rhode Island, work would come to a standstill before it ever started due to the inevitable dispute over who would erect the thing. The IATSE local insisted it was their job. The Carpenters' local insisted it was theirs. After a three to four-hour standoff where not a finger was allowed to be lifted by anyone, even civilians, the two stewards would oh-so-surprisingly come to the same conclusion: we, the promoters, should simply pay them both. One year the stagehands actually did the work. The next it was the carpenters. The bill, though, was always double.

Now back to the show.

On a good day, the lull presents itself around four or four-thirty. The early shift of the trades depart, their eight-hour day complete, generally after the unloading of the opening act who have learned that there is no point to arriving any earlier. The headliner's road crew hangs in anticipation of their paycheck's arrival for soundcheck about an hour later, finally popping open a beer or passing a joint to soothe their strained muscles and loosen up their brains with enough time to recoup before they have to get back to work.

Responsible headliners show up by about 5:30 or so, allowing themselves a good forty-five minutes to let the engineers try to equalize the hall and maybe rehearse a bit that's been sticky. In that case the opener is left with at least thirty minutes to get set up within whatever small footprint they've been allowed and they'll have the opportunity to at least run through the one minor hit that landed them on the tour in the first place.

For me, sound checks were the highlight of the day. While almost everyone but the engineers set off to the small humanity of a hot sit-down dinner, I'd make it a point to park myself about fifteen rows out, dead center, alone in my living room fit for fifteen thousand, the house lights full on and bright. I'd be treated to the headliner's hits multiple times – they had to be sure to get the money songs right – but it was also an opportunity to watch the creative side of the performance process first hand, particularly if it was early in the tour. Cues were still being confirmed. Recreating the recorded sounds of now-absent string sections or backing vocalists were being perfected to not disappoint with live renditions that appeared anything less than note-for-note. A solid setlist would be evolving, a secondary song which hasn't been delivering an adequate level of enthusiasm being replaced by another, less obscure fan favorite.

Satisfied that it's all as good as it's going to get, the musicians eventually retreat to their dressing rooms to relax and or limber up. Those that relax will generally indulge in their beverage of choice alongside a gluttonous spread that may never get touched until après encore. Those that limber are usually the drummers and the lead singers; a ninety to one hundred twenty-minute show will put the Steven Tylers and David Lee Roths of the business through as much physical stress as an NBA point guard that never sees the bench. And though it's tempting to follow "limber up" with "shoot up" for more poetic effect, in reality, it seemed that heroin was pretty much passé by the early '80s, the more energizing effects of cocaine making it the candy of choice during the era's scene.

Typically, arena dressing rooms are locker rooms. The only reason these fifteen to twenty-thousand-seaters were ever constructed in the first place was because of sports. NHL teams play 41 home games a year, as do pro basketball squads. Take all of your rock shows, throw in Ringling Brothers, Disney on Ice, some monster trucks here or there and all of those events may add up to only a small fraction of the dates that fill the hall from sports. The bottom line is that the overhead is paid by jocks, and the buildings that they perform in are designed to accommodate their home teams' needs and wants. So for rock bands, you try your best to dress up the locker room and make it look at least a little bit homey – a few sofas, a coffee table, end tables, an incandescent lamp or two to distract from the fluorescent overload and the equipment cubbies with their smell of sweat that has seeped into the surroundings. Some live plants are always a good idea to assist in clearing the air. Areca palms are perfect.

While you would assume that as a promoter, it would behoove you to be a good host, to make the best impression you can so the agents and artists learn to trust you, become loyal, and hire you to promote the band year after year when they return to your market, many promoters thought like Frank and cut corners in order to maximize the meager profit they were allowed. And so was born the concert *rider*, the part of the artist's performance agreement that lists everything they feel they need and must be provided in order to put on a proper show – from major technical requirements to transportation to catering – plus that infamous contractual list of incidentals and indulgences that needs to be delivered to the dressing room to satiate the bands' appetites and egos. The originality of their requests is often amusing, confusing, and sometimes considerably costly to fulfill, often necessitating a treasure hunt. They quite often involve alcohol.

Jorma Kaukonen, the extraordinary guitarist of The Jefferson Airplane and jam band Hot Tuna, chose 100-proof Smirnoff Vodka. I think that maybe he needed to be really lit in order to last through those legendary six-hour sets that he put me and countless fans through.

J. Geils, the Boston boogie band's namesake guitarist, always requested a bottle of 18% Thunderbird, a cheap white wine which, despite its lowbrow price, was extremely difficult to find. The 14% alcohol version was readily available and a staple of almost any local liquor store, but the more potent 18% strain was a rare thing. On the road, I'd have to search the seediest parts of whatever town we were in to procure J's screwtop poison. The upside of The Calderone being located in past-its-prime Hempstead was that Thunderbird 18 was fully stocked just down the block. I'd buy and store a case or two to keep on hand so I wouldn't be caught short. I have heard that once asked by an interviewer why, since the band had finally broken nationally with their first #1 hit "Centerfold" and he was now a bonafide rock star who could be drinking the world's finest wines, he instead requested a brown bagger. J. replied with shameless honesty to the effect of "I never want to forget where I came from...because I could be back there real soon."

Ted Nugent, on the other hand, insisted upon elusive vintages of Chateau Lafite Rothschild, maybe a hundred bucks a bottle even then. He also had a jones for an obscure root beer from his home state of Michigan, which I couldn't locate. I heard

While Ted Nugent's contract rider demanded decades-old vintages, Mr. J. Geils was a simple man.

that after continued frustration with promoters' lack of success in supplying the sweet suds, Ted eventually bought the soda company.

Sound checks over, the doors typically open at 7 p.m. for an eight o'clock show, giving the venue a good hour to profit from inflated concessions and the bands to sell exorbitantly overpriced T-shirts. As the PA begins blaring random background music, the crowd streams into the arena from all sides, racing to their seats underneath the brightness of the full-on houselights, either descending the steep steps towards the floor with enough dexterity not to tumble headfirst or ascending to the nosebleed sections by bounding the stairs two at a time, only slowing once they finally realize just how far from the stage their ticket is taking them.

Soon beach balls begin to bounce from row to row, primary-colored pie slices pinwheeling with each landing as the audience attempts to bat them higher and higher. A few stray Frisbees fly, careening around the room and bonking the inattentive in the back of the head. Joints are lit by the brave or foolish who are confident that here inside the venue, they are beyond the arms of the law. Many in the audience have already been primed. While pot is the overwhelming choice of Deadheads and the fans of jam bands, for metal music, it's beer. For Southern Rock, it's harder stuff, bourbon and sweet Southern Comfort. The hall quickly becomes one big party in anticipation of the evening's entertainment.

The IATSE show call being 7:30 to 11:00 p.m., at which threshold the crew goes to time-and-a-half or even double-time pay, the opener is off the stage by about 8:45, so the headliner can hit it at nine or nine-fifteen. That allows the stars at least ninety minutes to do their thing, including the inevitable encores brought on by the mass ignition of cigarette lighters. (Another victim of modern technology, lighters have been coldly replaced by the flashlight app on smartphones). The main spotlight operators take their place at the back of the hall, seemingly a mile from their targets, and those manning the smaller stage spots scramble up rope ladders like sailors to their crows' nest, perching themselves at the corners of the lighting trusses.

Suddenly the hall goes dark and the crowd roars...

Since it's only the opening act, the enthusiasm dissipates rather quickly, unless the audience is really lit or the band is actually a draw in their own right. More often than not, it's a baby band, a new act that the headliner's booking agency takes the opportunity to expose to the tour's huge audience in the hopes that enough people will pay attention to build the act some buzz. By this time, the eclecticism of the festivals of the sixties and of FM radio in the early seventies was already fading, and rock began splintering into buckets of specific tastes. Audiences began to expect the opener to adhere to the headliner's genre; there was no point in booking The Ramones in front of Fleetwood Mac. But all too often, that's exactly what happened, due to either someone's lack of common sense or maybe a perverse sense of humor. Plenty of great young singer-songwriters had to perform to hostile audiences precisely because of that kind of incongruity, attempting to be heard above boisterous boos while not losing faith in their own talent and mission. The most committed of them would play to the one person in the audience who got it, happy to have won over even a single new convert.

The opener leaves the stage, never seeing flame beckoning for an encore. Even if they did, there is no time. The band crews scurry out to do the set change, the opener's gear literally thrown in the garage to be dismantled and repacked to set off to tomorrow's gig. The black sheets that have covered the headliner's stacks are now drawn away and the audience begins to get some idea of the aesthetic of the show to come, be it spartanly spare or a bombastically cluttered stage. Details are attended to, connections are confirmed and blocking is taped fresh or repaired. With a good fifteen minutes to spare, all is ready, and the PA now primes the audience with tunes that the more creative artists have specifically chosen, though, on occasion, it's nothing more thought-through than a crew member's personal mixtape.

Suddenly the lights go out again, and the crowd roars…

I'll usually accompany the Road Manager as he escorts the band to the stage, he and I illuminating the way from the vomitory to the stage and then up the half dozen steps from the concrete to the deck with our Maglites. We want no artist injuries before the show even begins. I'll return to the stage when they're about to finish, but once they're up, I back off and disappear to make my rounds of the arena.

Perhaps the intro involves controlled feedback. Maybe a disembodied voice recites a poem or parable. Often the band appears one at a time, each virtuoso taking their turn to assemble for the full-on rush of the delivery of the evening's first hit or the opening cut from their latest record release. In any case, the audience is on its feet and in ecstasy and stays that way through the first three or four songs until the band decides to slow the pace with something softer and more cerebral or heartfelt, and the fans settle down. A good setlist has been agonized over to get it just right, to take the fans on an emotional roller coaster with never a chance to descend into boredom, ideally leaving the crowd wanting more once the house lights have been turned back on.

For me, it's time to cruise. I wander throughout the front of the house, viewing the performance from all vantage points, in my head critiquing the sound mix from each position, maybe standing still at some point to actually watch the band perform one of my own personal favorites if they are in fact an act that I'm fond of. I'll check out the show from the pit for a few moments, just long enough to get an in-my-face view of what's happening on stage but not long enough to incur damage to my eardrums. I never ever wear earplugs. I make my rounds for almost the first full hour before heading towards the administrative offices to check on Pam.

Pam rarely sees any of the show. She generally arrives around 6 p.m. to check on sales at the box office, submit a final guest list and grab a bite of dinner with me. After the band takes the stage, her real work begins as she prepares the night's settlements. Coming in, she has already accounted for all of the promoter expenses, minus any incidentals that were paid for with my day's petty cash. Once the box office closes, she first settles with the venue; their rent or participation as a percentage of the gross, plus any reimbursements for outlays not included in the contract, come right off of the top. Once in agreement and with those figures in hand, she moves on to settle with the Road Manager, sometimes the artist's Personal Manager if the gig has been important enough for him/her to show up. Most of the time, it's all pretty routine, but on occasion, it can get contentious if gray areas develop.

I'll head to the side of the stage, talk with the techs to make sure the show is going well from their perspective, then to the dressing rooms to check on the catering, get any messes cleaned up that were left behind and make sure that whatever else is supposed to be there is there when the band comes off – often that's when they eat their dinner if they intend to stick around long enough to unwind or do a few meet and greets.

After the encores, the legendary load-out begins. The instant the house lights go up, the band, lighting and PA crews scurry again to the stage, this time to break it down. Everything has to go out the door in the exact reverse order that it came in.

Once again, the coffee flows. The entire process takes about three hours – considerably less than it took to set up – and the rigging guys are the last to leave, though they'll be the first to unload tomorrow when they'll do it all over again in another venue in another state, or maybe even in another time zone.

Pam's left to go home if we're local, to the hotel if we're in Maine, Providence, Syracuse or some other foreign market where Freefall has been awarded the show. Maybe she and Mark will stop for drinks with the band's manager or go off to the suite of one of the band's entourage to socialize. I remain at the venue for the duration, not to leave until the last truck has rolled out the door.

The end of the evening is always a bit melancholy for me. Though both physically and psychologically spent, I'm nonetheless sad to let it go. Like the lead singers that pass through, I've become a junkie of the adrenaline high that comes with making thousands of people happy by having thrown a great party, sending them home with their own priceless memories. But now it's time to come down.

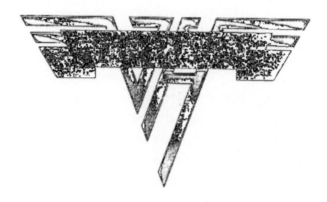

RE: VAN HALEN

Dear Purchaser:

Attached is a rider containing provisions to assure you of a smooth
and professional theatrical presentation. All provisions are spelled
out in great detail in order to prevent any misunderstandings and
to present to your customers the finest in contemporary entertainment.

Any immediate questions can be answered by calling Van Halen
Productions at ████████████.

All provisions must be adhered to strictly. Please feel free to
contact us at any time should there be any questions.

Looking forward to a successful show.

Sincerely,

Harvey Schaps/Tour Manager
Patrick Whitley/Production Manager

12

Bustin' Balls About Brown M&Ms

CONCURRENT WITH AEROSMITH'S APOCALYPSE was the ascension of Van Halen, picking up the Massachusetts-bred band's slack – not the Stones connection, per se, but as America's biggest, baddest rock & roll band, complete with their own version of a winged logo, this one setting flight from L.A.'s Sunset Strip instead of the suburbs of Boston.

As it happens with many young rock bands, especially harder rock bands, Van Halen is said to have come together through the networking of local players, attending each others' gigs with an eye to replacing their own weak links. Obviously, guitarist extraordinaire Eddie and Alex on drums were kin, but supposedly bassist Michael Anthony was the winner of an all-night audition, and that the brothers found it cheaper to hire frontman David Lee Roth than to continue to rent his PA system.

When we put our July 1980 show with Van Halen at Nassau Coliseum on sale, no one was at all aware of the level of popularity that these guys had achieved. In March of 1978, little more than two years prior, Freefall had hosted Van Halen as the first up on a three-act bill at The Calderone, opening for the late Ronnie Montrose's band and the still relatively unknown – at least on the East Coast – headliner, Journey. Even with all of that talent appearing on the same stage, the evening failed to sell out. So despite Van Halen's second album being as critically acclaimed and commercially successful as their first, we were still skeptical about them trying to fill Nassau Coliseum's 16,000 seats in support of their third, *Women and Children First*. We couldn't help thinking that we were setting ourselves up for a losing proposition, maybe it being a bit too early to be taking a big chance on booking the band into such a large venue. But the agents at Premier Talent were adamant, and they were right. To our amazement, the show sold out in less than three hours.

An early version of the excessive productions that came to represent the pinnacle of the '80s hair band heyday, this was to be the first of Van Halen's annual record-setting headlining tours, each successive outing bigger and laden with more hardware and wattage than the one before it. And along with this new level of spectacle suspended from the ceiling came a higher level of professionalism on the floor.

The band's manager, Noel Monk, may not have been a Leber-Krebs protégé, but he was cut from that same cloth, recognizing that rock and roll had left the realms of tie-dye and entered the new era of suit and tie. Noel meant business; he left no invoice unturned to get to the true net profit of a show so that Van Halen got the most of their 90/10 split, and when it came to marketing their image, he realized that what most of the world would see as excess the kids would see as cool. They realized that paying for destruction of hotel suites and dressing rooms was actually an investment in their brand and that it wouldn't be long until they would be able to afford to do it just for fun.

Despite ensuing years of their own Aerosmith-worthy dysfunction, it appears that Noel's early lessons in economics served the band's long-term finances well, each member remaining flush (at least publicly) throughout their periods of breakup. Ever the philosopher clown, David Lee Roth was recently quoted in Forbes stating that "Money can't buy you happiness…but it can buy you a yacht big enough to pull right up alongside it."

The Van Halen tour's Nazi-finance zeitgeist was matched only by its state-of-the-art and over-the-top production values, inspired sound and lighting effects conjured up by Pete Angelus, the first and only official tour Production *Director* I ever encountered. Pete's effects supported the young stars on an entirely new level for live rock performances. And screwing it all together for 100 or so gigs each tour was a top-of-the-line crew.

The Van Halen team was a regimented organization, a sharp contrast to the loose, seat-of-the-pants sidekicks that most bands had carried from the sixties into the seventies and which was still much in evidence in the early eighties with Aerosmith's bunch the poster children. I was taken aback when they descended upon us like Star Wars stormtroopers, commanding immediate control of every aspect of the event and doing virtually whatever they wanted, when they wanted, house rules be damned. As I said, that's not the normal situation in a union arena like Nassau Coliseum. Typically, you have to beg and then bargain to get anything to actually happen in a timely fashion, overtime pay funding union downtime at a retreat in Vegas. That day, though, I think the Locals were in awe of the Van Halen crew's confidence and efficiency, and even they thought better of flexing their muscle.

The captain of this team of uber-roadies? A young Scotsman named Patrick Whitley.

Not much older than I, Patrick (never "Pat") was a true professional – a rarity in the business. Completely in command from the moment he set foot in the arena, he effortlessly received respect, not least of all because he seemed able to keep his cool under almost any circumstance, regardless of how crazy things could get. Tall and trim, a youthfully freckled strawberry-blond, Patrick was almost exclusively extremely serious. On the long days of touring, there are constantly moments to try any man's patience, but Patrick had a maturity that many older veterans of the road often lacked; he faced the unexpected with poise and competence.

Patrick and I were of like mind and attitude – both moderately obsessive-compulsive – and so we formed a unique esprit de corps, which made life easier for both of us. When you're stuck working intimately with someone for the better part of 20 hours straight in an effort to leave twenty thousand people speechless, if one of you is off your game or worse yet, one of you is an asshole, you can develop a mutual loathing, spending the day counting the minutes until the whole ordeal is over. And so that day proceeded perfectly, the production's precision everything that the band and its management demanded. Refreshed by each other's work ethic, pride and commitment to detail, by the end of the engagement, we parted as newfound friends.

The band, on the other hand, was a young act in love with themselves, and ringleader Roth was the quintessential narcissistic lead singer, in that way not unlike Mr. Tyler. (Classic rock riddle: How many lead singers does it take to screw in a light bulb? One. He holds the bulb and world revolves around him.)

David Lee also relished living up to his growing reputation as being every bit the able horn dog. Still in his late-twenties, Roth's stage attire consisted of a bare chest atop painted-on leather, satin or the occasional cheekless chaps, going commando for the world to bear witness to his manhood. Whether the phallic bulge was real or a ripe cucumber, only the lucky ladies could say for sure. But David knew he had the world by the balls and he strutted his stuff to make sure that we all knew it, too, offstage as well as on.

In fact, David seemed to never be offstage.

While heading across the cavernous garage for the big black stretch that was to whisk him to his hotel following the final encore, he passed by Pam and without breaking stride, he scooped her up and twirled her around, letting out one of his patented good ol' boy hollers, loudly and lasciviously, which was magnified by the vastness of the space.

"Whoooooooweeeee! Now *that*, my boys, should be on the rider!"

Ah, yes, the rider, the now infamous Van Halen rider.

I've given you a taste for the craziness that concert contract riders had become, containing not just the items actually necessary to deliver a proper performance but also the eccentric demands added to test the willingness of promoters to indulge artist egos. Van Halen, it seemed, was so enjoying their status as rock's newest prima donnas that they were intent on setting the bar and then taking it higher for outrageous requests.

This, their breakout tour, memorialized them as "the band that made you remove all of the brown M&Ms." I, of course, complied – a contract is a contract, right? But, as insane as the directive seemed, and legal commitment aside, the request was easy enough to fulfill, and apparently, getting it done was one of the small details that cemented us on their list of preferred promoters. It turns out that it wasn't about ego or ballbusting at all. It came down to an extremely logical rationale: If we, the promoters, were attentive enough to follow through on such a seemingly insignificant detail, chances were that we'd get all of the big things right. And to stage a successful Van Halen show, everything had to work, and it had to work perfectly.

The band became ever more creative as their popularity and power multiplied. On the next tour, in the spring of 1981 to flog *Fair Warning*, we produced their second US tour date in Portland, Maine, and upon receiving the contract, it was evident that they were taking their mischief up a notch. One of the first items on the catering list was "one platter of Coney Island Whitefish." At warm-ups in Nova Scotia and New Brunswick, Canada, I was told that the Canadian promoters apparently didn't know what to make of it and had just completely ignored the request. In Providence, where New England's Brooks Brothers-styled Don Law was the dominant promoter, I was told that a deboned fillet was offered up to the new rock gods.

But being a New York native, I was quite aware that Coney Island whitefish are, in actuality, not fish at all. The term is Brooklyn borough slang for used condoms found on the beach, left behind from sandy, late-night assignations, usually under the hardwood cover of the boardwalk. With that knowledge, I gave the showrunner fifty bucks of my petty cash and sent him to the nearest Walgreens to purchase the most colorful assortment of prophylactics he could assemble, which we then artfully displayed as if they were petit fours on a Viennese table. For added effect, I had the kid visit the bakery to buy a cheesecake, placing it side by side with the condoms as my own inside joke to see if the band and crew were as clever and savvy as they thought themselves to be. I never found out, though, because the "white fish" disappeared before the band ever arrived, the crew each grabbing a handful in the hopes of product testing after the show. But the news that we "got it" trickled up to the band and their management, and we once again won credibility and kudos.

That night in Portland, as Patrick and I stood together to watch the last of a half dozen tractor trailers be loaded, locked and driven to the next city, we said our goodbyes until we would meet again when Van Halen were to visit us back home on Long Island in July. Patrick floated the idea of my someday working directly for Van Halen, acting as an advance man scouting the scheduled performance venues for him in order to head off any possible production problems. I said I was flattered and that I would think about it, though I never seriously did. I still had no real idea of what I wanted to do with my life, but I knew that it didn't involve living on the road for six months at a stretch, especially not with these unpredictably crazy characters.

By the time Van Halen's *Diver Down* arrived, they were arguably the hottest rock band not just in America but in the world. Premier Talent now awarded Freefall the mid-tour, three-day stand at Cobo Arena in downtown Detroit on August 13, 14 and 15, 1982. It was a market and facility we had never worked before, but we obviously welcomed the opportunity. Apparently, the local promoter had gotten himself in legal hot water with an array of charges and at the moment, he was an untouchable, so the band was giving us the dates that would have been his as a "Thank you" for all of our hard work, and for our faith in Van Halen's ability to sell ever-more tickets.

This was possibly the largest rock concert production ever taken out on the road up until then, an estimated 1.4 million watts of lighting, 10,000 watts of sound and 170 tons of equipment overall. But there was even more significance added to this particular run by the fact that *Life* Magazine was covering the Cobo shows for a photo spread that would appear in their November issue, under the title of "Rock's Rowdiest Rogues Go on Tour." And so Van Halen was going to make sure that they more than lived up to their already larger-than-life reputation for outrageousness. They had set the tone months before, when the itinerary was being booked, wryly alluding to their uncontrollable libidos by christening this outing as *The Hide Your Sheep Tour*.

I had never taken up Patrick on his offer, as much as it extended an incredibly exciting opportunity. But appreciative of his obsession with avoiding surprises, I arrived in Detroit two days early. The first was to get settled and to meet with the band's security director, Ed Anderson, the next to actually manage the load in and stage set up, this go-round being simply monstrous and more complicated than ever before. Having a day ahead of the first show to set up was an uncommon and welcome luxury, but I should have known from the moment I walked into Ed's hotel room that I was going to pay for it.

After first connecting with Ed via phone to get his room number, I bounded upstairs to his floor above and strolled down the quiet hall, ready to get the ball rolling. I knocked on his door and instantly heard the pitter-patter of small feet in response. The knob turned from the inside, and the door opened. I was greeted with a friendly chorus of "Come on in!" but no one to attach it to until I glanced down to see the smiling faces of two welcoming little people, Ed in the background unpacking his bags. "Say hello to Tweedledum and Tweedledee!" Ed shouted. In unison, the duo thrust their hands towards me in greeting to my puzzled expression. I was told the dwarves were there to serve as David Lee's bodyguards for this weekend in photo-op heaven.

The setup day should have been a leisurely, stress-free affair without deadline pressure, but no such luck. Nothing went right from the moment I entered the hall; it was as if I had never done the advance work that I had labored over for weeks and weeks before. The band crew was late and they were testy, despite a rare day of rest. The building staff and Locals seemed unaware of what was required despite my numerous discussions with the venue covering every detail. The catering appeared even later than the crew, and when it finally showed, the coffee was cold and the juice was warm. Everyone in Detroit connected to our shows seemed

Van Halen's sense of humor knew no bounds.

Munchies

    Potato chips with assorted dips
    Nuts
    Pretzels
    M & M's (WARNING: ABSOLUTELY NO BROWN ONES)
    Twelve (12) Reese's peanut butter cups
    Twelve (12) assorted Dannon yogurt (on ice)

intent on being thoroughly uncooperative. The concert business being the cutthroat enterprise that it was, my best guess is that we had been set up to fail, likely by the pariah promoter we had replaced. I guess he held the position that we, the out-of-towners, had stolen these shows from him, and so he had put the word out to fuck Freefall and the band, who would then ultimately blame us. His plan worked like a charm. The Van Halen people quickly became frustrated, and even Patrick showed me little sympathy.

While the 12th proved to be as unlucky as one would expect the 13th to be, we did manage to get through the load-in and set-up, though barely. But when I arrived back at Cobo the next morning, I discovered that I had been relieved of most of my normal duties and relegated to taking charge of finding acceptable strippers for the first evening's backstage party. This enviable task took the better part of the day as "acceptable" was the operative word, and it turned out that none of Detroit's exotic dancers were considered to be top-shelf. We had tapped the building staff to contact the local blue establishments for prospects who were willing to awake mid-morning and make their way to Cobo's load-in door to be interviewed. Some were summarily dismissed. Others were made to audition, gyrating right there on the ramp, flashing a bit of T&A while the crews voted on the talent's assets and abilities. I thought that several of the ladies would do just fine, but for a variety of reasons, Ed still found them to be lacking. Finally, three young women were selected for the gig that would likely be the highlight of their careers.

Once offstage, David Lee and the rest of the boys were ready to show *Life*'s cameras and readers just how crazy their world could be. The dressing room was transformed into an impromptu strip club, every bit as debauched as the band's haunts at home on Sunset, complete with blinding strobe lights, pounding power pop and limitless alcohol overflowing as the girls did their thing for a packed room of friends, crew, posers and press. The lenses from *Life* were licking it up.

By the second show, things had settled down to a dull misery for me. I had been stripped of authority and was now little more than a spectator with an All-Access Pass. The first highlight of the circus that night was the dessert. We were told that it was Ed's birthday, and so Pam located a Trojan cake big enough to hide the enormously endowed dancer who popped out and performed as part of the package. With cellophane-thin flesh-toned tights but a no-hands-allowed contract, the boys got riled and worked up with no outlet for their enthusiasm. Real cake flew, and all egged on Ed to woo the young lady that was the Trojan's filling, David Lee and I two of the loudest cheerleaders.

The party quickly moved to the Renaissance Center hotel so both band and crew could partake in more fleshed-out festivities. We were also staying at the Center, and at Ed and Patrick's invitation, Pam and I decided to pass by Van Halen's floor. The scene was not as raucous as backstage at Cobo the evening prior, nor as spontaneous as at Ed's party ending just an hour before, but it no less reeked of booze and sleaze. Here, everything could, and eventually did, move behind closed doors.

As the elevator peeled open, we were greeted by a spectrum of legs – form-fitting spandex or denim or unabashedly bare – punctuated by sparkling stilettos and calf-accentuating wedges. The walls of the halls were lined with scores of prone young women dressed their best to display their assets, presumably with the hope of spending some quality time with Eddie, Alex, Michael Anthony or David Lee, himself; drinking, smoking, getting high and reliving the band's glories from earlier that evening, the mood was convivial and the crowd quite content to wait their turn for a possible private performance of their own, as periodically a band member's door would open and one or another of this happy harem would be summoned inside. Realizing that there was nothing going on here that we wanted to be part of, we pushed the Down button and called it a night.

On the 14th, all hell broke loose.

The band was intent on giving *Life* everything they came for, wanting the photographers to capture the pinnacle of the rock and roll lifestyle, the "Rogues" going wild. That meant a carefully orchestrated, full-scale trashing of the dressing room. Minutes before they were to hit the stage, the food began to fly. Cold cuts, coffee and crudités, and even the bowl of brown-free M&Ms were used to decorate the walls, floors and ceiling. Eddie's brother Alex took the show outside, playing a crazed ninja with a Samurai sword, bisecting six-packs of soda and beer in the arena's halls, spraying the place with explosions of sugary suds and foam. For me, it was the straw that broke the camel's back.

Seeing my utter disgust, Patrick knelt to pick up the broken pieces of a dish, looked my way soulfully and tried to cajole me into helping. "Come on mate...lend me a hand, won't you?" To him, I guess, it was all in a day's work. To me, it was the final humiliation of this lost weekend in Motor City. As I knelt down to help my friend, I looked him in the eye and sighed.

"I'm sure glad I never signed on to this madness full time."

In the months that followed, I filled in to help Mark and Pam with one last Aerosmith gig and a few more Ramones shows, but this run had put an end to my infatuation with rock on the road. I had had enough of catering to the ever-bigger egos of far too many not-so-nice people. Patrick? From what I can see, he still lives this crazy life, and he must have developed an affection for the less stable performers. He appears to have become quite the go-to guy for mega-productions supporting the likes of Guns N' Roses,

Kiss, Mötley Crüe and other high-octane hard rock and metal bands, each with their own unique craziness. But for me, these unbearable four days had felt like a life sentence. It did, though, have its redeeming moments. Well, at least two of them.

On that final evening, I got to enjoy a laugh at Eddie's expense, which is ironic, because at the time he was actually the most normal and nice of these four sophomoric psychos. While looking for Pam amongst the arena's administrative offices, segregated from the backstage goings-on, I stumbled upon Eddie on the phone in tense conversation with his sitcom wife, Valerie Bertinelli. Eddie was pleading with her to "give me a break, baby..." for what seemed a typical husbandly indiscretion or oversight, probably something as mundane as "Why haven't you called me all day?" As much as I felt empathetic towards the guy, it was also somewhat gratifying to see the newly anointed guitar god, the heir to Hendrix, groveling at the long-distance feet of his young bride. There is a certain vindication in knowing that at the end of the day, all guys are subjected to the same kind of relationship shit, no matter how rich, how adored, or how critically acclaimed. As it seems that almost all Hollywood romances sooner or later come to an end, so did theirs, but Eddie and Valerie made it all the way to 2007.

And despite my desperation for it all to end, Van Halen provided another one of those magical musical memories, just like the Aerowives had in Hartford. Midway through the second evening's set, I stole myself away from the backstage bullshit and wandered out front for a minute to actually watch. I climbed atop a forklift parked just off stage left, Eddie's side of the stage. I sat on its roof, powwow style, and leaned back to take it all in, finding some peace in their earsplitting assault.

A darkened stage came alive with Alex's pounding pedals and flailing sticks, quickly giving way to the unmistakable opening notes of "Little Guitars." A sole spotlight picked up Eddie, shirtless under Pollack-inspired overalls, picking at a ukulele-sized version of a caramel-colored, burled wood Les Paul, and the band took off. David Lee appeared and, with his infinite energy, shook, shimmied and karate-kicked his way to driving the jailbait wild, once again in revealing spandex. Even staid bassist Michael Anthony got into the head, the usually more-sedentary support player bopping as he banged out the rhythm. Each struck their finest rock star poses, and the spectacle ended with Eddie's riffing stopping on a dime as the hall simultaneously plunged back into darkness. It was all over in less than five minutes, and even I gave them a standing ovation.

Forging A Metal Masterpiece

Watching AC/DC open the Grammy Awards 35 years after I met them was more déjà vu than Memory Lane. Brian Johnson's vocal cords displayed no less power and his pitch remained perfect (at least to my ears) as he growled his way through his predecessor Bon Scott's signature "Highway to Hell." His hobbit-like frame still stood firmly in command of center stage, the same black tee and denim form-fitting his now sixty-plus frame, the same black work boots and Andy Capp cap serving as vertical bookends. Angus Young refused to hang up his English schoolboy outfit despite his increasingly crinkly kneecaps, and he duck-walked with all the energy of the bouncy Chuck Berry imitator that I led onstage with my

Maglite back in 1980. Ripping through power cords, Angus gripped tight to his high-slung Gibson SG just as he had in the months before the world would wake up to Back in Black, the exquisite Aussie metal masterpiece that had just been released and would go on to be one of the biggest-selling records of all time.

As much as Freefall was lucky enough on more than one occasion to be at the right time and the right place with breaking artists – Van Halen's rapid rise from third-string at The Calderone to arenas across the U.S. a perfect case in point – we were just as often a little bit too early. Mark had presented AC/DC at The Calderone some months before I arrived on the scene, in what turned out to be one of lead singer Bon Scott's final live appearances before he died alone on a roadside in a friend's Renault, presumably a casualty of one-too-many nights of over-the-top partying that was ruled by the coroner as "death by misadventure."

Few groups are able to move past the death of a lead singer, particularly one with as distinct a personality as Scott had. But the survivors quickly recruited British bar band frontman Johnson and headed into the studio to write and record *Back in Black,* and that summer, they began their tour to support it. Just as Premier had insisted with Van Halen, AC/DC's booking agency, ATI, was confident that Back in Black would launch the band to new heights in the U.S. So instead of allowing us to make the safe bet and book them to now headline The Calderone, whose 2,435 seats we were sure could be an instant sellout, the agency instead insisted they play for us at Nassau Coliseum, a leap to 16,500. As great as the record sounded, we felt it was too soon. Unfortunately, this time we were right. By the day of the show, we had sold not even 5,000 tickets, and we had no share of the concession revenues to fall back on.

Despite the soft sales, AC/DC arrived with their army of crews and equipment, rolling down the ramp into the Coliseum's garage as day broke on the morning of the show. One by one, each truck carefully backed into the vomitory to be unloaded. I quickly realized that The Calderone could not have supported this new spectacle; the always high-wattage band had stepped up their game considerably. Countless cases were ramped to the floor, along with gargantuan sound and lighting rigs, amps upon amps, and The Bell.

AC/DC's new set piece, Hell's Bell, was British-forged bronze and easily weighing a ton or more. Hidden from our view as it nestled in its huge custom road case, we assumed The Bell to be just another benign prop until it quickly became evident that it could crush any one of us in an instant. Four Teamsters together managed to dislodge it from its designated packing position within the Jenga-stacked semi, and at least as many stagehands had to gather on all sides to guide its wheels down the ramp, slowing the cube's descent until it reached the industrial gray concrete floor. I followed as they towed it towards the front of the stage, the ramp at the rear too steep to push it up.

We called in the forklift to provide the necessary muscle to actually get the thing onstage. With sputters and whirs, the driver positioned his prongs dead center under The Bell's case. He pulled back the black ball-headed lever and with a groan, the fork lifted The Bell, raising it about a foot above the stage as all present crossed their fingers and held their breath that the machine and its operator wouldn't topple face forward. The lift gently lowered the case to the deck, drew back its forks and there The Bell sat to the relief of all. Until the case promptly dropped, its castors cracking through the stage in unison as it came to rest flush and immovable. Its massive weight concentrated on its narrow wheels was apparently too much for the Coliseum's stock staging.

As well planned as every detail generally is with a show of this size, this surprise put all but the AC/DC crew in a panic. Its castors wedged in the deck, its mass unable to be tipped it was impossible to reinsert the forks, the only way the Locals thought it was ever going to be moved again. Minds great and small gathered around, alternating between brainstorm and hopelessness, but now almost three months and several dozen dates into the tour the roadies had apparently seen it all before, and they knew that the solution was really quite simple.

With little fanfare, the case was unclipped and lifted from its base to reveal The Bell in all of its bronze glory. Forged by John Taylor & Co. Bellfounders, this bell was in fact, one and the same as that heard on "Back In Black." A scaled replica of Taylor's Dennison Bell in the company's hometown of Loughborough, the AC/DC bell's toll was supposedly recorded and subsequently reduced to half speed by the record's engineer in order to achieve the more dirge-like sound heard on the album.

As we stood by, a heavy gauge cable was lowered from the ceiling and clipped to The Bell's cannon. When the winch reversed, the cable pulled taught, and The Bell tilted to its rear. As it cleared free of the case, the bronze swung gently to and fro, finally settling enough to allow the crew to guide it as it was slowly hoisted to its place of honor high above, ready to toll for the band's opening of "Hell's Bells." The punctured stage was replaced, avoiding any unfortunate missteps or possible misadventures by Brian while he belted out AC/DC's new signature song and the band's older, equally rousing anthems.

Showtime came around and I headed to the arena locker rooms to help escort the band. Leading the charge were a slight, boyish Angus, still youthful enough to carry off his Ashfield Boys High uniform, and barrel-chested Brian, the recipient of Bon Scott's torch, both bursting at the seams with bravado. Though we

Conflicting sources stated the bell's weight anywhere between 1,000 and 2,000 pounds, but the road case settles it: 1300 kilograms equals 2,866 pounds!

braced ourselves to lose a mild fortune, we knew we were about to witness something big, something destined to become the defining tribute to those classic *Spinal Tap* clichés-to-come of sex, drugs and rock and roll. And it all broke loose with The Infamous Bell, whose great weight sent it sinking straight through the stage, launching AC/DC to sales of over 200,000,000 records. *Back in Black* alone accounts for more than a quarter of them. Not bad for a band born on the border of the outback.

I was able to track down the British maker of the road case for The Bell, who added even more color to the *Hells Bells* legend.

"I went over to measure up a couple of times for the flight case when it was in this state [as seen in the foundry photo] before the inside was spun and tuned, and then we collected it when it was finished. As I recall, it weighed in at around 1100kgs. This original bell was only used for the *Back in Black* tour…and then a fiberglass copy was made…[The original bell] was so heavy [that] when Brian hit it, it didn't swing, and you could not hit it hard enough to get a sound out of it…[But] when we had it at the factory to finish the flight case we would hit it with the forklift… to sound lunchtime!"

Ain't Nothin' Like the Real Thing

THE BEST CLASSIC ROCK, particularly when played live, was and still is defined by the rare combinations of talents and temperaments that work alchemy to create unforgettable music that becomes iconic, historic and evergreen. When one or more of the band's beloved lineup departs to seek their own individual stardom, the magic is lost. Almost always, at least as far as the audience is concerned, the main ingredient is the lead singer. Conversely, more often than not, The Voice can't achieve the same level of success when it goes solo.

Sammy Hagar may have shocked the world when he actually made Van Halen 2.0 work for a while, but it was really an entirely different deal. Today the only band almost everyone wants to see has David Lee Roth at the microphone.

Journey have just never been the same without Steve Perry. Guitarist Neal Schon and crew drafted a close facsimile and carried on, selling out summer stints in amphitheaters, especially when they became a nostalgia act. But if Perry ever decides to come out of retirement I think the band would probably ditch their innocuous sound-alike and book themselves into stadiums.

Death is a different story; a band's afterlife without its singer can be acceptable, though it's usually decidedly different. Brian Johnson was a more marketable frontman than Bon Scott, and with him, AC/DC immediately released a mega-selling masterpiece that has allowed the band to have legs for decades. When Brian finally had to bow out at the last minute because his ears were shot, it took the likes of Axl Rose to save the day, on leave from his own platinum-plated reunion with Slash and Duff after the three of them floundered without each other for almost twenty-five years. The Grateful Dead may have died with Jerry Garcia in 1995 (admit it, Jerry was not just the lead guitarist; he was also the lead singer, at least to those of us who weren't true Dead Heads), but his fellow trippers went on as they splintered and regrouped into numerous different configurations, each playing to far smaller crowds even though continuing to make tons of money due to their fans' Deadication. The Doors, though, truly died with Jim Morrison.

Along with introducing me to Tull, my brother had also turned me on to Yes. Though both are now considered purveyors of "art rock" or "prog rock," the two bands couldn't have been more different. Tull's Ian Anderson painted pictures of cynical intellectualism with a mastery of metaphor and set them to either updated blues beats or Old English folk. Yes' Jon Anderson penned ethereal, incomprehensible verbal landscapes set against his symphonic band's lushly layered electronic arrangements.

Despite the disparate approaches to their art, I loved my Andersons almost equally. But both singers took divergent paths once they peaked in their artistry and sales. Ian knew that he was the Star but remained insecure enough to still need his band's moniker, so he just replaced his supporting players one by one, on and on, eventually keeping the brand for himself. To this day, many casual fans still think that he, personally, is the "Jethro" in Jethro Tull. I guess that Jon did not have that same luxury or hutzpah. In 1980 Jon quit Yes rather abruptly, along with keyboardist Rick Wakeman, and he left a vacuum at the mic stand with disastrous and lasting results for both the band and himself.

At my virgin Yes event, I was treated to a start-to-finish performance of the four album-side suites of *Tales From Topographic Oceans*, prededed by the entirety of the immensely melodic *Close to the Edge* capped by encores of their early, more traditional singles-length "Roundabout," and "Yours is No Disgrace". I was so enthralled that to this day I remember every song, though that could be because there were only nine of them. Call me a geek if you'd like, but I greatly admired their musicianship and melodies. They also happened to provide a wonderful setting for being stoned. Delta T and I subsequently saw Yes again at Nassau in 1976 and once more in '78 at The Garden as they pushed *Tormato* to less than enthusiastic critical and commercial success. If the band themselves considered "Don't Kill the Whale" to be the strongest effort to designate as their new record's single, we knew that they were in trouble, but we hung in there hoping that they would turn things around. They didn't.

Fast-forward four years and I'm once again working with one of my all-time favorite bands, or at least 3/5 of them. *Tormato*'s album and tour had been the last hurrah for Yes' classic lineup of Anderson, guitarist Steve Howe, bassist Chris Squire, drummer Alan White and Wakeman. Though *Tormato* fast went platinum, its sales just as quickly stalled. While Anderson and Wakeman walked, setting out to seek new inspiration, the remaining Yesmen carried on with an extremely interesting and incongruous choice of replacements.

In 1979, "Video Killed the Radio Star," a prescient piece of new wave synth-pop released by the duo of Trevor Horn and Geoff Downs, also known as The Buggles, became an international new wave hit. But before earning their immortality two years hence for their song being the first music video clip ever to be played on MTV, their new manager, and Yes', had the bright idea that integrating The Buggles into one of prog-rock's most successful acts would be a convenient, if not sensible, solution to the problems of his suddenly incomplete superstar client. The result was Drama.

Drama may have sported classic Yes cover art by the otherworldly illustrator Roger Dean, but the album sounded little like what the real world was used to. Though all band members received songwriting credit, the influence of The Buggles was unavoidable. Making matters worse, while Downes' keyboard skills were adequate and his look innocuously rock, Trevor Horn's voice was nothing like that of Jon's, and his Elvis Costello style stood in stark contrast to the trippy visual brand that Yes had been consistently crafting for more than a decade.

The tour came to Long Island in October, and the troubles to come with the affair were evident early on, the show being a slow sell from the start. For one thing, Nassau was following little more than a month after the band had played three sold-out performances at Madison Square Garden, little more than twenty miles away. Secondly, the album had *only* been released two months earlier, not enough time for the disc to build steam even if it had been outstanding (which almost everyone agreed it wasn't). Thirdly, the *album* had already been released two months earlier, enough time for everyone to find out that it was a solid departure from what the fans had known and loved and that Horn and Downes were not Anderson and Wakeman. This band wasn't Yes anymore; it was now *The Yuggles*.

Nonetheless, the hybrid group set out with high hopes and big egos. The show was in the round, carrying its own rotating stage to be constructed in the center of the arena, like a circus, and the catering called for strictly vegetarian fare. Some weeks before, at the Providence Civic Center, I had to negotiate the usual union nonsense that came with the custom set-up. At Nassau, I didn't have that difficulty; if the band brought the stage, then the stage was gear and the IATSE guys handled it, case closed. But where the caterers in the Providence were easily able to accommodate the dietary demands of Steve Howe and company, the same variety of culinary skill was decidedly lacking in the Coliseum's house catering and concessions firm. "Tell them to eat cow" was the response I received just days before the show and weeks after I had submitted the catering rider. Ordinarily, the concessionaire's contract with the building would have forbid any sort of outside food service from setting foot in the place, but this time they finally admitted that they couldn't handle the order and so had to let it go. They did, however, refuse to allow any outside caterer to use any of the building's facilities or equipment.

Scrambling for alternatives, I approached a vegetarian café not far from our office and not so wittily named The Asparguy. The restaurant's young Chef Sean assured me that he was up to the task of feeding the finicky band and was thrilled to take on the challenge in spite of his lack of experience. When presented with the fact that he would not have a real kitchen at his disposal, the novice also assured us that he would be able to assemble the necessary portable appliances along with the wares and utensils required, in addition to all of the requested flesh-free ingredients.

When The Yuggles hit the stage, young Chef Sean went to work attempting to concoct his colorful creations. As was pretty typical, performers eat their dinner following their finale, preferring not to work on a full stomach or, worse yet, under adverse gastro conditions. While the band struggled to win over the crowd with half a dozen new tunes that no one recognized or cared for, along with less as many standards and a few forays into virtuosity that were leaving people cold, Chef Sean struggled with his toy kitchen set, his small electric cooktop too tiny to orchestrate the myriad of dishes he had planned and a short supply of key ingredients forcing him to compromise his recipes. The smell of sautés and simmers gone wrong filled the air as the poor boy juggled his pots and pans in a rush to produce a meat-free feast worthy of a Michelin star. I could see that the meal was heading for a disaster worthy of the evening's ticket sales.

After finally delivering to the crowd what it had been patiently waiting for all night, a de rigueur encore of "Roundabout" and "Starship Trooper," The Yuggles were ready to chow down after their almost two-hour performance. Sean plated their portions carefully as each band member entered, the chef waiting with anticipation for their reaction to his efforts. Knives and forks carefully dissected the greens, yellows and purples; first bites were taken and…immediate reactions were universal. Not ones to trash their dressing room, as Van Halen likely would have, in their quiet English way, The Yuggles one by one just got up and walked out, heading off to the hallway while leaving their lightly touched plates to be cleared. Chef Sean was crestfallen and embarrassed that his big opportunity to cater to the stars had crashed and burned. His inexperience had provided neither the ingenuity nor the improvisation necessary to pull it all off.

After the *Drama* tour played itself out, whoever remained and was still calling themselves Yes fired their misguided manager and The Buggles went their separate ways. In early 1981, the band's new manager-with-bad-timing released a statement that Yes no longer existed. Trevor Horn found his true calling as a producer, most prominently as a svengali to Seal, and Geoff Downes would walk with Steve Howe to join John Wetten, late of even earlier prog-rockers King Crimson, and drummer Carl Palmer of ELP to launch their new prog-pop band, Asia.

On that evening in 1980, The Yuggles were no more satisfying for Yes' fans than Chef Sean's sad attempt was for the band, sending the crowd home hungry after being fed the first of many watered-down versions to hit the road for decades to come. By 1983, there was already a new Yes: this version, with Jon back in front, was another New Coke – same name but a very different taste. An unknown Trevor Rabin assumed guitar responsibilities and took the sound in a more radio-friendly direction just as Howe and Downes were doing with Asia, generating Yes' first bonafide #1 single, "Owner of a Lonely Heart." But the accolades and sales were short-lived, and though Jon has stayed with varying formations of the band for several decades, it seems to me that he became tired of chasing past glories and has pursued more idiosyncratic solo projects. But many fans never forgave him for that first breakup, for leaving Yes and allowing it to fall prey to someone outside's desperate and horribly gone wrong experiment at reinvention.

Today Yes is just one of many classic rock brands that tour as little more than tributes to their best selves, often led by the member who possessed a savvy attorney that was able to procure for his/her client the rights to the name. In addition, full-fledged tribute bands consistently sell out sizable venues playing note-for-note recreations of the FM hits that I grew up on, be it The Beatles, Led Zeppelin, The Grateful Dead, Pink Floyd, or Yes, even while the surviving members tour in their own varied reconfigurations.

But personally, I'm a purist, and I can't bring myself to indulge anything short of my own measures of authenticity. I'd rather listen to the live records left behind to remember those priceless moments of magic the way that I first experienced them. For me, nothing comes close to the real thing.

©Bill O'Leary/Timeless Concert Images

Steve Howe seems to be the current owner of the Yes brand. Here he performs with The Yuggles at a sold out Madison Square Garden, a little more than a month before playing to our half empty hall at Nassau Coliseum.

AEROSMITH

December 4 & 5, 1979
Broome County Arena
Binghamton, NY

December 6, 1979
Cumberland County Civic Center
Portland, ME

Tuesday, December 4, Binghamton

Steven Tyler directing Jimmy Crespo during
rehearsals the evening before the opening concert of the
Right in the Nuts tour.

Wednesday, December 5, Binghamton

Steven seemed in fine form for the first performance of
the tour. The next night we wouldn't be so lucky.

© Ron Pownall

Thursday, December 6, Portland

Steven backstage, about an hour before the fall.

Thursday, December 6, Portland

Brad Whitford keeps riffing as Tyler lies on the stage.
The show does not go on.

PINK FLOYD

February 24 through 28, 1980
Nassau Coliseum
Long Island, NY

Roger Waters at his most militaristic, acting out both the yin and the yang of the Wall's protagonist, Pink.

David Gilmore high atop The Wall delivering one of his breathtaking Comfortably Numb guitar solos.

Roger indulging Pink's Oedipal complex on "Mother,"
accompanied by one of The Wall's unprecedented props
and effects.

The band waves good night amidst the wreckage of The Wall.
Brian and his doody-brown Buick LaSabre await.

VAN HALEN

August 13, 14 & 15, 1982
Cobo Arena
Detroit, MI

Friday, August 13

David Lee Roth getting costume adjustments prior to
the start of the band's three-day stand at Cobo.

Friday, August 13

Eddie Van Halen fiddling with his little guitar.

Saturday, August 14

Ed Anderson's birthday bimbo popping from the Trojan cake. That's me in the green Polo shirt, standing by as she pies Ed in the shot above, then I'm egging Ed on below with the help of David Lee Roth and the crowd.

Saturday, August 14

Tweedledum and Tweedledee standing guard over David Lee
to make sure that the groupies don't get carried away.
(Dave is autographing the young woman's blue jeans.)

Saturday, August 14

Dave holds court in the hall with his Detroit harem during the after-party on Van Halen's floor at the Renaissance Center Hotel.

Sunday, August 15

Alex Van Halen plays Samurai with Coors Light and soda backstage as the rest of Van Halen are trashing the dressing room for Life Magazine's cameras.

Dave's cheekless chaps always drove the ladies wild.
Goodnight, Detroit!

15

Ritchie's Revolving Door

RITCHIE BLACKMORE IS DIFFERENT. First of all, he's a guitarist, not a singer, and he's been able to remain the Star despite having no vocal abilities. Unlike others, he's also never tried to base his present on his past with Deep Purple. Instead, Ritchie has always tried new things, and hence his post-Purple Rainbow was never a band in any traditional sense. It always seemed more like a project, morphing through several hard rock styles while more than two-dozen associates came and went through eight records and numerous tours over two decades.

Delta T's repertoire was heavy with metal. When they weren't banging out Black Sabbath, they were playing Deep Purple, Paul effortlessly reproducing Ritchie's riffs from a Carlo Robelli knockoff of a Fender Stratocaster. "Smoke on the Water" was an obvious cover. Walk into any Sam Ash or Guitar Center then or now and chances are someone will be picking at an electric guitar, "Duh Duh Duh – Duh Duh, Da Duh – Duh Duh Duh, Da Duh…" no matter whether beginner or shredder. But Delta T went deeper, Purple's killer live album *Made in Japan* becoming the backyard band's bible. (Just for the record, I think that the "Smoke" version on *Japan* is far superior to the studio version on *Machine Head*, with the band not editing out what sounds like Ritchie popping a string, which just makes it all the more authentic and even charming, if one can use such an adjective in regard to rock of Ritchie's type). The funky "Strange Kind of Woman" was also one of Delta T's staples and they delivered it capably. "Child in Time," with its interlude of guitar and vocal interplay, was a much more difficult attempt; no one in Delta T could come close to singer Ian Gillan's higher register.

Early '74 had been an amazing initiation for us, as in little more than a month, Nassau Coliseum treated us to Yes, Black Sabbath and Deep Purple, Delta T's three favorite bands and biggest influences. Burn was the album Deep Purple was promoting, along with a new lineup, what's become known by Purple fanatics as the Mark III incarnation. Jon Lord remained on the Hammond B3 organ, and Ian Paice still played drums, that evening sporting on his back a slap at Frank Sinatra who was to play the hall for multiple nights just a week or two later, a bold silk-screen declaring "Fuck Old Blue Eyes." But a more blues-based David Coverdale had replaced Gillan on vocals, and in bassist Roger Glover's shoes now stood younger Glenn Hughes presenting the double threat of also being a vocalist with an extraordinary range. Glenn had a waif-like look with waist-length hair that rippled like a wispy wave when he tossed his head with classic rock star theatricality. This was just one of the many lineups to come for Deep Purple over the next 40 years.

Ritchie would last only one more year with Deep Purple before creating Rainbow, essentially commandeering the Ronnie James Dio-fronted Elf who had toured with Purple as their opening act. Ritchie's reign over Rainbow became characterized by his fickle tastes and excessive demands dictating who was

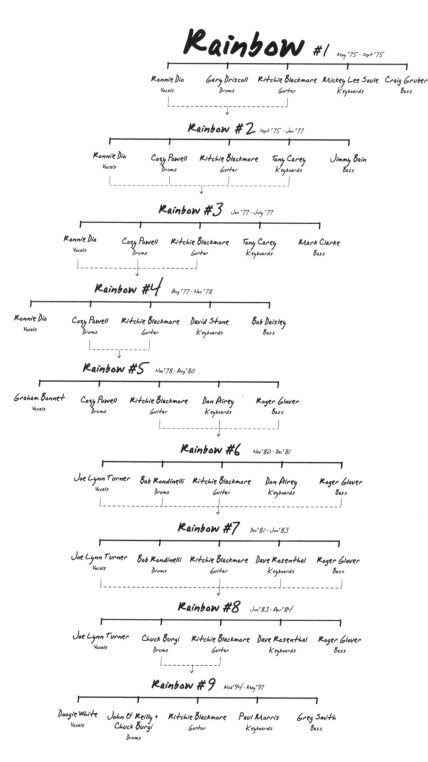

Rainbow #1 May '75 - Sept '75

Ronnie Dio	Gary Driscoll	Ritchie Blackmore	Mickey Lee Soule	Craig Gruber
Vocals	Drums	Guitar	Keyboards	Bass

Rainbow #2 Sept '75 - Jan '77

Ronnie Dio	Cozy Powell	Ritchie Blackmore	Tony Carey	Jimmy Bain
Vocals	Drums	Guitar	Keyboards	Bass

Rainbow #3 Jan '77 - July '77

Ronnie Dio	Cozy Powell	Ritchie Blackmore	Tony Carey	Mark Clarke
Vocals	Drums	Guitar	Keyboards	Bass

Rainbow #4 Aug '77 - Nov '78

Ronnie Dio	Cozy Powell	Ritchie Blackmore	David Stone	Bob Daisley
Vocals	Drums	Guitar	Keyboards	Bass

Rainbow #5 Nov '78 - Aug '80

Graham Bonnet	Cozy Powell	Ritchie Blackmore	Don Airey	Roger Glover
Vocals	Drums	Guitar	Keyboards	Bass

Rainbow #6 Nov '80 - Dec '81

Joe Lynn Turner	Bob Rondinelli	Ritchie Blackmore	Don Airey	Roger Glover
Vocals	Drums	Guitar	Keyboards	Bass

Rainbow #7 Dec '81 - Jun '83

Joe Lynn Turner	Bob Rondinelli	Ritchie Blackmore	Dave Rosenthal	Roger Glover
Vocals	Drums	Guitar	Keyboards	Bass

Rainbow #8 Jun '83 - Apr '84

Joe Lynn Turner	Chuck Burgi	Ritchie Blackmore	Dave Rosenthal	Roger Glover
Vocals	Drums	Guitar	Keyboards	Bass

Rainbow #9 Mid '94 - May '97

Doogie White	John O' Reilly + Chuck Burgi	Ritchie Blackmore	Paul Morris	Greg Smith
Vocals	Drums	Guitar	Keyboards	Bass

worthy of being his bandmates in the studio and on stage, as well as having the last word on the varied creative paths the group would follow.

I first crossed paths professionally with Ritchie in the summer of 1978. Just three years after Rainbow's formation, they were already sporting a few replacements to their original roster. Rainbow were appearing at Suffolk Forum, first up on a double bill with REO Speedwagon. REO was riding high on the strength of their Top 40 album, *You Can Tune a Piano, But You Can't Tune a Fish*, with its easygoing power pop.

Earlier in the day, while unloading Rainbow's gear (the Forum being a non-union arena, the college-aged stagehands did double duty, standing in for the Teamsters, too) one of the roadies handed me a naked, cream-colored Stratocaster that had been sitting atop cases near the ceiling of the semi, exactly like the one I'd always seen Blackmore straddling in album photos and fanzines, and which he had played when I saw him onstage with Purple. I looked at the roadie with surprise. "No case?" I asked. I assumed that stars like Ritchie had expensive guitars, often vintage and likely quite valuable.

"Nah, Ritchie likes them to look banged up." My jaw dropped when I heard that, but my eyes then darted to the name *Carlo Robelli* in place of the famous Fender logo that would have straddled the straight edge of the headstock, just like Paul's. "He switches his *Strat* for a *Robelli* before he trashes it at the end of the show. Doesn't want anyone to realize it's not the real thing, though," the roadie admitted to me.

With essentially two headliners, the stage was packed with band gear leaving less than optimal room for Rainbow, forcing them forward more than they probably would have liked. Dio needed room to roam as he dramatically gesticulated to underscore the severity of his Gothic lyrics, and though Ritchie would stay fairly firmly in place, his antics towards the end of the show required space to spread out. The lights went out, the band took the stage and the music was loud and dirty, Ritchie's playing filtered through a fuzz box as he ground out his lumbering riffs and raucous yet eloquent solos. I watched Rainbow from the security pit, positioned directly in front of Blackmore, his white wedge-heeled boots just feet in front of my face.

Towards the end of the set, while segueing into tenuously-controlled feedback, Ritchie casually swapped his Fender for the fake and began to abuse the instrument with a vengeance. Holding the body, he banged its head to the ground before breaking its neck on the speaker stack beside him. He then tossed it to the floor and stomped on its body, pickups and strings. As the sonic chaos became deafening, I pressed my fingertips into my ears, just before Ritchie grabbed the guitar by what was left of its fretboard and began to windmill, finally letting it fly for the rafters. The instrument clipped the lighting truss, reversed its rotation and crashed directly in front of me, splintering and spraying its bits into the audience, one slice hitting me square in the chest. Yet another memento I didn't have the good sense to hold onto.

For poor Speedwagon, Rainbow must have been a tough act to follow. It was evident that Rainbow was whom most of the ticket buyers had paid their money to see, many leaving before REO even took the stage, and the rowdy remaining Blackmore fans had little tolerance for Kevin Cronin and his crew's tight but tepid set.

One year later, Ritchie had switched up Rainbow again; Dio had left and the dapper Graham Bonnet was now at the microphone. Roger Glover from Deep Purple had rejoined Ritchie on stage right to play bass, Cozy Powell was still on drums, and a newcomer now sat at the keyboards. Blackmore's creative direction had veered towards the more commercial, and a cover

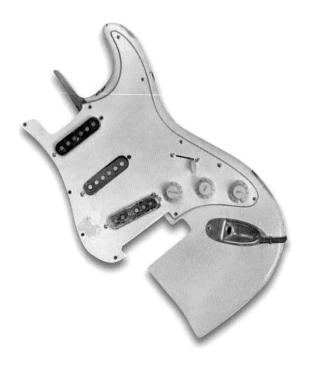

The results of one of Ritchie's nightly finales.

of superstar songwriter Russ Ballard's "Since You've Been Gone" became Rainbow's only real mainstream hit, ever.

Though still pre-MTV, video renditions of promising recordings were becoming a standard asset of record promotion, and Rainbow's label, Polydor, rented The Calderone to shoot a faux live performance of "All Night Long," a second pop-styled attempt at crossover success. A tall, lanky blond had been hired to shake her booty, ostensibly the muse that is keeping the singer up at all hours. For the better part of the day, we listened to the recording on endless repeat as the unplugged band postured and lip-synced for the video crew, and as catchy as the song was, we grew bored of it quickly. But lucky for us, the day's monotony was broken by the dancer's continual wardrobe malfunctions. Occasionally her hot pants needed to be peeled from her bottom as they rode between her cheeks, and her sequined tube top was apparently a size too small for her uncontrollable breasts. Over and over, the director called "Cut!" only to reshoot with the same result of un-airable areolas rendering the take useless. An unintended parody of classic hair band excess and sexism, the version that was ultimately released to television and which can be seen today on YouTube is far less entertaining than its outtakes.

Just three months later, Rainbow was back at The Calderone, for their third headlining appearance in just four years and with Germany's Scorpions opening, a much more compatible bill than REO Speedwagon had provided. After a typically loud and dramatic performance, the beaten Robelli laying in splinters on the floor, Blackmore stalked offstage after flipping his pick to the front row. He marched through the backstage door and stood by my side at the theatre's electrical panel, his black satin uniform clinging to his sweat-soaked torso.

After several moments Ritchie craned his neck back around the door jam to peek at his fans, unconvinced that the audience was deserving of more, their reaction to his new personnel and uncharacteristically top 40 sound not what he had hoped. As the rest of the band waited in the wings with us, I looked to him for instruction. "Ritchie, whaddya want me to do?" With a still stoic face (Ritchie almost never smiles) he ordered me to repeatedly dim the houselights in an effort to whip the fans into believing that the legend was returning for one more. He ultimately decided that their enthusiasm lacked the necessary intensity, and without a word, he abruptly made an about-face and called it a night, leaving me to deal with his fans' disappointment. I turned the house lights on full and left them there, waiting out the applause as it morphed into boos and the fans finally turned their backs to head for the doors.

While decidedly British, Ritchie has often made Long Island his home base, and on occasion, he would appear at shows by other artists I was presenting in the clubs, I guess to keep abreast of what was happening in rock's underground. Despite his well-earned reputation for being difficult, he would never ask for star treatment; in fact, he wouldn't even announce himself. He would simply show up, pay his cover charge and drift to the periphery of the room. Just as on stage, he was always clad in black, except for a white leather biker jacket that, for a while, he seemed quite fond of. He was rarely bothered by autograph seekers; his dour persona no doubt scaring off any with thoughts of approaching him.

On my next round with Ritchie, Rainbow had finally graduated to full-size arenas and Nassau Coliseum, though again with a co-headlining bill, this time with The Pat Travers Band opening the show. (Does anyone remember, "Boom, Boom, Out Go the Lights?" I didn't think so.) This Rainbow team once again was the product of comings and goings, Bonnet now replaced by New Jersey native Joe Lynn Turner and Cozy Powell losing his place to Brooklyn's Bobby Rondinelli. Ritchie

Ritchie with Rainbow at The Calderone Concert Hall, cradling his creamy Stratocaster.

kept Rainbow alive for a few more years but continued to run through yet more personnel changes, finally shelving the band to rejoin Deep Purple in 1984 for a reunion of the classic *Made in Japan* lineup. This time that band stayed intact for almost nine years, far longer than it had the first time, until Blackmore finally again walked out.

Ritchie then brought Rainbow back to life one more time with an entirely new cast, but only briefly, as he began to focus his interest and talent on Renaissance and medieval music, a passion he shared with his new young girlfriend and vocalist, Candice Night. Ritchie soon killed Rainbow's resurrection with the birth of Blackmore's Night, a full-fledged immersion including period instrumentation and costumes. Since beginning the troupe in the late '90s, no less than another two-dozen different player have accompanied Ritchie and Candice. In 2008 Ritchie married Candice. She is his 4th wife.

16

Breaking Contracts & Picking Up the Pieces

I OFTEN TELL PEOPLE THAT I learned more about business from Van Halen than any MBA program could've taught me, our legal obligation to segregate the brown M&Ms so preposterous yet so profound. But at earlier times in my brief career in the entertainment business, I found myself dealing with the ethical dilemma of knowingly not complying with contractual demands, instances where I was forced to compromise against my own juvenile but usually sound judgment. Two pickles in particular still stick in my craw – one with Judas Priest and a second with The Allman Brothers Band. But before I get into it, I need to alert fans of both that they won't find any dirt on either act; this chapter is more of a reminder that as often as not, we can avoid problems by not creating them ourselves.

On the 5th of July in 1980, we were presenting Judas Priest at The Calderone, and as the weeks wound down to the date of the show, ticket sales failed to come even close to break-even, despite budding superstars Def Leppard on the bill for support. Judas Priest quite specifically required two Super Trouper spotlights, those carbon-rod burning behemoths that could throw a white-hot beam a few hundred feet and still singe your eyebrows. It was a fairly standard request for any act working beyond the clubs – that's why we owned our own "reconditioned" pair of spots housed in the projection booth in the nether regions of the theatre. I had chiseled a new opening through the six-inch thick cinder block to accommodate our second light, chipping away Shawshank-style with nothing but a carpenter's hammer and a screwdriver. But one of our Troupers had burnt out the preceding month during a performance by Triumph, a Canadian hard rock band on tour trying to crack the U.S. market, though not succeeding. Following that loss, the expense of having the Trouper repaired had not been budgeted, leaving us with a sole spot whose own health now came into question as I realized that the pair were likely older than I was. With an impending second loss in a row approaching, Mark had no intention of laying out the cash now to fix them even though contractually committed, and I was not to let the band know in advance.

Dreading the confrontation that I knew was inevitable, I came clean to Priest's Production Manager the moment he entered the theatre. First off, I respected that no one likes surprises. Second, I already knew that the guy was difficult from having worked with him at Nassau Coliseum less than five months earlier when local favorites Twisted Sister had stepped up their game to the arena level. Not surprisingly, the bad news resulted in a rant that was entirely justified by our knowing non-compliance. And to make matters worse, he and I both knew that on the day after Independence, neither of us could conjure up the necessary expertise or parts to put the Trouper right.

Def Leppard were early in their career and led the way with a harder rock set than they would ultimately become known for, and the lone spot was holding up for them, following lead singer Joe Elliot from stage right to stage left and highlighting him dead center. Until it didn't. My worst fears were fully founded as the surviving Trouper snuffed mid-song and Elliot sunk into the wash of the multicolored par lamps illuminating the stage from above, now just another marionette filling in his part of the band's heavy metal mix.

As the opening act, Def Leppard had no complaint about the failure. They packed up and shipped out to the next gig without a word, like most fledgling bands just happy to have been paid to play. But as Judas Priest took the stage, it was evident that something was missing, the silent spotlights leaving leather-clad and chrome-studded Rob Halford to stalk the stage in obscurity. As it should, the show went on nonetheless, but the PM made sure to let me know with a nonstop string of expletives that I'd never work in the business again. Obviously, he had little control over my career prospects, as I went on to produce almost 60 more events, many of them far bigger productions. But I forever felt guilty, unable to shake the memory of my wholly-avoidable train wreck. Look, I'm still talking about it 35 years later.

With the Allmans at Nassau Coliseum, the issue was more one of egos than economics. The Allmans had been off the road a few years, so their appearance was an easy sellout. Brother Duane and bassist Berry Oakley had eaten the peaches some years before to put an end to the original Allman Brothers Band, the lineup that became legend with *Live at The Fillmore East*. Then Dickey Betts took the opportunity to go center stage to make the Allmans more accessible with mainstream songs like "Ramblin' Man" and "Jessica," the rare instrumental that broke through on the Hot 100. Addictions, egos and infighting caused the band's break up in 1976, but that death was short-lived. A reconciliation of Gregg and Dicky followed in 1979 with a troupe that included lots of new blood, beginning the ABB's own revolving door of rotating players. That 1980 Allmans ensemble was what I would consider one of the weaker versions of the Brothers. Gregg and Dickey showed no particular inspiration as they walked through their hits, and though still displaying brief flashes of their southern bluesy brilliance, the Allmans seemed like they had lost their way. They now had a guy playing *keytar*, a white plastic keyboard with a shoulder strap whose novelty was thankfully fleeting, compromising the authenticity that the band had until then seemed to take so seriously despite its myriad of setbacks.

In addition to being Production Manager/Promoter's Representative and the Theatre Manager/Concessions Manager at The Calderone, I was also Freefall's Advertising Manager. The Promoter's Representative in me, once again studying the artist contracts in great detail, pointed out that Jack Bruce's agreement to be the opening act carried a clause demanding equal billing with the headliner in any promotion for any event in which Bruce would be supporting talent. (Though neither of us was destined for a legal career, Pam and I had become adept at reviewing performance contracts, some easily 50 or 100 pages long. We were skilled at uncovering potentially problematic clauses buried deep within the densest legalese.) The Allman's contract – as did that of virtually every arena-level headliner – precluded any such equality. Clearly, the Allmans were the star attraction, and no opening act, no matter how respected, seminal or successful, was going to have their name equal in size to that of the Brothers. A conundrum of conflicting contracts, instead of throwing it back to the agents or managers to duke it out, Mark decided to flex some muscle of his own and insisted that I simply ignore Bruce's clause, return the document signed and intact and then, worse yet, instructed me to omit the artist's name from our advertising altogether.

John Scher represented Jack Bruce as the ex-Cream bassist's manager. As a concert promoter, Scher controlled the market in North/Central Jersey, and he was then beginning to make moves into artist management, much as Bill Graham had been and Mark would himself be in the next few years. Scher possessed vastly more clout within the industry than Mark did, and they had been quietly waging a personal feud, finally prompting a confrontation that left me sandwiched in between.

Scher inevitably saw the advertising that we were running and recognized that Jack Bruce's name was nowhere near the same size as that of the Allmans; in fact, it was nowhere to be found. Despite his demand being both impractical and unreasonable, Scher threw a fit and lodged a formal complaint with Premier Talent, Bruce's booking agents and one of Mark's biggest supporters. In response, Mark had me sign my name as Ad Manager to a letter he wrote in defense of our non-compliance, a missive laced with passive-aggression and no logical legal standing. Though no one was about to litigate the matter – everyone knows that with lawsuits of that sort, the only winners are the attorneys – in the long corridor from locker room to the stage, I took the heat for our lame response.

Jane, a top executive at Premier, stopped me in my tracks. "Gregg, you know that you're wrong, right? You don't have a leg to stand on. You even left Jack off of the passes, for God's sake!"

Indeed, earlier in the evening, we had been forced to add a bold "JB" with a Sharpie to our preprinted backstage passes when Bruce's road manager had realized the slight. Scher had overheard my exchange with Jane and gloated over the awkward position he had put us (actually me) in, notching one in the win column of his ongoing rivalry with Mark even though his client had been rendered anonymous to the general public. Following on Jane's heels, he got in my face himself, his "So there!" smirk saying more than any words could.

These scenes may seem insignificant to many who do business in a certain way, believing that everything is still negotiable even after they have signed on the dotted line. But for me, whether it's a handshake or a voluminous document, an agreement made in good faith is binding on both parties and should be executed down to the detail, even if it involves something as seemingly insignificant as brown M&Ms.

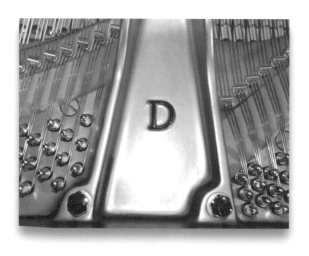

17

A Few Notes About Pianos

IN ADDITION TO FREEFALL PRESENTATIONS, Mark owned Earth Music, a keyboard company that Joey had helped him build into a profitable sideline from promoting. Organic keyboard instruments are a tricky business: expensive to buy, difficult to maintain and almost impossible to sell for anything close to what you originally paid. Not unlike a top-of-the-line foreign sports car. It made sense for most guitar-based bands – and even quite a few piano men – to rent instead of own, and once they made that decision, they would often turn to Earth Music. Pianos and organs were the assets of the company, and they turned a good profit if you could keep them out on the road and working.

So back to the ABB for a moment: *Enlightened Rogues* had been released in February of 1979, and for the second leg in support of that record, the Band needed a full nine-foot Steinway Model D concert grand. (It's actually 8-foot 11-3/4 inches, but who's counting?) Earth Music happened to have one available. The only problem was that the Allmans wanted it in white, and ours was classic black lacquer. So I had to find someone to refinish it – a customization that apparently no one had ever asked Mark for in the past. A classic "piano finish" is one of the marks of hand production that make Steinways so damn expensive, and to strip and refinish it in a different color was a sacrilege that should have cost a small fortune. But via the Yellow Pages, I found a local shop that said they could do the job – supposedly professionals – with pick up and delivery included for what I thought to be quite a reasonable cost.

But then I waited for the Steinway's return. And I waited. And I waited some more. Finally, in late December, the Allmans' tour was about to begin with an unofficial opening performance at The University of Maine's out-of-the-way campus in Presque Isle – a paid rehearsal for the band's official first date, a day or two later downstate in Augusta. Arrangements were made with the band crew to detour to Long Island to pick up the piano at The Calderone on their way north. I didn't tell them that it wasn't ready yet, that the piano had still not been returned to us. I sweated out each day the Steinway wasn't delivered, ultimately being forced to demand that it come back to us no later than the day of the Allmans' scheduled pickup. It finally arrived that morning and Carl, The Calderone's caretaker, took receipt.

As the Allmans' equipment truck and crew were scheduled to arrive early evening, I got to the theatre late afternoon and made my way through the dark and empty house, the familiar odor of the musty upholstery of its old and empty seats soaking the still, stale air. Up on stage sat the huge, sea blue, riveted road case, front and center, lonely and abandoned. I figured that I had better have a look to see what Earth's thousand-plus had gotten us before letting the Allmans take it away.

I had been working with keyboards for a while by then, first under Joey's tutelage and more lately on my own, mostly doing pick-ups and deliveries and arranging maintenance work through third-party specialists like the ones I had contracted for the refinishing. Learning to unpack and set-up the thousand-pound Steinway all by myself had been a must. I had become quite adept at it, even on occasion being timed by stopwatch to challenge my own previous record.

When a grand is going on the road, it is packed within a massive vertical coffin on wheels, the piano lying on its side, straight edge to the floor, resting on the form-fitting foam that coats the interior of the case. The first order of business is to butt the case to a wall and to lock its wheels in place so that the thing doesn't roll away or, worse yet, fall over, its one-ton weight crashing down to crush you. You unlatch and remove the broad side of the case that reveals the bare bottom of the piano. The legs and pedals have been stowed within a smaller case designed specifically to accommodate the keyboard's dismembered limbs, each with its own foamed cubby. You remove the piano's three legs and pedals from their nests, and carefully screw in the leg that supports the treble end of the keyboard and the one that holds up the narrower, rounded end, which I refer to as the nose. Once those legs are attached, you unstrap the monster and slowly pull it towards you by that treble leg to start gently lowering the piano to the ground. You gather all of your might underneath until the solitary, centered leg at the nose touches the floor, the piano now resembling a beached tanker listing to port, the bulk of its weight still being supported by the case. You then dash to the bass end of the keyboard, placing its unattached leg within reach before heaving up the corner yet to have its leg attached. You lift until the treble leg touches down, and with lightning speed, you move the third leg into place and screw it in, finally rolling the ship several feet away from the case. Once confident that you've succeeded, you collapse and wipe your brow, thanking the Lord that you have neither destroyed an extremely expensive musical instrument nor gotten yourself killed. With composure regained, the pedals go on and the diagonal lyre braces are put in place to hold them firm against heavy-footed players.

The Allmans' refinishing job had been done half-assed at best. In fact, the piano hadn't really been refinished at all – the slackers had simply spray painted the Steinway white, and sloppily at that, the new color still wet in spots where the paint had pooled. It seemed evident that they likely hadn't even touched the job until a day or two before delivery, but there was nothing that could be done now, the band's crew would be arriving imminently.

But again, I waited, and I waited and I waited. About 11 p.m., I rummaged a mover's quilt from the backstage basement and curled up next to the Steinway on stage to nap, a loose cushion from the front row serving as a pillow beneath my head. About two in the morning, I awoke to a pounding on the back door; the Allman crew had finally arrived for the pickup. I groggily sent the Steinway off for the long overnight road trip to Presque Isle, hoping that no one would notice its less than stellar condition. I went home to get some sleep before I made my own way to Maine the next day by air.

With a population of fewer than 125 people per square mile, Presque Isle is literally in the middle of nowhere, situated at the tip of the horn of northern Maine, a bike ride from New Brunswick, Canada, just about as far north as you can possibly get in the continental U.S. east of the Mississippi. I set out early the next day, starting with a shuttle flight to Boston, where I laid over for a few hours to connect with a commuter prop to take me the second leg. We touched down at Northern Regional Maine

Airport late afternoon and I checked into a vintage hotel on Main Street, just down the block from the college. Arriving at the field house, I found the load-in and set up complete; our big white elephant assembled – minus a small but important detail.

"We're missing the lyre braces, my friend," was the sarcastic greeting of the keyboard roadie with a good-old-boy scowl and sneer.

I froze. Though I had put the thing together to avoid just this kind of surprise, I had neglected to check on the accessories. Apparently, the careless refinishers had forgotten to replace the braces in their cubby when they returned the sloppily painted piano. And now Gregg Allman would have no use of the pedals – no una corda, sostenuto or sustain – to add nuance to his bluesy expression when he sat behind the ivories.

I had to quickly figure out how to fix my faux pas, which was not going to be easy considering my geography. Bereft of any special services for musical instruments, and this being long before the advent of big-box warehouses, my alternatives were limited to an old-school hardware store about to close its doors for the day. My mind raced as I scanned their wares spread across creaky, well-worn hardwood and dripping from pegboards stretching from floor to ceiling. I caught sight of a bin of dusty wooden dowels, and in an ah-ha moment, I bought a variety of circumferences to improvise with onstage, along with a roll of duct tape and a can of high gloss white spray paint.

Back at the venue, I tried each dowel until I arrived at the proper fit for the slots. With a handsaw, I cut two of equal length and quickly doused them with the white Rustoleum to match the Steinway. Once reasonably dry, I secured each piece in place with the duct tape, which I then also painted white. Despite being shaky, the dowels did the trick, and with a restrained foot, Gregg got through his piano bits that night with a minimum of compromise.

I promised the band that I'd ship the missing parts to wherever they were upon my return to Long Island, and I learned that the devil is in the details, that not a single one can go unchecked, and that my ability to improvise was once again one of my biggest talents. Two pennies and a dime had done the trick.

Going forward a year and back to the Allmans' Nassau Coliseum gig: touring pianos need to be tuned before every performance, as did the big black one now set up again on stage right for Gregg. A local tuner was on hand, a guy that I regularly hired at both the Coliseum and The Calderone. The bands universally thought he did a great job, but God, he liked to talk, and if you let him yap, it would take him twice as long. I paid him by the job, not by the hour, so I usually didn't care, and knowing his M.O., I would steer clear while he went about his work. But that afternoon, I let my guard down and got dragged into conversation while he delicately twisted and turned the instrument's pegs and plucked at its strings. All the while, the Allmans' production manager was watching us like a hawk, perched stage left. When he apparently realized that the tuner and I weren't about to break it up, he flew over in a rage.

"What the fuck are you doing? This thing's gotta be perfect by soundcheck, and how the hell is that gonna happen if all this guy hears is your bullshit? Leave him the fuck alone and let him tune the goddamn thing!" The PM was obviously way more high-strung than any Steinway would ever be, but he was completely justified in questioning how the tuner was going to get it in tune if he wasn't 100% focused on his task. I slunk away sufficiently warned, and my tuner got back to his tuning, getting it right as he always did and as I knew he would.

But the point was well taken, and to this day, I am diligent not to distract highly-trained specialists from doing their job, especially those responsible for unforgiving precision.

Today, I politely try to avoid participating in small talk with young Katie, who cuts my hair.

"Just Call Me Dick."

So I'm sitting in the windowless, penitentiary-green Manager's office in the Calderone one day in June of my junior year at college. I'm musing that if I'm making $30,000 by the time I turn thirty, I'll consider myself a rich man. Then Mark rings me.

"I just got a call from a guy named Richard Wagner. A musician. He's moving to Boston and he wants us to take his piano up there for him."

I'm just twenty-one and up for anything. "No problem. What size?"

"Don't know, I think it's a grand. Here's his number. Just call him and take care of it. I don't need to be involved."

"Sounds good," I reply, quite pleased that Mark already has enough confidence to just leave me to it. (In retrospect, I suppose that Mark sensed a situation not worth his while and punted it instead of just saying "No.")

I call and I get the guy on the phone on the first try. "Hello, Mr. Wagner?" Wagner confirms that it's a grand piano. "When do you want us to come get it, Mr. Wagner?" I ask. "This Saturday? No problem!" I say, "We'll be there in the morning." To be safe, I figure that it will take three guys to share the lifting, driving, and for company, so I float a fee of $300 plus expenses and he readily agrees (which I assume means my quote is too cheap, but it's now too late to reconsider it). "Thank you. And please, just call me Dick," he says before hanging up.

So I enlist two of my buddies – Larry and Thierry – to assist me in this seeming no-brainer, a should-be-simple-but-long day of schlepping a boxed-up piano from Manhattan to Boston, then immediately turning around and coming home. We get an early start so we can beat the traffic into the City. We rent a U-Haul big enough for a grand like the one Earth owns, the one we leased to the Allmans, and we gas up the truck and head west with our pickup address in hand and about a hundred bucks out of pocket.

We breeze into Manhattan and head to the address Dick's given me, which had seemed an odd one from the start because it's on the Upper East Side. We arrive at a boxy but elegant white brick apartment house, mid-60s-modern, a red and gray uniformed doorman standing watch behind the thick sheets of glass at the entry. I had expected that we were headed to a recording studio or a warehouse. Why the hell are we coming here to pick up the piano? (I do not have a good feeling.)

There's nowhere to park on the street, and we're certainly not going to spring for a garage, even if we could find one that would take our U-Haul. So we troll the surrounding blocks until

we spot an opening. "Looks kinda tight. Whaddaya think?" I ask
Larry, who's been behind the wheel. "A piece of cake!" he tells us
with what amounts to misplaced confidence. Larry has to parallel
park, so I jump out to spot him. "Cut it now, cut it now!" I yell as
Larry backs up. But as he glances at his left side-view, so he doesn't
hit an oncoming car, he clips the passenger mirror on the vehicle
beside him on the right, ripping it from its mounting with the
screech of metal on metal, the mirror crashing to the asphalt and
shattering on impact. I immediately do 360-degree surveillance to
see if anyone has noticed. We seem to be in the clear, but we gotta
book, or else someone will figure out it was us. I jump back in
the cab with "Let's get outta here!" – my panic this time trumping
my responsibility, and we take off. We weave a wider circle, but
without luck, we head back to our address and double-park out
front. Larry and I leave Thierry behind to make sure we don't get a
ticket or, worse yet, get towed. It's now about 10 a.m.

The doorman calls upstairs to the apartment and gets the
green light from someone to let us up. We cross the marble lobby
with its brightly polished brass accents, we get in the elevator and
I take a look around. How the hell did someone fit a grand piano
in here? (I'm feeling worse.)

We get off the elevator and look for the apartment. The
corridor is lined with a rich piled and patterned carpet (not great
for the castors that'll be carrying over a thousand pounds), but it's
long and straight and wide. (Good! No tight corners to navigate.)
The walls are fairly freshly painted (Better not bang them.), and
the building is odorless, not like outer-borough apartment houses
where you're instantly immersed in the sordid smell that results
from the combination of the cooking of countless ethnicities. (I
tend to get nauseous with that sort of thing.) We find the right
apartment and push the black button beneath the peephole,
which results in a classy "ding dong" instead of a more ordinary

"bzzzzzz." We hear the shuffle of slippered feet headed our way, the dialogue of the television blaring behind. The door unlocks and slowly opens.

"Who're you?" she demands, looking frizzy and fried with an unlit cigarette in the hand that's resting on her hip, sweat pants slouching below a navel revealed by a too-small tank top that's stressing against her uncupped nipples.

"We're here to move the piano. I spoke with Dick," I say.

"You guys don't look like movers. He hired a couple of college kids? What the fuck?" she asks with disgust as she surveys us head to toe. "Dick's not here now, but come on in." She leaves the door wide open as she turns and leads us within a sprawling apartment. (This being Manhattan I now imagine it wasn't really sprawling at all. But for three college guys coming out of 60 square foot dorm rooms, anything larger seems enormous.) Against the far wall are several guitars nesting neatly in their stands, while front and center on the parquet wood floor stands the grand – all eight-feet-elevenand-three-quarter-inches of beautiful black lacquer, this one a Baldwin, sheet music spread open on the rack above the ivories.

She plops down on the couch, lights her cigarette and pours vodka from a half-full bottle of Stoli into an already wet glass, mixing it with orange Crush before asking, "Didya bring any boxes?"

"Whaddaya mean? Boxes for what?"

"Well, yer' moving us to Boston, right? We have to pack all of this shit into something, don't we?" She sweeps her arm before her, the now burning butt tracing the room from left to right. I notice all of the hastily assembled heaps representing someone's lame attempt at organizing a complicated life. Clothing in a lump over here, disheveled bedding over there, books in haphazard stacks toppling to the floor, and countless other less-thematic piles strewn randomly around the room. (Now I'm starting to panic.)

"Uh, Dick never said anything about MOVING him – and you, I guess – to Boston. We're not professional movers. We're just here for the piano." I'm hoping that the *Three Stooges* appearance of the duo of Larry and I will convince her without further debate.

"Well, that's not what he told me," she says decisively. "Dick should be back soon, though, so you can sort this shit out with him." She's all the while absently perusing LPs in a plastic milk crate at her feet, not really purging or even sorting them, just kind of moving them front to back. She suddenly pulls one out and hands it to us. "This is Dick's latest record." It's *Fearless*, the recent release by Tim Curry, a.k.a. Dr. Frankenfurter from *The Rocky Horror Picture Show*, the cult flick that I had seen repeatedly at midnight showings while in high school years before people started dressing the parts and throwing stuff at the screen.

We look at her quizzically and she answers our question before we can ask it. "Yes, it's *technically* Tim Curry's album. But Dick plays guitar and co-wrote almost the whole thing. It's a terrific record. Have you heard it?"

"Yeah, well, I've heard 'I Do the Rock.' Great song," I reply.

"Oh, yeah, well…Dick didn't write *that* one," Dick's Chick replies with disdain as she looks away and takes a deep drag on her cigarette.

I try to get her back on track and explain that since all agree that at least the piano is going, we might as well start preparing to do that. Then it hits me like a ton of bricks. "I don't suppose that you have a case for the piano, do you?" I ask. She laughs a small laugh that sounds more like a single snore.

"A case? I don't know what the hell you're talking about."

That's just what I was afraid of. I realize now that, at the very least, we have to go back to Hempstead, back to The Calderone, empty our Steinway from its case, and bring the big blue monster back here so we can use it to move Dick's Baldwin to Boston. (We're in deep shit now and it's getting over our heads.) If all had gone as planned, we'd already have been on our way. "As *planned*?" Ha! Now facing another grand-sized fiasco, I realize that I had neglected to ask a few basic questions because it had seemed such a simple job. And I forgot that even though I had never heard of this guy, I was nonetheless dealing with an *artist*, and if I'd learned anything by now, I'd learned that most artists think that their wishes will be granted regardless of their impracticality.

I tell Dick's Chick that we'll have to retrieve the piano case from Long Island, but even so, I'm not sure if it will fit in the elevator. "Your problem, not mine," she tosses off as she lights another cigarette and returns to her movie and breakfast spirits.

"OK…Well, we'll be back in a little bit. We gotta go check out our options. Hopefully, Dick'll be back soon, too," I say as she pays no mind and we head downstairs to figure out what we're going to do. As we descend in the lift, Larry says, "Chick's crazy. How the fuck are we going to move all of that shit for them? They didn't even start to pack!"

"Listen…We just gotta get the damn piano out of here. We're going to figure that out now, go get the case, come back for the piano and get on the road as soon as Wagner gets here. We'll deliver the piano to Boston and be done with it."

We exit the elevator and walk out in front of the building, for a fleeting moment floating Loony Tunes schemes of jerry-rigging a pulley system to lower the thing out of Dick's window. But we quickly realize that even if the three of us could lift the damn thing, the window was utterly too small.

"You guys need help with something?" It's the doorman, probably wondering if we're casing the place.

"Yes sir, actually, we do." I proceed to tell him our plight, our crazy plan, and he laughs.

"How the hell do you think they got it up there? The building has a service elevator."

The doorman takes us past the lobby, towards the rear and working innards of the building, leading us to a larger elevator with padding pinned to the walls that looks big enough to do the job. But just as I'm breathing a sigh of relief, the doorman asks: "Did you reserve it?"

"What do you mean, did we 'reserve' it?"

"Well, you can't just use the service elevator any time you want. You need to reserve it. People move stuff in and out all of the time, but if they didn't reserve the service elevator first, they'd be crashing into one another and gettin' into fist-fights. It can get ugly." We explain our sordid situation more fully and he laughs. Apparently, Wagner and Dick's Chick have quite a reputation in the building and everyone is glad to see them go. "Well, you're lucky – nobody else reserved it today. But I can only let you use it until five. On the dot, we shut it down. The residents want peace and quiet in the evenings."

Larry and I assure him that we'll be back well before five, thank him for his help and head back upstairs to see if Dick has returned yet. He hasn't. Dick's Chick invites us to "Have a seat, watch the movie." So we wait, but still no Dick.

"Listen, if we're ever going to move this piano, we gotta go. Please tell Dick that we were here and that we'll be back as fast as we can," I finally tell her and we get up to go. "Make sure to close the door behind you," she throws over her shoulder.

We hurry to break the bad news to Thierry that we have to go back to Long Island...but the truck is gone. In a panic, Larry and I head in opposite directions, one north and one south on the avenue, to see if Thierry is parked somewhere close by, but he's nowhere to be found. We regroup in front of Wagner's building to figure out what the hell is going on when Thierry and the orange and white U-Haul suddenly come rolling up.

"Where the hell were you?" Larry barks at Thierry as our third Stooge stretches to roll down the passenger window.

"Where the hell were you guys?" Thierry replies in his typically calm way but with more than a hint of resentment at being left on the street all of this time. "I had to move the truck, keep driving around the block, so we didn't get a ticket!"

We all take a deep breath and recount our last hour or so as we head east over the Queensborough Bridge. We calculate that even with no hiccups, we won't get back from Boston until tomorrow morning, but no worries. We're on an adventure and tomorrow is Sunday. We can sleep in until Monday.

Unfortunately, by now, the rest of the world has woken up and traffic is beginning to get heavy. We don't get back to The Calderone until around one or so. We relieve the case of Earth's grand – having to fully set up the piano in the process. We strap the case to the wall of the truck, grab some lunch, gas up (Now I'm in for a buck-fifty) and get on the road back to Manhattan, relieved that even though we know we've still got a long day ahead we're finally on our way. It's now about 2:30.

If you've ever driven the Long Island Expressway with any regularity, you don't wonder why it's been dubbed "The World's Largest Parking Lot." The entrance ramp dumps us into the right-hand lane and we sit, and we sit, and we sit. And then we sit some more, the three of us crammed side by side by side in the U-Haul cab's stifling, 100-degree early summer heat, the AC not working, our asses sticking to the molten black vinyl as we sweat it out to get back to Dick's place before five o'clock.

We finally arrive at the building around 4:45. (We're not dead yet, but it's not looking good.) This time Larry stays behind as Thierry and I bolt to the door.

The afternoon doorman knows nothing from the A.M. guy, but when we tell him that we're here to move Dick and Dick's Chick, he happily escorts us into the lobby and holds the elevator open. "But hurry up, guys. You've only got the service elevator for another ten minutes or so." (Don't we know it.)

"Ding dong, ding dong, ding dong..." We keep ringing the doorbell with no sound of movement from the other side. "I can't fuckin' believe that they would go out, knowin' that we were coming back!" Thierry says in disbelief. The clock is ticking and frustration gets the better of him. Thierry starts banging on the door with his fist. "If you're in there, open up the damn door!"

"Chill out, asshole!" we hear from inside, Dick's Chick's raspy, nicotine-stained voice unmistakable. "Where the hell have you been?" she demands to know as she lets us in. "I got tired of waiting and crashed for a while. Dick came back but had to go out again. You guys ready to move us now?"

The clock ticks five and it's over, at least as far as actually getting anything accomplished is concerned. Now all that's left is to figure out how to get out of this mess while trying to cut my losses; it was my cash that had paid our way this far. Suddenly we hear the knob turn and the door crack open. "Hey, here's Dick now!" Dick's Chick proclaims as Wagner walks into the room.

Dick's a stocky guy, a little taller than me, a good ten years or more older, with a handsome face. His features are large, and his shoulder-length brown hair seems to accentuate his nose, making it look larger than it actually is. He's dressed mostly in black on this glorious but sweltering June day, and he's not seeming too spry; a look of exhaustion is more like it. I imagine that he's been up a long time, I'm thinking that he's probably been in the studio for the better part of the past few days. (That's what musicians do when they're not on tour, right?) We introduce ourselves politely before the shit will hit the fan. His hand is rather large and solid, just like the rest of him.

"So, what's going on?" he asks matter-of-factly.

"Well, sir," I start, "there seems to be a bit of a mix-up. When we spoke on the phone, I thought that you hired us to move a piece of equipment to Boston for you. Your friend here somehow thinks we're moving everything." Just as Dick's Chick had done earlier, I sweep my hand across the room to reference its random piles, but my purpose is to underscore their hopelessness.

He sighs and mumbles a tired "I don't remember the conversation too well." He plops down on the couch next to Dick's Chick.

"Well," I say, "I thought we'd be picking the piano up at a studio, ready to be taken away. We got here to find ourselves at an apartment building, with no parking, a nine-foot grand with no case and a service elevator that we can only use until five o'clock, which came and went. Until now, you were nowhere to be found. On top of all that we've got your girlfriend over here insisting that we've been hired to move all of this stuff, which no one has even started to pack. We're not a 'moving company,' we're a keyboard service. I've already had to lay out a hundred and fifty bucks, and now it's too late in the day to move anything." I'm not a bold guy and I avoid confrontation at all costs, but I must sound exasperated, maybe a bit scared, and he's too tired to argue. Dick sighs.

"Listen, we must've miscommunicated," he says, "and I'm sorry I wasn't here sooner to help straighten it all out. Sorry for all of your trouble. This is obviously more complicated than either of us had thought. Tell you what. Here's two hundred bucks and let's call it a day." He finds four fifties in his wallet and hands them to me. Thierry and I stare at him in disbelief. I thank him and say that we'd be willing to come back tomorrow, but we were told that we're not allowed to use the service elevator on Sundays. Looking around at the room and surveying the disarray, he shakes his head. "Don't worry about it, guys. We'll figure it out."

We say our goodbyes, more to Wagner than to Dick's Chick, and as we turn to leave, he calls us back for a moment. "Hey, here, take a copy of my new record for yourselves and your friend. I think you'll like it."

"Thank you, Mr. Wagner, and good luck to you. I hope it's a huge hit."

"So do I. And please, forget Mr. Wagner. Just call me Dick."

My friends being good friends, they didn't ask to get paid, so Dick had made me whole and then some. Unlike so many of the performing personalities that I had already met, he had turned out to be a nice, rational, easygoing guy. We took the extra fifty bucks that he had given us and toasted Dick at a local Hofstra bar after ditching the truck.

As I began to write this bit, more than 35 years later, I realized that I knew nothing of Dick other than what little I had learned on our misadventure. But now, my curiosity was piqued and I wanted to get to know this mostly anonymous rocker that I had met all too briefly, this regular guy who took pity on a trio of young kids caught in a prickly predicament.

Obviously, this Richard Wagner was not the nineteenth-century composer whose "W" is pronounced like a "V" and with an "a" pronounced as a short "o," as in bog, cog, fog or log. *That* Wagner was responsible for the 18-hour *Ring* cycle of opera and its dramatic "Ride of the Valkyries." *This* Richard Wagner was a go-to rock guitarist who lent his lyrical axe to a host of rock luminaries, responsible for several of the 70's most memorable performances, though often un-credited so as not to damage the reputations of the lesser players who, while being official members of their bands, couldn't deliver the goods.

It was precisely because of the confusion caused by the name he shared with the celebrated nineteenth-century composer that he had taken to calling himself "Dick" instead of Richard. When Wagner released his eponymously titled solo album, Richard Wagner, more often than not, he would find it mistakenly filed in the record store's classical bins. Later in life, though, he seems to have embraced the connection and took to proclaiming himself the *Maestro of Rock*.

Early on, Dick saw regional success with The Bossmen and The Frost, his mid-sixties bands formed in Saginaw, Michigan. In '72 he tried to take a more progressive tack with the formation of Ursa Major, briefly featuring a young Billy Joel on keyboards. The band didn't click, but Dick's life soon took a turn when he bumped into producer Bob Ezrin.

Ezrin recruited Dick and fret-mate Steve Hunter to help record Lou Reed's less-than-enthusiastically-received second solo record, *Berlin*. Despite the critical and commercial snubbing the album received, Reed hired the duo for his international tour, which resulted in two recordings – *Rock and Roll Animal* and *Lou Reed Live* – which are still considered two of rock's finest live albums. The young maestro was specifically hired to fashion new, more majestic arrangements for Reed's dark Velvet Underground favorites, renditions more capable of commanding the festivals and arenas Reed was to play. Dick's reworking of Reed's music and the duos' dramatic, Allman-esque twin guitars gave Reed's repertoire more power and new color, seamlessly meshing metal, melody, funk and finesse. The tour was consistently sold out, and the audience's appreciation of the band's talent and taste is heard throughout the recordings. The pair's reward? To be fired by Reed, likely for standing in his light.

Luckily for Dick, Ezrin treasured the guitarist's talents and spread them around, introducing him to Alice Cooper and others. Dick played for-hire gigs providing ghost guitar work on a trio of Alice's albums – *School's Out*, *Billion Dollar Babies* and *Muscle of Love* – before their relationship blossomed into a full-fledged collaboration. A perpetual work-in-progress from the Frost days, "Only Women Bleed," which Dick finally finished with lyrics from Cooper, proved to be a publishing annuity that helped keep the guitarist financially afloat for decades. I've also discovered that Dick was responsible for the live-sounding solo, Steve for the studio licks, featured within Aerosmith's "Train Kept A Rollin'," tasty bits that I and most of the band's fans always assumed were the work of Perry and Whitford.

Dick also lent his guitar and pen to an eclectic cross-section of 1970's hitmakers, including Kiss, Peter Gabriel, Hall & Oats and Meatloaf, in addition to Mr. Loaf's fellow *Rocky Horror* alumnus, Tim Curry.

Called "the consummate gentleman axeman" by Kiss' Gene Simmons and acknowledged for his outstanding talent by numerous contemporaries, Dick was known as a self-deprecating artist who was content to take a back seat to the massive egos he worked for, just happy to play, *The Invisible Virtuoso*, as one rock writer christened him. "I'm kind of shy. Being a star is not a big thing to me," he admitted to an interviewer. As Dick got older, he gravitated towards nurturing newer artists, hoping to help them avoid many of his own mistakes. Making lasting impressions, Dick was said to be "one of the greatest people ever" by at least one appreciative young rocker that he mentored.

Dick performing with Lou Reed on the tour to be recorded for the live classic, Rock and Roll Animal.

After a string of major medical mishaps – a heart attack, a stroke, brain surgery – Dick passed away in 2014 at the age of 71 in Phoenix, still recording and playing live. In addition to Michigan and New York City, from what I can tell, Dick also lived in California and Nashville, but it looks like he never did make it to Boston.

19

Getting by with a Little Help from Our Friend

THOUGH I KNOW I pledged early on to avoid clichés, I guess no rock memoir can really be considered complete without at least a little bit about the drugs. Particularly blow. Snow. Rock. Nose powder. Along with sundry other less-than-legal means of mental enhancement and escape.

In college, all I'd ever done drug-wise was smoke pot and occasionally take a toot of Seth's free "speed" when the need arose. I wasn't a "head," nor were any of my friends. Smoking pot was just the same as drinking beer. In fact, we usually smoked pot when we drank beer.

At Hofstra, cocaine just wasn't on the menu. The only time I was ever exposed to it was an evening when my Tower C floor mate Michael dragged in some guy who claimed to be Mel Brooks' son, and he said that he had some blow that he wanted to share with us. I was skeptical of the whole opportunity. First, I had a hard time believing that the guy was Mel Brook's son, even though I gotta admit the kid was a dead ringer for the 2000 Year Old Man. Second, I was careful. I wasn't going to put shit up my nose that was coming from a guy I didn't know shit about. By then, the landscape was already littered with famous fatalities – Janis Joplin, Jimi Hendrix and Jim Morrison, with Belushi and others to follow close behind – and we had had an accidental overdose of one of our own. Alita, all of nineteen or twenty, had died doing a little too much of the wrong thing.

But in the music business of the late seventies and the early eighties, cocaine was part of the fabric of life on the road. Pot wasn't present (unless we're talking about the Grateful Dead or one of their several side projects), as work was to be done and it couldn't be done properly or safely while stoned. The same for booze, even beer, available only when accompanied by dinner. Instead, the more flush road personnel – the higher paid strata of specialists such as guitar techs and engineers in addition to the band's management appointees, the Tour Managers and Road Managers – would do a line or two now and again to fortify the faculties. But never before eating, always after. Unlike pot, cocaine suppresses the appetite, and food was just as essential to making it through the 20-hour days as stimulants were. Hence crews often referred to the pickme-up-powder as *dessert*. My own indulgences were usually the result of petty briberies offered up by the guys responsible for opening acts looking for a little more room to spread out onstage or off.

Once the headliner showed up, the dressing rooms were where the real action took place. I witnessed varying degrees of excess, with coke serving to entertain as well as invigorate. Stick figures were snorted in games of reverse Hangman. First names, and sometimes last, were spelled out in all CAPS and snorted one letter at a time. A single stripe was drawn across the cocktail table in a challenge to the entourage to inhale the entire length in a single snort. All with no fear of an overdose, nor of the police making an appearance to break up the festivities. Law enforcement's jihad against rock by now was so '60s. In the '80s, drugs were blandly accepted as part of the rock star mystique.

Not every artist was so stereotypical. I can't vouch for their one hundred percent purity, but the worst that the virtuous virtuosos from Yes ingested in my presence were the gruesome green vittles that made up the bulk of their contract rider demands. Van Halen, despite all of their well-earned reputation as rock's delinquents du jour, seemed to crave exclusively beer, bourbon and other spirits, though I can't attest to what may have accompanied their libidinous adventures behind those closed hotel doors. On the other hand, a lot of the harder rock bands like Aerosmith indeed had very visible appetites for opioids.

I was several years out of the business when Mark invited me to join him one evening to see a young Mötley Crüe as the opening attraction on Ozzy Osbourne's *Bark at the Moon* tour. Though Mark was not the promoter, he had a friendship with the band's management, and he saw an opportunity for face time with the Crüe and to foster some goodwill, all in the hopes of landing rights to the band in a market or two if and when they would become a headliner themselves. We were allowed to spend the evening in the pit and I once again subjected my cochlea to crunching chords and screeching solos at dangerous decibel levels, this evening to the strains of what would become hair metal classics including "Crazy Train" and "Shout at the Devil."

After the show we met up with the Crüe and their managers, Doc and Doug, for drinks at the John Peel Room of the nearby Island Inn, home of the decadent *Tipsy Sherry Trifle*, a huge layered dessert tureen that my mom and dad, my brother, sister and I would share in celebration of first communions, confirmations and graduations. Along with Doc and Doug were bassist Nikki Sixx and guitarist Mick Mars, lead singer Vince Neil and drummer Tommy Lee either calling it an early night or having better things to do. Heavy drinking ensued, and after several rounds, the two wandered off. I got up to pee, and upon entering the men's room, I found the duo of tattooed metalheads huddled over the urinal drawing lines on its flat porcelain top. "Want a taste, man?" they invited with their drunken L.A. drawl, and though it was tempting, I just couldn't say yes to sucking up snow mixed with the stink of stale piss and naphthalene cakes.

While I can't condone the recreational use of drugs, I obviously can't vilify it either. I understand the need of performers to augment their stamina through foreign means and/or to subsequently unwind post-performance with those same means or in combination with others. In the recording studio, despite time being money, the pace is relatively leisurely and while there is still pressure to deliver it is not front and center with no do-overs the way it is every evening onstage. But touring takes its toll, beginning with a hundred of hours of rehearsal (at least it should be), learning new numbers, relearning old hits and dusting off deep cuts. Once on the road, night after night is spent under the white-hot heat of hundreds of par lamps, posing and prancing while belting out fifteen to thirty songs back to back (the exact number depends upon the creative bent, whether you're Yes or you're The Ramones) usually over the span of almost two hours, with no break. Then there's the travel itself. No matter how big a star you are, you still live out of a suitcase, often sleeping in the bunk beds of a bus, each day waking in a new city, state or country, sometimes only recognizing where you are in time to deliver the obligatory "Good evening, Tallllaaahasseeeeee!" between the second and third songs of the set. It's grueling, debilitating work regardless of the amount of adrenalin released, the level of adulation received, or even how many panties and bras are tossed your way. Sometimes it just takes these guys and dolls something a bit stronger than a shot of B-12 to make it through the day.

The End of the Road

WITH THE *MYSTERY CLUB TOUR* closed out in Hartford, we parted ways with Aerosmith until the onset of winter, plenty of time for Steven and the rest to try to get their shit together in a more meaningful way in order to pursue a more lucrative comeback. It had been a tough few months for everyone involved.

Throughout it all, Tyler's health was of constant concern and it was necessary to ensure his stamina, especially in light of all he was doing to compromise it. Unfortunately, Mark's preferred method of placating Steven had been to allow him to indulge his vices. Not directly, of course, but along with Marion, the ganja king, we were shadowed by a second specialist. Wayne carried the harder candy, and whenever Steven or anyone else in the band wanted some, Wayne was there to satisfy their cravings.

To prop Steven up legally, though, we'd keep Tiger's Milk powder on hand, a popular brand of vitamin and protein concoction that we mixed with good old-fashioned cow's milk and raw eggs. He'd drain a full glass in a single gulp. Like many things that would pop up on contract riders, it was not easy to find, so we bought it by the case and it traveled with us, nestled among the guitars and amps.

On his more strung-out days, I'd have to find a local MD willing to give Tyler an injection of B-12 without a prescription, which wasn't particularly all that difficult. As we arrived at each club, I'd begin by asking around for a referral to an undiscerning doc; in the years bridging the '70s and the '80s, especially in the club world, no one would think to ask you why. But failing success at that, I'd resort to a local Yellow Pages and begin making calls. Once I revealed my purpose and the patient involved, I pretty quickly could find a taker.

For all not physicians or pharmacists (I assume that would be most of you), Vitamin B-12 is a key player in the function of the brain and nervous system, and given Tyler's habits, he could use the insurance as well as the benefit from the vitamin's pick-meup qualities. A B-12 fix would, though, entail taking Steven out in public during the daylight, and as you may imagine, he's not an easy guy to disguise. As the cabbies chauffeured us to the doctor's office, they knew something was up, and they would peer uneasily into the rearview mirror to peek at their otherworldly passengers. I would sit beside the driver while Steven perched on the hump seat in the back, looking waiflike while wedged between big Joe D. and breakfast boozing George. Tyler would grin all the way with the anticipation of a child on his way to the sweet shop.

After the run of club dates in June, the band gave it a rest until December. We were called back to manage two performances in Aerosmith's hometown, at Club Boston, later renamed The Metro, now a House of Blues, at 15 Landsdowne Street just outside the Big Green Monster at Fenway. Almost a year to the date of my first shows and Tyler's collapse on stage in Maine, these gigs went extremely well, and they provided me with my most personal moments with the singer since this entire affair had begun. I hope that the necessary statute of limitations has passed.

We were all staying at The Copley Plaza, in Back Bay, and one evening at about 2:00 a.m., the phone rang in my room, Tyler's unmistakable, raspy voice at the other end.

"Gregg?"

"Yeah?" I croaked, still in the deep sleep I had just recently started.

"Gregg, it's Steven, man. You up? Can you get hold of Wayne for me?"

"Steven? It's fucking two o'clock in the morning!" I snapped. "Why don't you call Wayne yourself? He's right down the fucking hall."

"I don't know what room he's in and...I don't know; I just don't want to go out... Pleeeaaase do this for me...." he pleaded. "Pleeeaaase Greeeegg..."

His calling me by name was particularly surprising. Even after almost a year of extremely close quarters and sharing all of the scrapes we had been through together I had been convinced that he still didn't know it. But he sure knew Wayne's name. It was on the tip of his tongue.

Repeated calls to Wayne's room elicited no answer, so I threw on some clothes and headed down the hall. I knocked on his door, lightly at first but with escalating urgency as I continued to receive no response. In retrospect, it didn't surprise me; at that hour of the morning, I could have been a narc, or worse yet, I could have been a buyer or seller who had a beef with Wayne and his illicit business as a middleman. Either way, his wealth, health and freedom could have severely suffered if he wasn't careful.

"Wayne! Open up! It's Gregg, man!" I finally shouted in a whisper.

I heard a rustling inside and eventually footsteps; the door finally cracked open, revealing Wayne's steely eyes and square jaw, shirtless, with beltless blue bellbottoms hugging his hips, obviously pissed that I'd woken him up.

"Whaddya want? I'm busy…" I quickly told him about Steven's call and request. "OK, come on in."

As I stepped inside the room, it was instantly apparent that I'd interrupted him and a mostly-naked young Asian woman whom I recognized not to be his wife. Wayne strode to the desk, lifted a large Ziplock bag that looked to be half-filled with talcum powder and he poured a small pile onto the hotel desktop. He scooped it up with a credit card and deftly dabbed it into a tiny origami envelope the size of a special-issue collectible postage stamp. Wayne then handed it to me and simply said "Here." Unfortunately, while he was willing to supply at this hour, he was not about to deliver.

"Wayne, I can't take it. That's not what I do!" I protested.

"Then you tell Steven to come get it himself. I'm not going out."

"Come on, Wayne, I can't have the hometown rock star roaming the halls of one of the finest hotels in Boston. I don't need him ending up on the front page of the fucking Boston Globe!"

"Sorry, man, he called *you*. Sayonara" he said as he dipped his head towards his roommate.

Knowing an argument was pointless, I offered a sarcastic "Thanks a lot" and trudged off, disgusted at being made an unwilling delivery boy. This was the first and last time I promised myself. Ever.

Arriving at Steven's room, I again quietly knocked. Steven answered his door almost immediately.

"Gregg, hey, man, what's up?" Really, I thought, he's asking me "What's up?"

"Well, for one thing, I am now. I ran by Wayne's for you."

"Oh yeah, right, thanks, man. Come on in."

Steven and Cyrinda were wide awake, fully dressed and watching TV overloaded hamburgers that they had ordered from The Copley's 24-hour room service. Replacing his more typical narcissism with some unexpected hospitality, he said thanks again and asked me if I was hungry and would I like to join them.

"Sure, I'll hang out a little bit," I said. I'd gotten out of bed, got dressed, woken up Wayne and come this far. I figured I might as well end up with a story to tell my kids someday. Someday when they were much older than I was then.

Cyrinda and I sat on the unmade bed as Steven pulled the room service table closer, grabbed a water goblet that he emptied and dried before flipping it over and wiping its base clean. He unwrapped the tiny wax package that Wayne had sent him and dumped the precious powder out in a lump upon the thick clear glass. He wiped the room service knife clean with the white cotton napkin and carved six long lines of diminishing length as they paralleled each other from the diameter towards the rim of the circular base. With a rolled Jackson, he snorted about a half of the first, passed the bill to Cyrinda to take her turn and then gestured for me to take mine. I'd like to say I once again declined, but, hey, it's not easy to be a saint in Sodom.

As I looked around the room, I couldn't help but smile. My surreal journey to get to this place had been an amazing thing. If a palmist had read me my future five years earlier, when I was just seventeen and straining to see from the cheap seats of Madison Square Garden, a paying customer, an outsider, that I'd end up

Steven & Cyrinda, circa 1979-1980

on the edge of a bed in a five-star hotel, shooting the shit with one of the biggest rock stars in the world (albeit one that was at that moment almost destitute) I'd tell them that they were fucking crazy. But my passion for music and a fairly big set of balls had put a series of events in motion that had landed me at the end of my rainbow. But now that my pot of gold was sitting in front of me, all I really wished for was to return to the comfort of my pillow for a good night's rest. It was becoming just another evening of working overtime, all still just part of the job. I stayed a while longer, watched some television, talked some small talk and pilfered a French fry or two while they finished their food and polished off the powder.

Mark held on to his role as the band's glorified foster father for another year or so as Aerosmith struggled to finish their next new album, *Rock in a Hard Place*, but the relationship was never going to work long term. Mark just couldn't convince the band to get a grip. It seemed impossible for Steven to focus on songwriting, and though CBS foot the reported $1.5 million it cost to make the album, the band continued to have money problems. At one point, Steven was so tight that he called Pam pleading for a loan of $100 so he could buy an anniversary gift for his folks, a birthday present for Nana, or some other more domestic need. Coincidentally, at that time, a gram of cocaine cost $100, too. Pam never bought his story, but she sent him the money anyway and thus began an almost weekly recital of ridiculous requests, one preposterous story after another as to why Steven suddenly needed a C-note to get by.

Eventually, Brad Whitford went the way of Joe Perry and was replaced by Rick Dufay. Freefall managed this now further-diluted version of the band through recording, and eventually, a new arena tour followed. An Aerosmith performance in Providence in November of '82 began my final round with the business.

For one reason or another, neither Mark nor Pam were present in Providence, most likely due to a conflicting promotion that they deemed more important than one more date with this still assumed-to-be-doomed quintet. And so I was left to do settlement – number-crunching that I was ill-equipped for. But there was nothing to fear, for Big Joe B. was by my side. Joe sat in on my reconciliation with the venue, a second set of eyes on the expenses and revenue, making sure that no one got shortchanged nor caught on to my ignorance.

Post load-out, I met Joe at his hotel room to recap and recalculate to be sure that everyone had received their due. Once all was reconciled, he broke out a bottle of Johnny Walker and we toasted to another night of survival. He told me that he had no idea where it was all headed, with Aerosmith still being in disarray and all, and that it was probably a good thing that I was getting off the road and onto a more stable career. We chatted for a while until we drained our heavy hotel tumblers and called it a night. We would meet up one more time a few months later in Syracuse for my final affiliation with Aerosmith and the last show of my all-toobrief career in concert promotion. Joe wished me well, we both knowing it was unlikely for us to cross paths again.

I've been frustrated in my efforts to discover whatever happened to Big Joe B., another unsung supporting player, another behind-the-scenes indispensable that got ground up by life on the road with madmen and geniuses. One of the few traces that I've been able to find is *The Joseph Baptista Memorial Scholarship Fund*, a permanently endowed financial aid award offered by Boston's Berklee College of Music. It was established in 1991, apparently the same year that Big Joe B. passed away, less than ten years after I last saw him. Now the school's financial aid department had no idea who Joe was, nor did they have any record of who started the scholarship. I told them that Joe was a good man, he was most deserving of the memorial, and that I imagined plenty of people owed him a lot. I know that I do.

It would be several years before we'd meet up with Aerosmith again, though this time only as guests. Having by then severed all ties with Leber and Krebs as well as with Freefall, the band had found new guidance from a young manager named Tim Collins. Collins' big idea was to impose some discipline, get all of the original band members to make up and clean up and put them back in the studio and on tour to reclaim their once and future stardom. He was successful on all counts, and Aerosmith's resurrection is one of rock's most unlikely happy endings. Their rebound album (or more accurately rehab album), *Done with Mirrors*, may not have produced a hit, but it showed that they were finally, truly back in the saddle. Collins had believed that there was still plenty of life in the old horse, but that Aerosmith would have to clean house in order for them to believe it themselves. By changing labels, leaving Columbia for David Geffen's new record company, and giving legacy producer Jack Douglas his walking papers in favor of upstart Ted Templeton, the same Svengali that was then guiding Van Halen to the top of the charts and ticket sales, the band once again had a shot at relevance within the hard rock marketplace. Mark, Pam and I visited backstage when they swung by New York, and for a second time, Steven remembered my name.

They had been one of the biggest bands in the world, and I think given a little time out of the limelight, the world actually began to miss them, either because of nostalgia, an antipathy on the part of hard rock fans for the synthesized "new wave" bands

My dear departed friend, Joe Baptista.

that were taking over radio, or both. Their original followers embraced them once again while they cultivated an entirely fresh audience to whom they were a novel and new old sound.

My personal relationship with Aerosmith has come full circle, I am once again one of those original fans, continuing to follow their career and see them perform. Though their legend has grown exponentially, their bodies have slowed down considerably, just like mine, and illnesses and accidents seem to multiply. Joe Perry has had a knee replacement, Tom has had a brush with throat cancer, Brad busted his head getting out of his Ferrari, and Steven seems to still take a fall at least once each tour. So far, it appears that Joey Kramer is the only one who has escaped physical mishap or compromise. I hear that he's started a coffee company on the side.

But regardless of what shape they're in, each time I see Aerosmith play together I'm reminded of why I still have such a very soft spot for them. From the beginning, their unique brand of garage rock gave the band an everyman quality that I couldn't resist, which was only magnified when their rocket to stardom quickly crashed amid their monumental fuck ups. And being on board for that plunge, holding on for dear life all the way down, is a ride I'll never forget.

Recalling Aerosmith's trials again reminds me of the universal truth that was evident even with the teenage Delta T: whether reaching the heights of stadium success or never leaving their parents' garage, drama is the stuff that rock bands always have and always will be made of. An assembly of disparate talents and temperaments finds a common cause and manages, hopefully, to make something more than just a lot of noise, to maybe even move us, before their own uncontrollable egos, insatiable appetites and irreconcilable differences cause their bond to break and the band to disband. And then with age hopefully comes wisdom and tolerance, and they reform for endless reunion and farewell tours that finally make them the fortune they're now mature enough to invest, hopefully wisely, so that they never have to play shitty clubs ever again.

Nurturing New Talent & Hawking Old Tees

WHEN MARK ARRIVED AT the office one day in the fall of '81 with the deadpan declaration of "I think you should start looking for other work," I was not particularly surprised.

With more than a dozen Aerosmith performances, 1980 had been a banner year for Freefall, and I produced almost 50 shows during those twelve wild months. 1981 was a different matter, with half as many events and not every one producing a profit. Aerosmith was still in denial of their dysfunction and sat out that year to instead begin on the long road to delivering a new album, all the more difficult without the contributions of Joe Perry and Brad Whitford. And despite some paybacks from a few baby bands that were finally breaking through, Mark's relationships with artists and their agents were softening. In addition, the entire concert industry was in a slump; a bad economy coupled with the rise of dance music were fingered as the culprits. By summer, my staff position had become unsustainable overhead. Freefall continued to pay for my services on a freelance basis for another year but finding alternative income was imperative.

Freefall's competition offered no opportunities for me. All possible positions were being held onto hard by seasoned vets of the venues and other concert promotion organizations who were now themselves struggling to make ends meet. A twenty-threeyear-old had no prospect of unseating any one of them. I turned to the record companies and talent agencies only to be offered bottom-up positions for as little as $6,000 to $8,000 a year, more modest sums than I was able to survive on. A brief stab at booking talent for clubs and colleges on my own just left me with a long-distance bill greater than any potential commissions.

I quickly decided it was time to put my formal college degree to work and to follow in my dad's footsteps, putting my rock dreams to bed to pursue a more stable career in the advertising business. That summer a focused effort put holes in the soles of my best dress shoes and landed me an entry-level position in an advertising agency paying a few thousand dollars more than ATI had offered me to start in the mailroom, and the next three decades are a blur of writing snappy headlines, winning accounts and keeping them happy.

Mark and Pam carried on with promoting for a while – dates with Asia, an offshoot of the breakup of Yes; Rush once or twice; finally capitalizing on U2's rise to arenas and a one-off with Duran Duran; and recouping their losses with AC/ DC's eventual and now iconic popularity. And there was the Jethro Tull show, the one where Ian Anderson turned his back on me. My new schedule precluded me more and more from participating, and so they turned to the established players, including my original mentor, Joey. Though if I could make it work, I still did – my three days at Cobo with Van Halen and my final gigs with Aerosmith had been brief sabbaticals from my desk job.

As the number of artists that Freefall was awarded became fewer and further between, new sources of revenue had to be found. So Mark and Pam took what they had learned from their trials with their quasi-management of Aerosmith and retooled Freefall to concentrate on artist representation. Freefall Presentations morphed into the Freefall Talent Group, first managing promising local favorites Twisted Sister and Zebra before adding Baltimore's Kix and TNT out of Trondheim, Norway.

I couldn't bring myself to fully separate from the scene, so I'd show up and assist in any way I could pro bono. Sometimes Mark would drag me along to entertain his "clients," as he had on the evening with Mötley Crüe. Of everyone involved, I was actually the most knowledgeable about the music itself and I connected with the artists. I was well versed in the biographies and discographies that were influencing young bands, and despite having no talent myself, I understood songwriting and instrumentation. I knew when a melody wasn't memorable, where a bridge was needed to break up the monotony. By then, I could listen to a recorded guitar solo and tell the difference between a Gibson Les Paul and a Fender Stratocaster, a Stratocaster from a Telecaster and a Rickenbacker from a Gretsch. I could instantly differentiate the acoustic being strummed, a six-string or twelve, a Martin, Taylor or Takamine.

A hard-working Long Island bar band, Twisted Sister belted out Bowie covers until they found their own sound and attitude. John "Jay Jay French" Segall founded the band in the early seventies, and after some early trials and errors, he brought on Dee Snider as lead singer, Eddie Ojeda on lead guitar and Mark Mendoza on bass, all of whom would remain the core for decades of reunions. In true Spinal Tap fashion, at one point, the band burned through four drummers over three short years.

With a do-it-yourself mind towards their career development, Jay self-managed the band, savvy enough to create their own t-shirt company in order to fully capitalize on the fans' insatiable appetite for Twister Sister merchandise. With singular focus, the band worked relentlessly, and by 1978 they had become popular enough to promote themselves into sellouts of The Palladium in New York City as well as our Calderone. Less than 18 months later, they sold out the better part of Nassau Coliseum's 16,000-plus seats. Mark began to take notice and to take the band seriously, and by 1981 he had taken over most management duties from Jay. Until my retirement, I suffered through what I considered to be their garish style and boorish rants. While I sat in the wings constantly checking my watch to make sure that we didn't run into overtime with the unions, the kids loved the act and Twisted Sister kept selling more and more tickets and t-shirts.

By 1984 Twisted Sister had moved beyond the beer-soaked bar rooms of Long Island and New Jersey to arenas all across America. Their third release of original material, *Stay Hungry*, their second on Ahmet Ertegun's Atlantic Records, had everything Twisted needed to catapult them to The Big Time – a major label push, the perfect level of outrageousness for MTV's video jukebox, the right timing with hair metal hitting its heyday, and sing-along songs that were simply irresistible. But subsequent releases saw their sales slide, and by 1987 Dee left the band. Throughout the next decade, he struggled at reinvention, first with the creation of Desperado, featuring guitarist Bernie Torme (a wonderful human being as well as a solid player) and ex-Iron Maiden drummer Clive Burr (a total nut job), followed by a darker turn with Widowmaker.

Despite the support of high-profile friends like Howard Stern, neither project struck a chord with either old fans or new.

Zebra was a three-piece; Randy Jackson on guitar and vocals and the primary composer, Felix Hanemann on bass and Guy Gelso on drums. Founded in New Orleans and earning a devoted following for their covers of hard rock/art rock stalwarts such as Led Zeppelin, Yes, Rush and the like, they found their way to a second set of fans on Long Island, sprinkling their sets with originals. The band produced a trio of albums; the first, produced by Aerosmith's long-time tutor, Jack Douglas, was one of Atlantic's fastest-selling debuts. Zebra went gold with little effort, moving more than a half-million records based upon the pent-up demand of the band's rabid following within the two markets. Sales of their next two were essentially dead on arrival.

But by the summer of '83, their Long Island base grew to such an extreme that Zebra was asked to headline a daylong free festival sponsored by WBAB-FM, the classic rock radio station that owned the 12 to 24-year-old demographic in the Nassau-Suffolk market and who was one of the band's biggest cheerleaders. The event was expected to draw 10,000 fans to a sports field at Suffolk Community College. Like Twisted Sister, Zebra had control of their own merchandise sales and they sensed a huge opportunity to capitalize on the crowds. Zebra's production manager, Marty, rang me up around midnight the evening before, realizing that they had no one to manage that effort and asking if I'd be interested. His timing couldn't have been better, as I had just taken a hit due to my naiveté. I had been introduced to Broken Arrow, a younger local band that had developed a small following by performing perfect renditions of hits by Tom Petty and similar musicians, as well as a few self-penned songs in the same vein. Fantasizing myself to be rock's next great impresario, I began discussions with Broken Arrow to take on their management as a side project for myself, an effort that went nowhere due to their difficult nature and my lack of both patience and experience. But at one of their shows, I had met a trio of fans who gave me a line on hot VCRs for a fraction of retail cost, and I had been taken for several hundred dollars. Long story short, I'm basically an honest guy, but the too-good-to-be-true deal was impossible to resist, and I learned a hard lesson with damage to my ego as well as my wallet.

Knowing that Zebra were in a jam, I struck a hard but fair bargain: I wanted ten percent of the gross for whatever I sold. Marty readily agreed, as 90 percent of something was better than 100% of nothing, which would be the case if I hadn't agreed to do the job. We met up early the next morning, crawling into the band's van to inventory what was on hand in dozens of cardboard boxes containing a wide variety of styles, themes and cuts, more than 800 shirts in all. I told Marty that we would keep it simple and sell with one-price-fits-all at $10.00 a tee.

As the stage was being set, I positioned the van at the single point of entry to the festival. I figured that I would get them as they arrived and I would get them as they were leaving – no one would be able to come or go without passing my wares. Big, bold signs covered every window of the van to provide eye-catching promotion as well as much-needed privacy inside. I was confident that I'd be dealing with plenty of cash, and I wanted to be the only person aware of it. My OCD told me to sort the mess

by both theme and size so that I could do transactions quickly – as I had learned with the beer at the Calderone, a captive audience meant that the faster you could serve, the more you could sell. Zebra wowed their fans with a great performance, and the crowd got themselves sufficiently loose to open their wallets. I sold out.

"How did we do?" Marty asked with the last fans leaving as dusk began to set in.

"I sold it all."

"What?"

"I sold it all. A little over $8,000 worth."

"You're shitting me! That's incredible! Where's the money?"

"In my pockets. I've got $7,200 in this one for Zebra and $800 in this one for me."

"Uh, you're taking $800 bucks? Isn't that a bit much?"

"Isn't that we what agreed on last night and again this morning?"

"Yeah, it was, but…nobody ever thought you'd sell eight grand of that shit. The band's not going to be happy."

"Listen, Marty, a deal's a deal. Second, the band should kiss my ass. They're $7,200 richer for playing a 'free' show, and that's more money than they usually make when they get paid to play."

"Yeah, I hear you, but I gotta talk to them. This is gonna be a problem."

"Your problem, not mine," I said, channeling Dick's Chick, as I turned to clean out the van of the now-empty boxes.

When all was in order, I strolled over to Zebra's trailer to deliver their cut. Mark must have seen me coming and stepped outside just as I arrived.

"$800, Gregg? Really, are you kidding me?

"Not at all. That was the deal."

"Well, the guys are pissed. They don't think it's fair."

"Well fuck them if they don't think it's fair. That's the deal you guys made, and I held up my side of the bargain."

Suddenly Randy Jackson appeared in the doorway. I always liked Randy. Unlike most of the singers I'd met, he had a modest demeanor and he always seemed able to keep his ego in check. "So Gregg, what's the story?'

I explained my side to Randy, not pleading my case but holding firm to my conviction and laying it all out as a fait accompli. "I'm not your fucking record label and I'm not your partner. Besides, I have *your* cash in *my* pocket. Do you want it?"

Randy smiled ruefully and said "Yeah, and thanks. You made us a lot of money today. We appreciate it." That was that and I think that everyone went home happy. (Maybe not Marty, though. I have a feeling he might have taken at least a little bit of shit.)

Kix, born in Hagerstown, Maryland in the late seventies/early eighties, became a Freefall client just prior to their fourth and most successful album, 1988's *Blow My Fuse*, coincidentally yet another release on Atlantic Records. The record featured the power ballad "Don't Close Your Eyes," preaching alternatives to suicide. Surprising since it focused upon such a touchy topic, "Don't Close Your Eyes" rose to #11 on Billboard's Hot 100 Singles chart and the album sold over a million copies. But while Kix was certainly talented, they were hardly unique, a poor cousin to AC/DC, with far less tongue in their cheek. Songs like "Bang Bang (Balls of Fire)," "Get it While It's Hot" and "She Dropped Me the Bomb" lacked the necessary melody and metaphor, and Atlantic dropped the band by '94.

TNT had a chance; in my estimation, they were the most technically talented of the bunch and to my tastes they were consistently solid songwriters, though never quite able to craft a killer hook. Their American lead singer Tony Harnell was one of the best rock vocalists I have ever heard, with a remarkable range and a classic rock star look and style. Lead guitarist Ronnie Le Tekkro was an amazing player, and at times ahead of his time, dabbling with synthesizers and a prototype of something called a "quarter-step guitar." Mark and Pam managed TNT through three albums on Mercury/Polygram – *Tell No Tales*, *Intuition* and *Realized Fantasies* – but American metalheads just couldn't fall in love with the Norwegians.

They certainly were a ton of fun to hang with, though; their idioms and idiosyncrasies a constant source of amusement. When in the States, they had little to keep them occupied outside of their work associated with the band, so Pam and I would often play chaperone to these fish out of water, showing them the sights in New York and introducing them to new foods via some of our favorite restaurants. It was one evening in Manhattan when we had Ronnie in tow that our car got towed, and we had to drag him with us to the West Side docks to free it. It was about 10 p.m. when the cab dropped us off, and the fine-paying line was dozens long. Ronnie, with his ass-length hair and purple velvet pants, stood out even in New York, and while he attracted his fair share of stares, he paid no mind. He was too busy checking out the scene, mostly an assembly of down and outers for whom the ransom was the last thing they could afford. As it came our turn, the victim in front of us was pleading with the teller to let him off the hook, a foreigner apparently in town claiming that his rental car had been yanked behind his back as he was exchanging words with the driver who had rear-ended him. Worse yet, his wallet was in the car, so he had no cash or credit cards on him to pay. The teller was having none of it, refusing him even access to the auto in order to retrieve his ID and money. Ronnie, witnessing the absurdity and injustice of the poor guy's plight, decided to stick his nose in. He sauntered past the "Stand Behind This Line" line and positioned his face less than an inch from the thick Plexiglas separating the suffering outof-towner from his tormentor.

"You're a waste of human flesh," Ronnie declared to the teller in his thick Norse accent.

"What did you say?" the incredulous civil servant asked for clarification.

"I said, 'You're a waste of human flesh,'" Ronnie repeated. He glared at the teller for several moments before stepping back in line with us to wait our turn. It didn't help the mistaken offender's case, but forever after "A waste of human flesh" became our code for people we considered assholes, and we began to use it as liberally as Ronnie. There were a lot of assholes in the music business, just as there are in politics.

You Can't Always Judge a Man by His Mascara

HAVING MOVED ON AFTER years of being in the thick of things, I lost touch with almost everyone except Dee Snider. I had known Dee when he was a star gazer. I was around when the rocket took off. And I was standing by when he floated back down to earth. Through it all, Dee and I developed an Odd Couple friendship; I think he appreciated that I wasn't particularly interested in his celebrity, that we just enjoyed each other's company like any other duo of suburban dudes despite our decidedly different appearances.

Twisted Sister has always been one of those bands that critics love to hate, but they are among the few to create anthems every bit as eternally relevant as Queen's stadium standards "We Will Rock You" and "We Are the Champions." "We're Not Gonna Take It" has been enlisted by numerous brands to hawk everything from motels to carpet cleaning to menstrual products. It found a recurring role on broadcast television as the theme to a geriatric *Candid Camera* hosted by the indomitable Betty White. And it gets hijacked time and again by politicians on all sides of the fence. "I Wanna Rock" saw a second life in video games, had its own good run of crass commercial exposure, and it was the centerpiece for *Rock of Ages*, one of Broadway's hottest shows and another misguided Tom Cruise movie. And both songs stand beside those Queen classics, forever rousing the fans to get behind the home team. "We're Not Gonna Take It" and "I Wanna Rock" are Twisted's own unique cultural contributions, songs that have become ingrained in the collective consciousness. You can knock Twisted Sister all you want, but you have to admit that we all know the words.

It was the video for "We're Not Gonna Take It" that made Dee's garishly painted face recognizable all across the land… and which landed him in front of the Senate Commerce Committee and Tipper Gore's Parent Music Resource Center – the infamous PMRC inquisition. The PMRC's self-righteous proposition was that "rock music was attributable to the decay of the nuclear family in America," and as such they were calling for an album rating system to be legislated so their social calendars would not be interrupted by the responsibility of monitoring their children's content consumption. "We're Not Gonna Take It" found itself dead center on their list of The Filthy Fifteen, in between Mötley Crüe's "Bastard" and the truly offensive "Animal (Fuck Like a Beast)" from W.A.S.P. Putting aside the fact that the lyrics to "We're Not Gonna Take It" are little more than a teenage tantrum against parental authority, the video is even less guilty of possessing any capability to corrupt. Basically it's a live-action restaging of the cartoon conflict between The Roadrunner and his indestructible nemesis, Wiley Coyote. Nothing except plenty of harmless slapstick ensues, but the video's premise of flipping the bird to the generation in charge was apparently more than the Washington wives could endure. If they ever actually watched it, that is.

Only three artists stepped up to the plate to defend their rights to free speech. Volunteering to testify were Frank Zappa, John Denver and Dee Snider, Dee being the only one of the three who had been personally singled out as an evil influence. Zappa's testimony was a case of conspiracy-theory paranoia, a rambling treatise on the perils of the interference of government in First Amendment rights and the self-interested complicity of the recording industry establishment. John Denver seemed on a Rocky Mountain high as he focused on the bigger issues of youth and society while basically kissing the Committee's ass. Only Dee, from all appearances the least likely to represent the voice of reason, did just that after first debunking the accusations thrust directly at Twisted Sister and himself.

"I am 30 years old; I am married; I have a 3-year-old son. I was born and raised a Christian and I still adhere to those principles. Believe it or not, I do not smoke, I do not drink, and I do not do drugs."

Dee went on to succinctly state the obvious: in the end, it was a parent's responsibility to nurture and mold their offspring, and that monitoring what they see and hear along with what they eat is a major component of that responsibility. And yes, if that means listening to forty-five minutes of heavy metal or rap to assure yourself that it won't induce your kid to commit rape or suicide, well, that's really a pretty small price to pay. Amen.

In time the PMRC lost its credibility, almost as quickly as Twisted Sister did with their fourth album. For the PMRC, it turned out, "offensive" rock lyrics proved to have no more negative impact on America's youth than does getting off reading the memoirs of Casanova or searching for Satan in the Waldoscape of a 15th-century triptych by Hieronymus Bosch. In Twisted Sister's downfall, I'm certain that their cover of "Leader of the Pack" had something to do with it. It also didn't help that in Dee's zeal to clear his name, the kids became disillusioned: they thought he was a demon, too, and they were really disappointed to find out that he wasn't.

It's interesting to note that the only song of The Filthy Fifteen that is still going strong almost four decades later is "We're Not Gonna Take It." Compositions by more mainstream artists who made the list, including Madonna and Prince, were B-Sides at best. The deep cuts from AC/DC, Black Sabbath, Def Leppard, Judas Priest, and Motley Crue that the Committee cited were rarely reached by the turntable's needle in the first place. And acts like W.A.S.P. and Venom were virtually unknown beyond their small tribes of hardcore fans – and still are. All the PMRC accomplished by calling them out was to give them more notoriety than they probably deserved to begin with. But "We're Not Gonna Take It" is still around and still going strong, with a ubiquity it never had even when it was charting in Billboard's Top 40.

Dee is an extremely talented guy who unfortunately never found his creative brother – no Keith, no Joe Perry, no Richie Sambora to his Jon Bon Jovi in Maybelline. So the fame faded and Dee moved on, forming new bands with more proficient musicians and trying on new personas. He went through a spaghetti western phase with Desperado, then tried his hand at much darker material with Widowmaker, in my opinion, both stronger efforts even though both failed to approach Twisted Sister's success. So Dee set his sights on new pursuits. *Strangeland*, a horror film he wrote, directed and starred in. Doubleday published Dee Snider's *Teenage Survival Guide*. A syndicated radio show, *House of Hair* and hosting gigs on VH1. Getting his Nashville on with *Gone Country* and trying to please the dour real estate promoter and future Cheeto-in-Chief, Donald Trump, on *The Apprentice*. Dee even landed his own reality show enlisting the participation of the whole family, *Growing Up Twisted*. Dee is nothing if not the ultimate survivor, and he has become extremely successful at creating a brand out of Dee Snider. And on top of his ongoing list of adventures, he finds the time to do a great deal of charity work, his most ardently committed causes being autism and The March of Dimes. Bravo.

Dee has also been a good friend. It's a casual friendship, but it's one that I think we can both count on despite its occasional hiatuses. Our families became close, the music business' insanity not getting in the way of the more important parts of life. For a few years, Dee and I had a friendly paddle ball game going every Sunday morning, just like a lot of the old-timers in Brooklyn and Queens. These days we don't get together too often, but when we do, it's a comfortable mix of nostalgia and "What's new?" Though he and Pam will invariably revert to shop talk, we trade the latest exploits of our kids with him and his wife Suzette, and he never fails to ask me how I'm doing. Not that Dee has no ego, but in my experience, he has never succumbed to what I term as Lead Singer Syndrome, always keeping his head on his shoulders and not up his ass. From the beginning, I've appreciated that he's shown me the respect of addressing me by my name. His bandmates in Twisted Sister thought it hysterical to call me Clark, as in Kent, for

For my 50th birthday Dee gave me a peculiar present –
a Johnny Cash box set. For several years its significance
escaped me until I discovered that The Man in Black had been
born on the same day as me: February 26th.

my decidedly buttoned-up looks that were so at odds with their over-the-top costumes and coifs. Dee has always just called me "Gregg" (yet, like everyone else, he tends to forget my third G).

At the surprise party that my wife threw for my fiftieth birthday, Dee honored me by telling a story of our vacation together on St. Bart's many years ago when we were both much younger. We had commandeered a sailboat that day – Pam and I, Dee and Suzette, and Rissa and Cary, another set of our long-time friends; three thirty-something couples partying on the high seas, captained by our tanned French chaperone, Pilou. We had anchored in the cove of a small island for some lunch and a swim when the wind whipped up and one of Pam's exorbitantly expensive beach towels flew over the side, a Saks Fifth special sporting a stylish abstract mix of black, blue and green. Hitting the water, it proceeded to sink as if it were lead, resting a good dozen feet or so below the waves on a bed of coral and rock, perfectly visible through the crystal clear Caribbean water. Pam pleaded with me to retrieve it, so without hesitation, I dove in with Olympian form and ballooned lungs, pearl diving deeper and deeper until I captured my prize and returned triumphantly to the surface, gasping for air. For reasons I still don't understand, the scene stuck with Dee all those years and he cited it as a testament to my courage and fortitude. Teetotaler that he was at the time, he apparently never realized that I was simply smashed and had been just as likely to jump into a pool of piranhas. And that's the crowning irony of the whole PMRC farce. The heavy metal monster who got called on the carpet by Tipper Gore and friends is not just a smart guy; he's also a nice guy, with far more integrity and a way better heart than many of the people America often chooses to represent us.

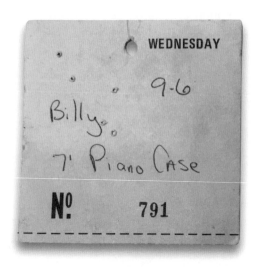

23

He's Always Just Billy to Us

THOUGH ONE OF THE most densely populated geographies in the world, Long Island has never been synonymous with great rock and roll. Our region is unfortunately far more renowned for spawning serial killers and sordid tabloid tales than we are for winning Grammys.

We've had our dalliances with dance-pop and divas (Mariah Carey and sometime resident J-Lo). We've had a few local cover bands that stepped up to the majors with their original material but fizzled fast (Twisted Sister and Zebra). Now and then, a few more mainstream rock talents rose to be middling stars but left little legacy (Foghat, Blue Oyster Cult). On the folkier side, we had Harry Chapin, a wonderful storyteller but a terrible driver whose career was cut short on the Long Island Expressway.

But we also have Billy Joel. He's huge, and he belongs to no one but us, just like Bruce Springsteen is claimed by Jersey. And just like Bruce, Billy has left a little bit of Long Island behind him as he's traveled all over the globe, even in Russia, right before the wall came down. Billy is the one thing that both Yankees and Mets fans can agree upon. And of course, we all just call him Billy, whether we've ever met him or not.

Billy made his presence known in a big way with *Piano Man*, his second album under his own name following his first real professional gig with The Hassles, a short-lived duo titled Attila, a brief flirtation with Dick Wagner and his Ursa Major, and finally his first solo outing, *Cold Spring Harbor. Piano Man* was followed by *Streetlife Serenade* and *Turnstiles* before Billy delivered *The Stranger* in September of 1977, the record which catapulted him to superstar status. Today, after fourteen albums and going on five decades of performing, Billy is one of the world's most popular attractions, currently playing for 20,000 Platinum Card-paying fans at Madison Square Garden every month from now through eternity.

Following the release of *The Stranger*, Billy performed a few random shows before closing out the year with a December gig at Nassau Coliseum, his first opportunity to headline in his hometown venue. It was also one of Brian's first shows as a runner for promoter Ron Delsener. More than two years before his escapade with Pink Floyd, it provided an early indication that the then-eighteen-year-old's chutzpa knew no limits.

The day before the event, Brian was browsing the bins in Sam Goody, one of the New York area's largest record chains. Announcements were made for an in-store contest asking "Who is The Stranger?" with the winning answer to walk away with a brand new video recorder. Already savvy enough to game the game, Brian figured, "That's easy! I'll just ask Billy tomorrow." And so he did.

The next day was the typical arena scene – non-stop action of load in, set up, soundcheck and performance. But the aftershow in the Coliseum's dining room was Billy's Big Day, a champagne celebration important enough to attract the president of Colombia Records and the legendary producer Phil Ramone who had guided Billy through the recording of *The Stranger*.

"Hey Billy, can I ask you a question?' Brian brazenly blurted as he tapped the singer on the shoulder. As Billy turned, Brian couldn't contain his excitement. With no further explanation as to who he was or how he came to be at the party, Brian confidently went on. "There's this contest that Sam Goody has, and they want everyone's answer to who *The Stranger* is. I figured if anyone should know, it would be you!" Brian took the flyer from his pocket and unfolded it in an instant, extending it to Billy.

Billy held the flyer in his hands, becoming visibly more upset as he read on, finally losing his cool. "You know, you write a fucking song, it can take a really long time to get it just right, you finally give birth to it and it becomes one of your children. Then suddenly some goddamn record store makes a contest out of your kid, minimizing the process and all of your hard work." He thrust the flyer back to Brian.

"Wow," Brian said, "I never thought of it like that." Then, without hesitation, Brian disregarded the Piano Man's indignance and went in for the close. "But hey, Billy, would you mind giving me the answer anyway, so I can win the contest, take home the video recorder?"

Billy ripped the flyer from Brian's hand and scribbled furiously on the back, the pen's ballpoint threatening to poke through the paper before he returned it and did an about-face.

Brian glanced down at the sheet and stared in disbelief. Billy had simply written: "There is no answer," and signed his name with a flourish.

That should have been the end of Brian's story, but the real irony is that when he returned to Sam Goody the following day, with the *only correct answer in the world, given to him by the singer that wrote the song*, no one believed him. They opted instead to award first prize and the runner-ups to winners of a random drawing of all the entries, despite the fact that they were all wrong.

After a February appearance on Saturday Night Live, Billy spent the Spring of '78 touring abroad – March in Europe, April in Australia and Japan – then taking the summer off before embarking on an extensive tour of the U.S. This leg of first-ever headlining in American arenas called for the biggest production of Joel's career, and to work out the kinks of both the rig and the repertoire Billy and the band camped out for three days in the Long Island Arena, also known as the Commack Arena, also a.k.a. the Suffolk Forum. The Arena was an old hockey hall that had its fifteen minutes of fame a few years before as the recording site for a number of tracks on the mega-selling *Frampton Comes Alive*.

On Day one, the trucks rolled in and the first order of business was piecing together the custom stage, then onto the lighting and sound, and finally the band gear. It was all done at a leisurely pace, involving a bit of trial and error, sharpies ultimately noting the correct connections and fittings on fragments of duct tape affixed to stage, equipment and road cases.

Day two was attended by a skeleton crew, a handful of us being asked to be available, just in case. Billy and his band arrived midday to give it a go and warm-up for the tour's first date, two days hence in New England.

On Top: Billy's answer to the big contest.

Below: The Stranger's producer, Phil Ramone, CBS Records' Walter
Yetnikoff, and Billy at the backstage party celebrating his arena debut
at Nassau Coliseum on December 12, 1977. (Brian swears that's his
head in the background between Phil and Walter.)

As the band took the stage, I took up my standard position for sound checks, in the center of the floor, an audience of one in an otherwise empty hall, a field of polished gray concrete between Billy and me. A kaleidoscope of color danced on the cement, pulsing from the trusses above the stage as the lighting designer practiced his cues. The band ran through some of the still new and less familiar songs featured on *The Stranger* as well as the album's first single, "Only the Good Die Young," all destined to be classics no matter how deep on the vinyl they were found. The band performed the hit repeatedly in pursuit of whatever perfection Billy had in his head, often stopping mid-stream to smooth a transition. I certainly didn't mind; as an alumnus of a dozen years of parochial school, that particular song had quickly found a place in my heart. I could completely relate to its chastisement of Catholic girls' chastity and its celebration of sinners forsaking sainthood.

Having never seen Billy perform previously, I expected to see him rooted safely behind the piano. But apparently, Billy was warming to his newfound rock star status; he was just twenty-nine and seemed to be having the time of his life. Microphone in hand, he sang to me alone as he prowled the stage, as comfortable in his role of frontman as he was as a piano man. At one point, Billy broke into "Shattered, " Mick Jagger and Keith Richards' odd, aggressively rhythmic rant from the Rolling Stones own summer of '78 hit record, *Some Girls*. It was a wonderfully spontaneous, unscripted performance by a gifted young man at the height of his confidence, taking a moment to simply have some laughs singing someone else's song that was far removed from the box he was already being put into by the critics and fans.

The third day was left to take it apart and pack it all up – making sure that everything found its proper place on the trucks and was ready to roll. But in their haste to get on, the road the crew left something behind. The semi's tail doors closed, latched and locked, they had neglected a slice of their staging resting against a wall, in plain sight but perhaps so obvious that it was easily overlooked. I'm happy to say that I'm the one who found it, and I like to fantasize that I saved Billy Joel from a career foreshortened by falling headfirst into a gaping hole, giving "Only the Good Die Young" an unintended irony. That December, Billy went on to play Madison Square Garden for the first time – three back-to-back and sold-out shows, the first of his now record-making tally that grows every month.

I next ran into Billy at a party several years later – a record release affair hosted by our local rock radio station, WLIR-FM, for Phoebe Snow's 1981 album, *Rock Away*, on which a number of Billy's bandmates contributed their talents. At the tiny, coffeehouse-style room just a few doors down from My Father's Place, the Island's equivalent to Manhattan's The Bottom Line, Snow gave a low-key solo performance that was followed by an open bar reception. Billy was by now a megastar, living a galaxy beyond even the superstars, and he was far cockier than he had been at *The Stranger* rehearsals. But when he overheard Pam's surprise that Billy was "much shorter than I imagined," he was quite visibly annoyed. He also, like everyone in the music business in the early '80s, was not immune to the indulgences of the decade. He spent a good portion of the evening not so subtly working the room in search of a little bit more of whatever was getting him high that night.

Though I'd seen Billy perform several concerts over the intervening years, it had been a lifetime since I had had the opportunity to see him up close and personal. My wife and I were to meet friends for dinner at a nice sidewalk joint near my home, her favorite in town, elegant yet comfortable, nouvelle Italian. As I reached for the worn iron handle on the weathered wood door, I glanced to my right and there was Billy, dining with a date and another couple, seated in the largely windowed alcove, his back to the traffic but his now bald and bearded style unmistakable despite his casual suburban camouflage of blue jeans and a button-down.

As I said before, Billy is one of ours. While I assume he's had his flings with LA and probably keeps a place in Manhattan, he's always called Long Island home. And no matter the escalation in the value of his address, from Oyster Bay to Lloyd Neck, from the Neck to Center Island, from Center Island to East Hampton, Billy has never given the impression that he's become too good for us. He doesn't hide behind massive hedgerows; he sits right in the front window. Everyone seems to have their own story of meeting Billy on the street, out and about as he tries to blend in and go about his life. While Billy occasionally makes the local headlines, it's usually for the same type of bad luck or bad decisions that we all fall prey to from time to time. And when Billy does wield his celebrity, it is almost always to champion a charity worth supporting.

We and our company were enough to fill two tables – and our party was feeling no pain. I got up to return some of my rented chianti and when I headed to the men's room, I faced Billy head-on as he was returning from the same destination. I instantly decided to engage him even though there was no chance that he would have remembered me. But with Brian as my role model, I said "What the hell!" to myself and "Hello!" to Billy.

The Piano Man gauged me with suspicion, a justified "Do I know you?" look, I suppose sizing me up to be a stalker or worse. But when I confidently extended my hand, he took it readily and shook it with vigor. Billy's own hand was sturdy and rough, again not what I had expected of him but maybe the result of hauling seines with the East End baymen whose plight had become one of his more recent causes. There was plenty that could have been said, but "Thank you" was all I could muster. Puzzled at first, he seemed to quickly recognize the depth behind my lame gesture.

Billy graciously nodded to acknowledge the simple appreciation of a stranger's hometown pride, and then he returned to his companions in the window for dessert.

Billy ate here.

The Italian restaurant where I accosted Billy. Home to a hearty mushroom risotto and an outstanding tuna tartar.

24

A Tale of Two Woodstocks

FOR ALMOST TEN YEARS of my advertising life, one of my clients was the Villa Roma Resort Hotel, an Italian take on the otherwise exclusively Jewish Catskill Borscht Belt. Once a month, I was required to schlep to the all-you-can-eat vacation spot located in Callicoon, New York, a three-and-a-half hour drive from my home. Villa Roma is nestled in a valley off the grid on a paved but severely potholed path just uphill then downhill from a poor man's farm, complete with a well-populated pigsty and various species of poultry running wild and spilling into the street. But several miles before leaving 17B for the back roads to the resort I would pass through the town of Bethel and the hamlet of White Lake, the actual location of the hastily relocated Woodstock Festival.

Once I discovered that the site of the legendary gathering lies less than a mile from the intersection of Hurd Road with the highway, whenever time would allow, I would make a quick detour to breathe in the air of the place where peace and love reigned for those three historic days in August of 1969.

On my first visit, a gray day in the dead of winter, I was struck by the vastness of the space, a natural amphitheater, a bowl with acres upon acres of grassland ascending from a picturesque pond below to a ridge a few football fields above. As I froze my ass off in the chill wind beside the commemorative plaque placed on the site by the then-current owners of Max Yasgur's famous dairy farm, I envisioned the half a million strong who were treated to an eclectic array of incredible music while indulging in all manners of mind alteration. The more modestly planned event had instantly transformed this unprepared rural town with a population of less than a few thousand into one of the largest cities in the U.S.

A number of winters later, in early 1994, I came to represent the Sullivan County Board of Tourism in their efforts to bring attention to the region's attractions amidst the death throes of their traditional vacation spot economy. The county was becoming deeply depressed; one after another, the great resorts closed their doors and lay desolate as tastes changed and keeping healthy was in, rendering obsolete the endlessly refillable platters of meats, mashed potatoes and fried everything. To me, the answer was obvious: plan an encore event to capitalize on the Woodstock Festival's 25th anniversary that would be rolling around in August. Who would need money for paid advertising with the endless free publicity that that would generate? I wasn't alone in my thinking; a number of professional and wannabe concert promoters had already expressed interest in doing just that. But the Catskill residents and their elected officials wouldn't even allow the idea on the table. Most of the folks affected by the infestation of hippies in '69 were still around, and they were damned if they were going to let it happen again. Every time I brought it up – and I was somewhat relentless about it – I was met with impassioned objections from closed minds that held nothing but antipathy for the now two-and-a-half-decade-old affair. I ended up creating an exceedingly brief and innocuous radio campaign that was more in line with the committee's conservative sensibilities.

As it happened, I was paying a call to Villa Roma on August 17th, the third day of the official anniversary. Stopping by the site to pay my respects on this day above all others was a must, Jimi Hendrix's "Star Spangled Banner" on endless repeat in my head on the drive up. At the resort, they told me that contrary to the county's earlier stance, they had at the last minute relented to allow Sid Bernstein, the all-but-forgotten impresario who had brought The Beatles to our shores, to mount a modest anniversary event but that his financial backing had fallen through. Now, even though still no official event was being held, several thousand people had descended on the site over the weekend anyway, getting back to the land to set their souls free and to connect with a piece of history that many of them were too young to have taken part in the first time. A small, makeshift stage had been erected, only about a foot off the ground, a wrinkled blue tarp stretched above in a valiant but doomed attempt to deter the inevitable rain, which arrived as if on cue. A number of the original festival's faded stars returned to play pro bono: Arlo Guthrie, Melanie, Leslie West of Mountain. Woodstock once again was a free concert.

That Wednesday, as I drove down Hurd Road's tree-lined length, I anticipated seeing the weekend's purists still lingering through the official end of the anniversary. But this gathering dubbed *Bethel '94* – Woodstock Ventures, formed by the same four organizers of the '69 event, held all licenses to the original festival's name, brand and images – had begun petering out on Sunday and now it appeared that only several hundred diehard pilgrims were still squatting on the site. It had been a weekend thing, and this being the more structured nineties, even aging hippies now had rent or mortgages to be paid, and my guess is that most people had to be back at work on Monday.

A few remaining campers lined the ridge, which besides being level, afforded a birds-eye view of the bowl and the pond beyond. There was no one performing below, and whatever rickety stage there had been was now gone. Instead, a small flatbed truck sadly stood where the original stage in '69 had been erected, the one from which Sly Stone, The Grateful Dead, The Who and Hendrix had wailed and worshipers were warned to stay away from the brown acid. Instead, there stood a PA system more in line with a high school gym, blasting the live recordings captured twenty-five years earlier.

*Woodstock's original memorial,
put in place on the event's 15th anniversary.*

The Woodstock Ventures people had avoided dealing with Bethel and Sullivan County almost from the start, early on pivoting to present the official Woodstock II about an hour and a half away in Saugerties. They again had lined up some of the hottest acts of the moment, most of which happened to be considerably harsher in tone than Crosby, Stills and Nash or Joe Cocker, the only returning originals. Mega acts Aerosmith, Metallica and Nine Inch Nails played to another overstuffed crowd – about 250,000 tickets had been sold and reportedly, over 350,000 people showed up. Like the first official festival, it got muddy and out of hand. But this time I imagine everyone made money. A reported ticket gross of almost $34 million was supplemented by major brand sponsorships, including Haagen Dazs, MCI and Pepsi. A $49 payper-view cable TV offer was available for those who couldn't or wouldn't deal with the hassles of actually being there and getting dirty. And, of course, there was $4.00 bottled water for the 350,000 lucky souls that were.

Fast forward: Michael Lang, the face of the '69 festival and its eponymous movie, pulled off another Woodstock windfall just five years later, but that 1999 version further buried the peace and love of the original and is now remembered mostly for its violence and vandalism. The bad vibes were enough to keep any other real anniversary attempts at bay until what would have been the Big One, the 50th, in August of 2019. Lang was determined to cash in one more time while anyone that cared about the history was still alive, but this time it crashed and burned before it ever got started. After a number of fitful starts and stops, lawsuits piled up on all sides before the festival was officially called off, and the Woodstock legend was muddied yet again.

25

Tossing 'Em Back with the Real Capt'n Jack

PARROT CAY IS A small volcanic atoll in the Turks & Caicos Islands, due north of Haiti, sitting at approximately 22° latitude, 73° longitude. Until the turn of the millennium, the place was populated by little more than tropical birds and spiny reptiles, with the island's most recent human residents being the eighteenth-century pirates who favored it as safe harbor between their next pillage and plunder. Today it is quite the chic resort destination, consisting of just 60-odd guest rooms and several villas, operated by an Indonesian concern attempting to recreate a South Pacific paradise in the Caribbean.

It is 2008 and Pam had planned a vacation as part of my fiftieth birthday celebration. The party she threw earlier in the month had been more shock than "Surprise!" Not that I was shocked that my wife would throw me a party, but I still can't get over how she had been able to keep it a secret so well for so long. God only knows what else I don't know.

After an uneventful flight from JFK to the T&C capital of Providenciales, we boarded Parrot Cay's private cruiser for a 40-minute trip to the resort. Clear skies and glorious sun reflected off the spectacular hues of blue and green, while white foam in the distance defined the reefs that protect these islands against the Atlantic's rollers from the north. We passed several large, but informal beachfront residences on the island's coast before the resort came into view, a promise of welcome rest and relaxation.

A planter's punch check-in and an afternoon of tropical sun had us ready for dinner and an early snore, but the occasion called for a toast to celebrate our escape from the distressful late winter weather back north. We meandered from the restaurant to the poolside bar, a zen-laden tiki hut no doubt imbued with impeccable feng shui. The bar was empty except for a grizzled seaman and a lazy retriever sprawled at his feet, an incongruous sight in this oasis of Gilt Group luxury. While Pam settled at the bar, I knelt to pet the pooch. An inebriated voice spoke out from above.

"She's a good old girl, my Pumpkin is."

Turning to reply I looked up to be met by the Cheshire grin of Keith Richards.

I had recently learned just exactly how clever my wife was. I knew that at this point, that after decades in the music business, Pam had become pretty well connected. And I knew that *she knew* that if there ever were a rock and roll personality that I would want to hang with, it would be Keith. But even she couldn't have pulled *this* off.

You'd think that someone like a Rolling Stone – especially one of the Glimmer Twins themselves – would have some sort of entourage, maybe a small posse, at least a dwarf bodyguard or two. But this evening, Keith was just a guy, alone at the bar looking for an interested ear. Pam and I recognized a once-in-a-lifetime opportunity and parked ourselves for what we knew was going to be one hell of an entertaining evening, and we ended up spending the next few hours with Keith all to ourselves. Shooting the shit, downing our respective indulgences, laughing and even singing.

I've met quite a number of famous and fabulous people, working very closely with many – as by now you know – and I've never been star-struck. But this was an entirely different sort of celebrity encounter, a sit-down-in-the-living room sort of thing where the public persona and myth got left behind, revealing the man with transparent glory. Gone were the constant stroking of the brow and tipping of fingers to his lips that appeared to display a premeditation in his replies to certain questions during recent interviews I'd seen. Tonight he was at home, and though we were random guests that he had just dragged in off the street, he treated us as if we were old friends.

Though he was already half in the bag, Keith was still quite lucid. He was often extremely witty, sometimes to the extent that you'd think his outrageous statements were rehearsals for a new career in comedy. The bits that follow are observations and quotes to the best of my memory. I qualify with "to the best of my memory" because that evening, I had no pen, no paper, no recorder to capture my own impromptu interview. And we were, after all, hanging with the legendary Keith Richards, which means the booze was flowing. And flowing.

Pam instantly found it natural to begin the conversation by suggesting that she and Keith knew someone in common – a Rick who was involved in the production of recent Rolling Stones concert tours. Keith couldn't make the connection: "Rick? Rick? Rick? No, I don't know that I know any Rick. But I DO know a MICK!"

Pam had seen the recent new U2 concert filmed in 3D. What did Keith think about that? The Stones had their own new concert film being released soon – *Shine A Light* – shot by Martin Scorsese over two nights at New York's intimate Beacon Theatre. Shouldn't the fans be able to see The Stones in 3D?

"3D? Honey, I don't need any fucking 3D! I'm ON THE STAGE, man, playin'!" he blasted back, furiously strumming an air guitar, the lit tip of his Marlboro dancing with the motion of his right hand. He then instantly lit up with glee to profess his affection for Martin Scorsese and his films. "Marty is the best, man. I'd do anything for Marty. I loved *Taxi Driver* – he used a lot of great Stones songs in that one."

"But, Keith, don't you appreciate where technology has brought music?" I countered. With this, he got extremely indignant.

"I don't give a shit about technology! It's all just ticky-tack, ticky-tack, ticky-tack..." he fumed while frantically tapping his fingers on the bar like an agitated elf banging a laptop. Keith hates the idea of digital downloading, and he contended that cassettes were the ultimate form for recorded music. Yes, *cassettes* and I thanked God he didn't say 8-tracks. But his devotion to such an obsolete audio format wasn't all that surprising. After all, Keith famously recorded the riff to "Satisfaction" one night in the mid-'60s while on tour, half asleep in his hotel room, on a shitty portable cassette recorder running on two double D batteries. He and cassettes go way back.

New music? Rap? To Keith, it's "all garbage. Oasis, U2... ha!" Forget that both bands had already been hugely popular for decades. And he was emphatic that rap wasn't even really music at all. "Ya gotta play, man. It's all about the live thing!"

For this reason, he liked Jack White, who I later discovered appears with the Stones in *Shine A Light*. "Now Jack, man, that boy can play!"

On all issues great and small, Pam was debating Keith, and he'd have none of it. So we soon moved off music for a while to get his take on more mundane matters. We had been aware that several celebrities had private homes on the island – the beachfront residences we had passed while arriving in the launch – and that actor Bruce Willis and fashion designer Donna Karan lived here. We now knew that Keith did, too, and that he occasionally wandered over to the bar, just like he had this very evening. "Why Parrot Cay, Keith?"

"I love the sand bars around this island," he replied without hesitation. "The little ones – the grandkids – they can walk out for a mile and it never gets above their knees." He paused to take a deep drag on his cigarette before breaking into a wide smile to deliver his punch line. "And if they're dumb enough to drown in that, then they don't deserve to live!"

Keith also liked the fact that the island had little or no law enforcement.

"Where else do you have homes?" I asked.

"London, Paris, a small place in New York, and in Connecticut. Connecticut, though, Connecticut is *HQ*." Then, sounding more like any typical American silver-haired snowbird in South Florida, he continued, "You know, I've worked all my bloody life to be able to flee the cold and wet up there and come to a place like *this* for four months of the year!" Whereupon he spread his arms wide to stress the scope of his paradise.

Keith hanging loose with Pumpkin's little brother, Rocket, on Parrot Cay, a month or so before he befriended Pam and I.

"Speaking of work, when *do* you think you will be working again?" I inquired. His recorded output is so rare that I am always interested in hearing about something new, either from the Stones or Keith alone. "Aye mate, that's the question!" he intoned in his best buccaneer banter. After a disgruntled and mostly incoherent commentary regarding his old friend and bandmate, we got the impression that if it were up to Keith, he'd be working all the time; he simply loves what he does. But with the sad state of the record business in 2008, he wasn't considering putting together a new Stones album. He was, though, working on a few new solo recordings of which he said, "I'm just going to throw them out there." Perhaps that's what I finally heard more than seven years later with the release of *Crosseyed Heart*, only his third album of original material outside of the Stones in over fifty years.

I was familiar with his first two solo works, and in an effort to impress him, I brought them up. *Talk is Cheap* and…I just couldn't remember the name of the second, and he had little patience for me to try. "*Main Offender*, man, that was the other one!"

His backing band, dubbed *The Expensive Winos*, was an assembly of some of the finest session musicians in America. I asked Keith if he had any thoughts of getting the Winos back together again anytime soon. "Ah, yeah the Winos! I've actually been talking to some of those guys lately. Steve Jordan, Waddy Wachtel, Bobby Keys…now those cats can rock!" At this point, he appeared to have a revelation and turned to me with surprise and delight, closing one eye to focus on my face. "Hey man, I didn't know you liked the Winos?!" I didn't feel it would serve any purpose to remind him that we had just met.

I did remind Keith, though, of another side project, a one-off tour where I saw Ronnie Wood and he perform at Madison Square Garden in the '70s in support of Ronnie's solo album,

Gimme Some Neck, and how he had played "Before They Make Me Run" which was his lone lead vocal on the Stones' own *Some Girls* album. "Ah yeah, The New Barbarians... "Before They Make Me Run." Man, that should be my fuckin' theme song..."

You had to wonder why he was here, at the bar, all alone, and you almost wanted to feel sorry for him, but nothing he said smacked of remorse. To the contrary, he'd flash his devious smile and go and say something else that was just so outlandish it made you realize that he was simply having the time of his life, today and everyday. It's obvious that he immensely enjoys being just who he is, no complaints, no regrets, no care for whatever anyone else may think of it.

All this time, the three of us became quite close, evolving into back-slapping bar buddies as the night wore on. And while making my mental notes of our wide-ranging conversation, I also made sure to soak in the sight of this Stone alone, all the traits and textures that are essential in describing his character. Even now, I can still see the smallest details that are usually otherwise only evident with the close inspection of an intimate portrait shot by the likes of Irving Penn or Annie Leibovitz.

It is obvious that Keith revels in the fact that he was the inspiration for Johnny Depp's Captain Jack Sparrow in Disney's *Pirates of the Caribbean* franchise and, at least on this occasion, he was fully dressed for the part. A trio of red, white and black bandannas surrounded his head, each knotted at back. A black cotton scarf was draped over a black jersey-sleeved tee hung above clam-digger pants boldly striped in gray and white and revealing his bony bare shins and calves. At bottom were anchors of fleece-lined black suede, the Ugg boots that are ubiquitous among teenage American girls, an incongruous choice of footwear for the 85-degree tropical heat. He accessorized his look with a mix of island beads and biker silver, including the big, bold skull ring that has forever been his trademark. A heavy-handed touch of eyeliner finished off his ensemble.

He chain-smoked Marlboros and chain-drank Bushwhackers, an island concoction combining vodka, rum and Baily's Irish Cream. "It may look like it needs some biscuits to go with it, but after a few, they creep up from behind and *WHACK* you in the back of the head!" Keith theatrically struck his cranium to dramatize the effect, this time his cigarette's ashes and sparks exploding with the impact.

Emaciated and waif-like, you wondered if Keith ever remembers to eat. When he stood, I realized just what a small guy he is despite his larger-than-life persona, much shorter than he appears on the stage or in film. He was organically tanned in that islander way, where the sun is simply a way of life, and his face was extremely weathered and worn, his deep creases and crevices no doubt the result of a lifetime of laughter as much as from drink and drugs. He hadn't shaved, his day-or-two stubble only adding to the overall appearance of a scurvied swashbuckler. His breath wore a permanent patina of alcohol and tobacco. He still seemed to have all of his hair, though much grayer than it generally shows in the media, and maybe a bit thinner. His fingers were gnarled like ancient olive branches, either from the onset of arthritis, fifty-odd years of wear and tear, or both. When I asked, "How old are you, anyway?" he didn't hesitate to tell us. As with everything else, his answer was honest and delivered with great pride.

"I'm almost 65, and I'm lucky to be here!" While I thought he was going to follow that up with a lament regarding the toll taken by his wicked ways, his explanation was more nostalgic. "I grew up with the bombs falling on me ya' know, back in London, in '43." Then upon further reflection, he let us in on his secret to survival: "Cigarettes, alcohol, cocaine, heroin...that's all fine, man. It's cheese that'll kill ya!"

At this point, I can't honestly attest to the sequence of events, but we covered a lot of ground that evening, and we were treated to scores of insights, opinions and absurdities before it ended. Here are a random few:

On wealth: "It's not about the money. I just love to play. People throw money at me every day. I just don't know how to spend it all!" (You get the distinct impression that he is clueless as to how much he may actually be worth, even though I imagine it to be in the hundreds of millions.)

On Phil Spector, and the legendary producer's then-recent arrest for the murder of a girlfriend: "Phil definitely did it, man, he always had guns around the house. There are bullet holes all over his ceiling. He'll beat it though; I'm sure he will." (Wrong on that one, Keith.)

On Ronnie Spector: "I fucked her."

On Johnny Depp: "My son [Marlon] introduced me to Johnny. He kept taking me out to dinner. It took a while for me to figure out what was up with all the free meals, until I realized that Johnny was studying me!"

On his appearance as Captain Jack's dad in *Pirates of the Caribbean 3*: "I got all of four minutes in the film," he declared with disdain, but then he proudly recited his one and only line. "It's not about livin' forever, Jackie Boy; the trick is living with yerself forever." (He didn't, however, explain what the hell it was supposed to mean.)

On Parents: At one point, I ran off to the loo for a moment and I returned to find Pam and Keith in serious discussion about the people that had raised them. The progeny of Greek immigrant parents, my wife is ever complaining about what she perceives as her second-class status within a devoutly patriarchal family. "Pom,

Pom, don't be so hard on your old man. Yer don't know how long he'll be around, ya know. I lost my Mum, Doris, just last year. She had cancer, and I was by her bedside in the hospital every day. On her last night, I played her a song, and you know what she said to me? She said, 'Keith, my boy, you're out of tune!' There she was, man, giving me shit 'til her last. But I miss her."

On the Caribbean Sea: "Europeans, Americans...we look at the sea as being the end of the world. These people [the islanders], they see it as a highway."

On the Caribbean sun: I guess he recognized from our paleness that it was our first day on the island, so he felt compelled to impart a little of his own parental advice, warning us to be mindful of the hazards of the ultraviolet, because, "Be careful, kids, yuz can really hurt yourselves out there!"

On self-defense: "I'm not a big guy, ya see, but I'm scrappy. Ya know how to get out of scraps?" Keith once again put on his best pirate voice. "Yer take yer knife, see, and lightly slice their forehead like this…" He demonstrated the carving with the side of his index finger. "It'll start bleeding like a bastard, ya see, and then the blood drips into their eyes, blinding 'em… That's when you kick 'em in the balls and run like hell!" Keith roared with laughter until his face suddenly snapped back to his sly grin. "I got me blade on me now. Yas want to see it?" Not waiting for our answer, with great pride, he brought forth what looked to be a six-inch switch that he'd been concealing in his pants. He flicked it open and ogled the blade in the bar light before safely returning the steel to its leather sheath.

On the Hells Angels and the recent report that they had put a contract out on the Stones after Altamonte: "Probably bullshit. That's all Mick's thing...he's such a media whore!" Then he followed with a sudden tirade of "Fuck the Angels! Fuck Sonny Barger [the Hell's Angels leader at the time]! Fuck Sonny Barger!"

On his fall from a palm tree in Tahiti the year before: "They flew me to New Zealand to patch me up. I was completely out and I put my life in their hands. I'm all better now, though, see?" And like a little boy eager to show off the scars of his latest two-wheel tumble, Keith gleefully removed the bandannas from his head and grabbed my hand. "Here, feel it, see for yerself!" he challenged as the pirate pressed my fingers and palm to his scalp and guided them from front to back and side-to-side to prove that there was no lingering damage where the wound had been. And indeed, through his thinning hair, I felt nothing out of the ordinary, which at the very least attests to the competency of his plastic surgeon.

One thing we never touched on that I really wish we had? The reports that Keith had snorted his father's cremated ashes; I can only imagine...

Somewhere along the way, Keith and I ended up singing "Only the Lonely" by Roy Orbison, but for the life of me, I can't tell you why. I also can't confirm one hundred percent that that was the tune; all evening, I had been matching his Bushwhackers with my own overflowing martinis. But when he broke into song I couldn't resist joining him, so I instantly leaned in to accompany his serenade to the bartender; two drunk buddies bent over the bar crooning like a pair of pining dogs. After all, how many people can say, "I once sang with Keith?"

Around midnight, probably for no other reason than to let the bartender go home, we said our goodbyes. Seeming to have no desire to turn in anytime soon, Keith pulled himself up off of his stool and in a quite gentlemanly gesture, gave us each a huge embrace, wrapping me then my wife in his thin arms and planting a big kiss on each cheek before releasing us. Neither Pam nor I thought to ask him to join in a selfie, sign an autograph or otherwise supply us with proof of what had been a truly surreal experience. We were simply saying good night to a new old friend.

Until we meet again.

Every evening thereafter, when we visited the same bar for our nightcap, we hoped to run into Keith a second time. But Pam and I knew that it wouldn't happen. Much of the evening's magic had been due to its kismet, and an encore performance would never yield for us the same wide-eyed wonder as the first. And I'm sorry to say that yet again, I have nothing to show, no trophy, no souvenir, no tangible evidence that any of this all happened. All forty-odd years of it. But it did. I was there. And I remember.

Immediately upon arriving home, back in the States, I began my sorting of our weeklong holiday's mail. A quick glance at the latest arrival of *The New Yorker* revealed a two-page spread advertising the luxury luggage of Louis Vuitton – featuring nothing but a photo of Keith in a hotel room strumming a vintage Gretsch, an LV guitar case by his side. Evidently, I mused, people really do just throw money at him. I later found out that our good-hearted friend had donated his modeling fee to charity.

Shine A Light was released just about a week later and there was an attendant plethora of press. In an Entertainment Weekly interview, there appeared a quote from Keith regarding Johnny Depp having "studied" him for his turn as Jack Sparrow, almost identical to the revelation he dropped on us at the bar.

When Keith's autobiography finally hit the bookstores, I quite expected to encounter passages that were likely to be iterative if not verbatim to those of our rendezvous on the island. But even though on that evening he must have been in the throes of its production, reliving his *life* for days on end, little of the wit or wisdom that he had rained on Pam and I seems to have made the final edit.

But perhaps the finest coda to this whole experience was to actually see *Shine A Light* in a theatre one month after our meeting. Scorsese captured the Stones up close and in your face, putting you "on the stage, man" right there with Keith, Mick, Ronnie and Charlie and their incredible supporting cast of musicians, now all literally larger than life. In the film, their age is evident, but their ability to still perform with the passion and intensity that they do is inspiring every time I view it. And while it's wonderful to see and hear many of The Stones' greatest hits, the moment I treasure more than any other is when Keith sings the plaintive "You've Got The Silver," a second-tier song from *Let It Bleed*. With the sole accompaniment of Ron Wood playing slide guitar, it is a stark and more melancholy version than the original recording, delivered by a man who has lived a lot of life during the decades in between. And standing alone at the microphone in the spotlight, Marlboro again dangling between his fingers as the ashes drip to the floor, his long gray coat blending into the darkness surrounding him, Keith looks every bit the scarred and scandalous pirate we shared the evening with on Parrot Cay.

Bits & Pieces

WITH TWISTED SISTER DISBANDED and the failure of Zebra or Kix or TNT to explode in America, Freefall began to freefall itself and Pam would soon be out of a job, too. But not for long. TNT's recording of *Realized Fantasies* had introduced her to producer Ric Wake, and for almost two decades, Pam went on to become his partner in their attempt to create a pop empire centered on the more polished sounds of the Top 40. They had a string of successes with megastars Mariah Carey, Celine Dion, Jennifer Lopez and others, but that is another story entirely, better left for another day and possibly another book. Here, though, are a number of bits and pieces from our story that couldn't fit neatly into any of the preceding chapters but which nonetheless I think are of interest to anyone still willing to listen.

Full disclosure necessitates I come clean about one more thing that I wish I had chosen to do differently. Fans clamoring to get backstage would often plead with us to get mementos signed for them, mostly record albums, but the occasional bra or panties made their way into our hands, too. I'd say, "We'll see what we can do," and hustle off with their hopes and take myself out of sight. "I'll be David Lee. You can do Eddie…" and we'd pass around the Sharpie until the evening's attraction had been fully represented by the indecipherable scribbles of stagehands and security. I'd march back out and proudly return the "autographed" item to its owner, who would thank me profusely as they gleefully skipped off with their trophy. Please understand that it wasn't about getting laid or paid; it was about making people happy, even thrilled, and I saw no harm in the deception if that was the result. But…I wouldn't be surprised to find any number of those forgeries for sale online, so caveat emptor.

Just as I had gotten myself in to see Led Zeppelin and Eric Clapton by pretending to be someone's son, as soon as I was a "suit," I learned that I could work it to my advantage. By showing up in a three-piece, handkerchief popping just so from my pinstripe's breast pocket, I would often be granted access to wherever I wanted to go, no questions asked despite no backstage pass. Who the hell would show up to an AC/DC concert at Madison Square Garden dressed for Wall Street? Had to be someone important, right? Yeah, right.

Post-rock, I've always worked in Manhattan, so I was wearing one of those suits when I visited Dee and Twisted Sister at Radio City Music Hall one evening in January of 1986, and by chance, I had the pleasure of sharing a deserted dressing room with Ahmet Ertegun. Ahmet is considered to be the father of the modern record business, a champion of outsider artists when everyone else thought rhythm and blues was only for blacks and that rock and roll was just another juvenile fad. Aretha Franklin, Ray Charles, Otis Redding, Led Zeppelin, Crosby Stills, Nash & Young and Genesis were his children, to name just a few. And Ahmet's dedication to personal style was as devout as his passion for the music. As well-tuned as his ears were, Ahmet's eye understood that finesse was the key to dressing well. He looked like a million bucks that night, as I imagine he did every night, naturally, and with consummate class.

So here we were, two suits brought together by cross-dressers. Before walking out, Mark had introduced me by nothing more than a first name, and a bit intimidated at being alone with the legend, I expected an awkward silence. Instead, Ahmet broke the ice with a bit of small talk followed by a few questions about my connection to the band, smiling all the while and seeming sincere in his interest. He then shared a joke with me, something involving B.B. King and Bo Diddley, roaring with laughter as he delivered the punch line of "Bo don't know diddly!"

Ahmet passed away some twenty-odd years later from injuries sustained by a fall backstage at The Beacon Theatre for one of those Rolling Stones shows that Scorsese filmed for *Shine A Light*.

In Providence, Ted Nugent's equipment trucks broke down en route and arrived just three hours before the show instead of when they were supposed to arrive, 8 hours earlier. After a lot of sweat and nails bitten to the quick, the show went on, on time, and it culminated with Ted clad in nothing but a loincloth falling into the crowd – again and again and again – to shoot the cover of his second live album, Intensities in Ten Cities.

A brief tradition brought The J. Geils Band and us together several times for New Year's Eve, and they caught me off guard one year with a last-minute request for a balloon drop. Though more populous than Presque Isle, Portland, Maine, particularly on New Year's Eve, wasn't a place one could simply make a phone call and order up an elaborate stage effect. So, yet again, I improvised. I was able to buy an old parachute from the local airport, and I ordered an oxygen tank and a couple of kids who agreed to fill a thousand or so balloons in exchange for free tickets. You may be saying, "Don't you mean helium?" No, I mean oxygen. I needed the balloons to eventually fall. One balloon at a time, the kids filled the massive satin sheet. We rigged the corners and hoisted it to the rafters high above the stage. At the stroke of midnight, we pulled the knots loose and despite my fears of malfunction, the scheme worked like a charm, raining a rainbow of jellybeans upon the crowd as we rung in '81 with J., Peter Wolf, Magic Dick and the rest of the band, batting balloons in a celebration of our gigantic house party.

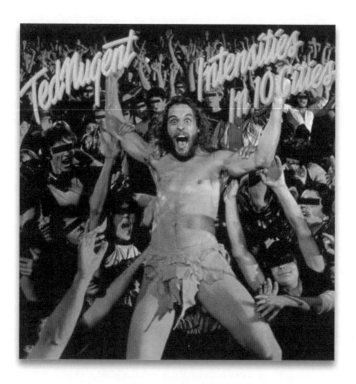

We had to keep prying Ted back from the crowd
until the photographer called it a wrap.

I met my third Mötley Crüe member almost twenty years after the John Peel Room Incident. In Miami, Pam's later partner Ric had us out for a day on his boat bombing around Biscayne Bay. One of our fellow seamen, an A&R guy for a metal-focused indy label, knew the Crüe's drummer and had heard that he was holed up at the moment in the new home of Puffy, a.k.a. Puff Daddy, P. Diddy, Diddy, and Sean John. (Who knows what the hell the hip-hop mogul may be calling himself when you read this.)

The 17,000 square foot mansion was on exclusive Star Island. Puffy had just purchased the home for $20+ million from Tommy Mottola, the former CEO of Sony Records and ex-husband of Mariah Carey. Tommy Lee was staying as a guest. We identified the house from the water and tethered ourselves to the pilings. The record guy rang the drummer on his cell, telling Tommy that what had earlier been a loose plan to just drop by was now a very real boat at the dock. Not long after, Tommy Lee strolled briskly down the long walk from the house. He was wearing only board shorts, which left visible almost every other inch of his emaciated body, covered head-to-toe and side to side with a montage of tattoos in varying bad boy themes surrounding the gothic-lettered MAYHEM, the centerpiece of his ongoing body art project. He hopped onto the boat for a polite chat, quite civilized despite his look and reputation. But before long, Ric's voluptuous Argentinian girlfriend latched onto the rock star, convincing him to join her on a quick jet-ski jaunt, the two zigzagging across the chop with her thong-tied, all-but-bare-ass thrust high in the air seducing Tommy Lee to catch her. It looked like he had plenty of experience at that, which was no surprise given his now very public exploits with Pamela Anderson on Nevada's Lake Havasu.

Meanwhile, the lord of the manor deigned to say hello, sauntering down to the dock, decked out in white (his own fashion label, I presume), his black skin standing in stark contrast. Puffy said a round of hellos, gave a quick hug to Ric and retreated to the house. Meanwhile, Tommy Lee and ChaChaCharo had returned and were now toweling off.

"Is this the real life, or is this just fantasy?" Freddie Mercury famously asked. I may worry more and more about income disparity in the world, but it was certainly nice to pretend that I was one of the chosen ones, even if just for an afternoon.

My Father's Place was next to the trestle of the Roslyn viaduct. The parking lot was right under it. No matter what act you were there to see, the pigeons would still shit all over your car. Michael "Eppy" Epstein was the proprietor, a wide man with wide smile sporting clogs before Crocs were even a glimmer in celebrity chef Mario Batali's eye. Unlike Hammerheads, Speaks or Detroit, My Father's Place was Long Island's equivalent to Greenwich Village's The Bottom Line – a higher class "venue" than a club – and Eppy was known to nurture talent young and old, supporting them in their bids to win hearts, minds and ears and move on to a career of playing much bigger stages.

The Police.

Pam and I saw them at MFP when they first came to the U.S. We went to the 11pm show. Pam fell asleep. The Police became one of the biggest bands in the world.

Eddie Money.

He only had one album, so he played everything I wanted

to hear. Shortly before he passed away, he was doing GEICO commercials.

Peter Tosh.

I didn't see the show, but I hung outside with a few hundred other people for several hours. It had been rumored that Mick and Keith would show up. They didn't.

Papa John Creach.

Eppy hired me to videotape the show. We had presented Charlie Daniels that same night at Hofstra. Charlie showed up to fiddle with Papa John during his late set. It was quite the hoedown and I was on stage right next to them all night to capture it. I occasionally wonder what happened to that video. I never got to see it.

Lou Reed.

Dick Wagner and Steve Hunter were not with him.

According to Larry: "While dancing, my eyeglasses fell off my face and ended up in a million pieces after being stomped on by me and many others. With all the peanut shells on the floor, who knew that it was my glasses that were making that crunching sound!" According to Michael: "Lou came out for an encore, played the opening riff to "Sweet Jane," and then stopped and walked off. There was damned near a riot, which may have had something to do with Larry's glasses getting broken."

The Clash invaded America with a week-long residency at an old Broadway dancehall known as Bond's because of the big neon signage left behind by the men's store that previously occupied the space. The run sold out instantly, and apparently, twice. Somehow the shows had been vastly over-ticketed, causing the NYPD to cancel the third night and forcing the band to extend their stay for 17 performances in order to make good to every ticket holder. Larry, Bruce and I had tickets but were turned away, being told that they'd be honored on a subsequent evening. Not ones to waste the train fare into Manhattan, we headed to the Village to bum around, drink some beers and have some laughs. On the way back to Penn, we came upon a corner cathedral on Sixth Avenue, the directory in front of the Rectory obscured by a sign pasted over its glass. "This Sunday The Rev. Pooker T. Littlehead Preaches: The Wages of Sin Will Earn You An Eternity in Hell!" We loved it so much that we took it home on the Long Island Railroad with us and Larry and I displayed it in the front bay window of our apartment for the entire neighborhood to see. For months.

Ironically, not long after our theft, the church was deconsecrated and transformed into the infamous Limelight niteclub, quickly becoming notorious for the decadence of drug use and sexual antics that its more spirited patrons were prone to committing in the century-old Gothic structure's dark corners. I was inside only once to see Dee perform with Widowmaker, one of his post-Twisted Sister projects. As my brother-in-law and I leaned on the bar and ordered our first of several rounds, two steel cages descended from the ceiling in the middle of the room, each containing its own scantily-clad dancer writhing and clawing the air like a pair of irascible lions. Whatever they were getting paid, I imagined that they'd be taxed on it in Purgatory.

Folksinger Louden Wainwright III was performing in the Hofstra Rathskellar, and I had invited my friend Tom from Delta T to see the show. Louden's big hit was a ditty called "Dead Skunk (in the Middle of the Road)," and you may remember him as Captain Spalding, the singing surgeon who occasionally appeared between scenes on TV's *M*A*S*H*. Midshow I spied Tom chatting up a chick at the back of the room and I wandered over to see what was up.

"Hey Gregg, meet Suzzy!" Tom enthusiastically slurred.

She gave me her hand, which I raised to my lips and lightly kissed before replying, "Your name's Suzy, right? He's just really fucked up?"

"No, actually it is Suzzy," she corrected me, and I walked away thinking that they were both very fucked up.

Many years later, I found out that her name was indeed 'Suzzy,' that she ended up having a daughter with Louden just a few years after our introduction, and that she achieved more than moderate musical success of her own as one of the The Roches with her sisters, Margaret and Terre.

I'm with Keith on having little love for the "ticky-tack, ticky-tack…"

In this day and age, I constantly get questioned as to why I still buy compact discs when streaming can satisfy virtually any craving on demand without wasting precious closet space. Well, I really like CDs; therefore I find whatever space I need to devote to my obsession. I find my music to be much more accessible when it's right in front of me instead of drifting in the cloud.

I'm also very interested in what an artist has to say or play over the course of much more than three and a half minutes. Some of my favorite songs have never made it into even rare rotation on the radio. The backstory is of great interest to me, too, the liner notes giving hints to motivations and influences that resulted in the works I'm listening to.

In my youth I started with vinyl but briefly got led astray by my brother and Louie to try eight-tracks, even replacing some of my records with the new "higher-tech" format. It became quickly apparent, though, that 8-tracks were the spawn of the devil. Albums as they were created never seemed to fit correctly on an 8-track. A slow fade-out and subsequent fade-in were necessary when a longer song needed to be carried over from one of the four programs to the next. Occasionally songs were simply cut short to fit, or conversely, there would appear long periods of silence if there wasn't enough material to fill the space. They thought nothing of mixing up song sequence in order to structure the timing to best technical advantage, creating havoc with concept albums by bands like my beloved Jethro Tull, Pink Floyd and Yes. And worst of all, inevitably, the player would eat the quarter-inch tape that wound back and forth on the spool inside, requiring hours of delicate work trying to rethread the tape in order to save my investment. I quickly fled back to vinyl until CDs came on the scene, and I've been a follower ever since.

Vinyl loyalists deplored the CD's sharp-edged sound, preferring the more lush, full-bodied tones of traditional LPs. Some suggested that lining the CD edge with a Sharpie felt tip trapped in the music's inherent richness, though I can't say that I ever tried it myself. They lamented the loss of vinyl's beloved cracks and pops and the home remedies we created for fixing the scratches and gouges that created them.

CD size was an issue for vinyl lovers as well. The new format not only turned song lyrics and album credits to even-smaller-than-agate birdshit, but it put severe new limitations on album art creativity – no more pop-ups, pin-wheels or zippers – and you certainly couldn't use a jewel case to de-seed when in the process of rolling your own. Now there was no more Side One, Side Two, no A Side or B Side, no White Side and Black Side. And while the CD's digital replication allowed for almost twice as much music as could fit on the much larger vinyl LP, it wasn't always welcome. It seemed hard enough to create a record where all 8-10 songs were keepers. With now having the ability (or responsibility, since CDs were, of course, priced much higher than most LPs) to give fans more value by including 12, 14, 16 or more songs, a lot of shit started appearing that we wished had stayed locked in the vault.

All that said, I learned to love the CD. Its smaller size proved efficient when your album collection, like mine, grew into the hundreds or even thousands. (I've just learned that Jimmy Page's music collection includes almost 6,000 CDs and over 4,000 LPs. I assume that space isn't a problem for Jimmy either.) Its portability meant you could now have your music in a single format both at home or on the go. Its virtual indestructibility made it immune to the carelessness of wives, girlfriends and terrible two-year-olds. "Shuffle," the ability to randomly play the songs on an album, enabled me to give a fresh twist to old classics, and multi-disc play made every party mix unique.

Alas, my way of life is being severely threatened in the face of the digital revolution. "They're packing it in. Everyone's downloading," said the stock boy at the Virgin Megastore in Times Square, now more than a few years ago as I watched the fixtures being loaded out the door. But even downloading quickly became passé, and Spotify is now the master of music's destiny. But I haven't given in. I still scour the meager CD offerings on display at big box stores for newer releases and classics that I never got around to buying, and when all else fails, I order from Amazon, though grudgingly.

But before you assume that I'm a Luddite mired in an endless replay of *Rock of Ages*, be aware that I maintain my own somewhat extensive CD collection that my wife views as a massive waste of both money and space. But I have to have my music at my fingertips and be able to touch it.

I still subscribe to the louder and harder the better, but I also have a softer side that appreciates good unplugged fare as well. I have buddies whose palates prefer the pre-Beatles style of the fifties and early sixties, particularly doo-wop and rockabilly bands. Others have matured towards cool, sometimes even improvisational jazz. I know a few sophisticates who claim that they actually enjoy classical compositions. My kids and their friends have been weaned on rap and top 40-style R&B. But for me, rock still rules.

I try to keep my collection limited to one-tenth of Page's, at about 600, via conscientious effort at purging to make room for new sounds. Choosing what's to go is often a painful process, but I have developed my own set of criteria for who gets voted off of my island. There are records that I thought would have great promise but didn't deliver; these usually stick around for a while, receiving repeated listens in the quixotic hope that I've been missing something. There are albums that have had their moment but by now have lost my interest; I simply can't justify their waning nostalgic value. Then there are those that fall into the often-embarrassing category of "What the hell was I thinking?"

Prince is one of the few talents that actually may have left me starstruck had I ever worked with him, but that opportunity never came to pass. I was, though, once in the same room with the Purple One, The Polo Lounge at the Beverly Hills Hotel. In early 2005 Pam and I had gone west with our young boys for her to take her own star turn with a guest appearance on the Ashton Kutcher/ Mila Kunis teen-com, *That '70s Show*. She'd won the appearance as a raffle prize at one of the endless string of charity functions that have seemed to control our calendar for the last twenty years. Episode #175 was entitled "20,000 Light Years from Home," after the Rolling Stones song.

On an afternoon off from Pam's taping, we had wandered over to see if the legendary inn was as ominous as the picture painted by the Eagles in "Hotel California." It wasn't. The Polo Club was lush with foliage and plush with velvet, and at about 3 p.m. it was all but empty save a few regulars at the bar. The restaurant itself was closed, so we sat in the cocktail area, ordered alcohol for two and French fries for four, and just as our food arrived, so did Prince in all of his own velvety plushness. His arm entwined with that of a stunning young woman, he was led to a table in the middle of the otherwise empty hot spot, where he graciously motioned for his date to be seated first, and proceeded to dine in privacy and elegance as if he were actual bloodline royalty.

It was one of those moments where I couldn't help but reflect on my own life and its vastly different direction. You see, Prince, Madonna, Michael Jackson and I were all born within 6 months of one another, and after each rose in their own supersized way, I tracked my smaller life in tandem with theirs, matching my more mundane milestones against their very different roadmaps. Today, Madonna and I are the only ones still standing, though I'm not quite sure of the significance of that coincidence.

Yes, one by one, my idols are dying or retiring, and at the risk of sounding old, I am having a hard time finding adequate replacements, though I try to keep my ears open. I don't intend to ever stop going to sweaty clubs or cavernous hockey arenas to see someone I want to hear, and better yet, I'd love to get involved in presenting live music once again, to be the one throwing the party. I want to organize a rock festival with cheap tickets, an event that exposes new bands to new eyes and ears, where the folks attending never know who they'll be seeing and hearing before the artists take the stage. They just show up because it'll be a nice day in the sun and on the grass, and if you have the right head, it'll always be plenty of fun. Sort of a watered-down Woodstock with just the right vibe every weekend. Are you in?

Keeping Score

CREDIBILITY IS AT THE core of an exercise like this. I have to ensure that you believe that I didn't just make this stuff up. So, in addition to what few photos I've been able to include, which document that I was where I said I was, what follows is the best accounting I'm able to make of the actual dates of events. It wasn't easy. At the time it was all happening I was conscientious enough to keep a running log of the shows I was producing, though not compulsive enough to note their exact dates. So from the fall of 1979 through the end of 1982, I at least knew the *order* in which the performances took place. From there on, others' internet obsession has enabled me to fill in most of the blanks. I can't guarantee that the people who've posted the data, have any better memory than I do, but more than a few citations were supported by at least one irrefutable source.

In addition to the official websites of dozens of the artists listed, fan-created sites and blogs, the most helpful sources for verification were *setlist.fm, concerts-db.com* and *lookatstubs.com*. In addition, I've poured over whatever images I've been able to find on Google of tickets and backstage passes, as well as vintage newspaper ads and posters in an endless search for third-party mementos of my shows.

The List has been of immeasurable help in reconstructing just what went on, and, in many instances, it has enabled me to resurrect even more memories of people, places and events. Little by little, and occasionally with a sweeping rush, sights, sounds, dialogue and emotions came pouring back with old scenes replaying themselves in tremendous detail, the colors and smells as vivid as the music. Then again there are also shows that are still a total blackout. Damned if I know why.

1976

Orleans	Hofstra Adams Playhouse – Sept. 1976
Nektar	Hofstra Adams Playhouse – 10/2/1976
Roger McGuinn	Hofstra Coffeehouse – Fall 1976
New Riders of the Purple Sage	Hofstra Coffeehouse – 11/4/1976
Hot Tuna	Hofstra Adams Playhouse – 11/11/1976
Ambrosia	Hofstra Adams Playhouse – Nov. 1976

1977

Johnny Winter & Muddy Waters	Hofstra Fieldhouse – 2/27/1977
Renaissance	Hofstra Fieldhouse – April 1977
The Outlaws	Hofstra Adams Playhouse – Spring 1977
Dave Mason + Jennifer Warnes	Hofstra Adams Playhouse – Spring 1977
Quicksilver Messenger Service	Hofstra Coffeehouse – Spring 1977
The Kinks	Hofstra Fieldhouse – 5/4/1977
Procol Harum	Hofstra Adams Playhouse – 5/11/1977
Nektar	Hofstra Adams Playhouse – 10/7/1977

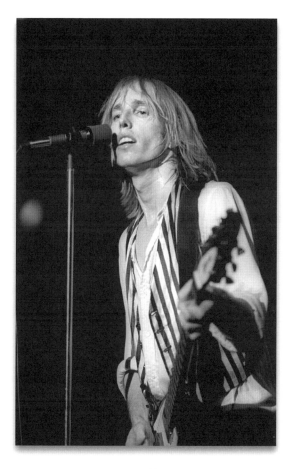

Tom Petty and The Heartbreakers at
The Calderone Concert Hall, opening for J. Geils Band
on July 28, 1978.

Jerry Garcia Band	Hofstra Adams Playhouse – 11/21/1977
Hot Tuna	Hofstra Adams Playhouse – 11/23/1977

1978

Louden Wainright III	Hofstra Rathskeller – Feb. / Mar. 1978
The Charlie Daniels Band	Suffolk Forum / LI Arena – 4/28/1978
Hot Tuna	Hofstra Adams Playhouse – 5/15/1978
Hot Tuna	Suffolk Forum / LI Arena – 5/19/1978
The Charlie Daniels Band	Hofstra Adams Playhouse – 6/9/1978
Papa John Creech + Charlie Daniels	My Father's Place – 6/9/1978
Blackmore's Rainbow + REO Speedwagon	Suffolk Forum / LI Arena – 6/10/1978
Dave Mason + Walter Egan	Suffolk Forum / LI Arena – 7/6/1978
Alvin Lee	Calderone Concert Hall – 7/23/1978
J. Geils Band + Tom Petty & Heartbreakers	Calderone Concert Hall – 7/28/1978
David Bromberg Band	Calderone Concert Hall – 8/26/1978
Billy Joel (Tour Rehearsals)	Suffolk Forum / LI Arena – Sept. 1978
Little Feat	Calderone Concert Hall – 10/5/1978
Twisted Sister	Calderone Concert Hall – 10/28/1978
Bill Cosby	Calderone Concert Hall – Nov. / Dec. 1978

1979

George Thorogood & The Destroyers	Hofstra Coffeehouse – Jan. 1979
Henry Paul Band	Hofstra Playhouse – Feb. / Mar. 1979
Jorma Kaukonen	Hofstra Fieldhouse – 2/24/1979
Elvis Costello & The Attractions	Calderone Concert Hall – 4/10/1979
Cheap Trick	Calderone Concert Hall – 4/14/1979
Emmylou Harris	Calderone Concert Hall – 5/25/1979

© Christopher J. Davies

Carlos Santana gets spiritual at The Calderone Concert Hall on November 24, 1979.

Graham Parker & The Rumor	Calderone Concert Hall – 6/6/1979
Rainbow (Video: All Night Long)	Calderone Concert Hall – July 1979
The Beach Boys + Chicago	Aqueduct Racetrack – Summer 1979
The Beach Boys + Chicago	Monmouth Racetrack – Summer 1979
Stephen Stills + Orleans	Belmont Park – 6/24/1979
Blondie + Rockpile	Belmont Park – 7/8/1979
Jorma Kaukonen	Belmont Park – 7/15/1979
Talking Heads	Calderone Concert Hall – 8/18/1979
The Charlie Daniels Band + Dave Mason + David Bromberg + Todd Rundgren	Belmont Park – 8/21/1979
Joe Jackson	Calderone Concert Hall – 8/31/1979
Stanley Clarke & Chick Corea	Hofstra Adams Playhouse – Sept. 1979
McGuinn, Clark & Hillman	Hofstra Coffeehouse – 9/9/1979
Dire Straits	Calderone Concert Hall – 9/10/1979
Ramones	Club Detroit – 9/13/1979
Ramones	Club Detroit – 9/15/1979
David Johnson	Club Detroit – 10/3/1979
Chuck Mangione	Calderone Concert Hall – Oct. 1979
Brand X	Hofstra Coffeehouse – 11/5/1979
Jefferson Starship	Calderone Concert Hall – 11/11/1979
Aztec Two-Step	Hofstra Coffeehouse – 11/17/1979
Merle Saunders	Hofstra Coffeehouse – Nov./Dec.1979
The Henry Paul Band	Hofstra Coffeehouse – Nov./Dec.1979
Pat Metheny Group	Hofstra Coffeehouse – Nov./Dec.1979

Jorma Kaukonen	Calderone Concert Hall – 11/21/1979
David Bromberg Band	Calderone Concert Hall – 11/23/1979
Santana	Calderone Concert Hall – 11/24/1979
Blackmore's Rainbow / Scorpions	Calderone Concert Hall – 11/30/1979
Aerosmith (Tour Rehearsal)	Broome County Arena – 12/4/1979
Aerosmith + Scorpions	Broome County Arena – 12/5/1979
Aerosmith + Scorpions	Cumberland Co. Civic Center – 12/6/1979
Ramones	Hammerheads – 12/13/1979
David Johansen	Club Detroit – Dec. 1979
David Johansen	Hammerheads – Dec. 1979
.38 Special	Club Detroit – Dec. 1979

1980

Ramones	Club Detroit – 1/6/1980
Aerosmith + Mother's Finest	Nassau Coliseum – 1/13/1980
Aerosmith + Mother's Finest	Cumberland Co. Civic Center – 1/20/1980
Aerosmith + Mother's Finest	Syracuse War Memorial – 1/22/1980
Twisted Sister	Nassau Coliseum – 2/8/1980
Edgar Winter	Club Detroit – 2/10/1980
Pousette-Dart Band	Hammerheads – Feb. 1980
Edgar Winter	Hammerheads – Feb. 1980
Pretenders	Club Detroit – 3/21/1980
Plasmatics	Club Detroit – 3/22/1980
Jerry Garcia Band	Calderone Concert Hall – 2/29/1980

Cheap Trick	Calderone Concert Hall – 3/28/1980
Johnny Winter	Hammerheads – April 1980
Rick Derringer	Hammerheads – April 1980
Aerosmith	Speaks, Island Park, NY – April 1980
Aerosmith	Club Detroit – April 1980
Aerosmith	Hammerheads – April 1980
Aerosmith	Fountain Casino – April 1980
Aerosmith	The Soap Factory – May 1980
Aerosmith	Emerald City – May 1980
J. Geils Band	Cumberland Co. Civic Center – 5/2/1980
J. Geils Band	Providence Civic Center – 5/3/1980
David Bromberg Band	Club Detroit – 5/8/1980
The Plasmatics	Calderone Concert Hall – 5/17/1980
Gentle Giant	Calderone Concert Hall – 5/24/1980
Aerosmith	Mr. C's – June 1980
Aerosmith	Uncle Sam's – June 1980
Aerosmith	Stage West – 6/11/1980
Aerosmith	Stage West – 6/12/1980
Triumph	Calderone Concert Hall – June 1980
Blue Oyster Cult	Hammerheads – 6/19/1980
Blue Oyster Cult	Club Detroit – 6/22/1980
Judas Priest / Def Leppard	Calderone Concert Hall – 7/5/1980
Ian Hunter & Mick Ronson	Hammerheads – July 1980
Devo	Calderone Concert Hall – 7/25/1980
Van Halen	Nassau Coliseum – 7/26/1980
Hall & Oates	Calderone Concert Hall – 8/14/1980
Journey + The Joe Perry Project	Nassau Coliseum – 8/16/1980
Journey + The Joe Perry Project	Providence Civic Center – 8/17/1980

Southside Johnny & The Asbury Jukes + Todd Rundgren + Rick Derringer + Pure Prairie League + The Good Rats + Al DiMeola	Belmont Park – 8/23/1980
J. Geils Band	Augusta Civic Center – 8/29/1980
Pretenders	Hammerheads – 9/1/1980
Yes	Providence Civic Center – 9/8/1980
Ted Nugent + Humble Pie	Providence Civic Center – Sept. 1980
Ted Nugent + Humble Pie	Nassau Coliseum – 9/14/1980
Steve Forbert	Calderone Concert Hall – Sept. 1980
AC/DC	Nassau Coliseum – 10/8/1980
Yes	Nassau Coliseum – 10/19/1980
Leonard-Duran II (Closed Circuit)	Calderone Concert Hall – 11/25/1980
Aerosmith	Club Boston-Boston – 12/1/1980
Aerosmith	Club Boston-Boston 12/3/1980
Alvin Lee Band	Calderone Concert Hall – Dec. 1980
Allman Brothers Band / Jack Bruce & Friends	Nassau Coliseum – 12/27/1980
J. Geils Band	Cumberland Co. Civic Center – 12/31/1980

1981

Allman Brothers Band	Calderone Concert Hall – 1/12/1981
Jerry Garcia Band	Calderone Concert Hall – 2/14/1981
Jorma Kaukonen	Calderone Concert Hall – 3/12/1981
Nazareth + April Wine	Calderone Concert Hall – 3/15/1981
Ted Nugent	Syracuse War Memorial – Mar. 1981
John McLaughlin, Al Dimeola & Paco DeLucia	Calderone Concert Hall – 4/17/1981
.38 Special + Willie Nile	Calderone Concert Hall – 4/22/1981
Rainbow + Pat Travers	Nassau Coliseum – 5/2/1981

Van Halen	Cumberland Co. Civic Center – 5/16/1981
Blue Oyster Cult	Hammerheads – 6/12/1981
Beatlemania (10 Shows)	Calderone Concert Hall – June 1981
Andre Segovia	Calderone Concert Hall – Summer 1981
Evelyn Champagne King	Calderone Concert Hall – Summer 1981
Marcel Marceau	Calderone Concert Hall – Summer 1981
Dizzy Gillespie	Calderone Concert Hall – Summer 1981
Santana + Gary U.S. Bonds	Nassau Coliseum – 7/11/1981
Ramones	Hammerheads – 7/15/1981
Van Halen	Nassau Coliseum – 7/18/1981
Rick Derringer	Hammerheads – July / August 1981
Joan Jett & The Blackhearts	Fireman's Memorial Park – 8/15/1981
Adam & The Ants	Calderone Concert Hall – 9/11/1981
Southside Johnny & The Asbury Jukes	Calderone Concert Hall – 9/25/1981
Journey + Loverboy	Nassau Coliseum – 10/10/1981
Journey + Loverboy	Providence Civic Center – 10/11/1981
Devo	Calderone Concert Hall – 11/8/1981
Susie & The Banshees	Malibu Beach Club – 11/12/1981
U2	Malibu Beach Club – 12/13/1981
Rossington-Collins Band	Calderone Concert Hall – 12/19/1981
Joan Jett & The Blackhearts	Calderone Concert Hall – 12/26/1981

J. Geils Band	Providence Civic Center – 12/27/1981
J. Geils Band	Cumberland Co. Civic Center – 12/31/1981

1982

Pretenders	Calderone Concert Hall – 1/28/1982
Bobby (Weir) & The Midnights	Calderone Concert Hall – 2/6/1982
The Ramones	Hammerheads – 3/6/1982
Blue Angel with Cindy Lauper	Hammerheads – March / April 1982
Billy Idol	Malibu Beach Club – 4/29/1982
Ian Hunter	Hammerheads – 5/8/1982
Leslie West & Corky Lang	Hammerheads – 5/28/1982
The Stray Cats + Dave Edmonds	Malibu Beach Club – 7/15/1982
Steppenwolf	Hammerheads – Summer 1982
Santana	Calderone Concert Hall – 8/6/1982
Rick Derringer	Hammerheads – Aug. 1982
Van Halen	Cobo Arena – 8/13/1982
Van Halen	Cobo Arena – 8/14/1982
Van Halen	Cobo Arena – 8/15/1982
Aerosmith	Providence Civic Center – 11/9/1982
Ramones	Hammerheads – 11/26/1982
Ramones	Hammerheads – 11/27/1982

1983

Aerosmith	Syracuse War Memorial – 2/24/1983

Shows That I was Happy to Pay For...
Plus Plenty That I Didn't Have To

1973

Jethro Tull / *Passion Play*	Nassau Coliseum – 9/1/1973

1974

Yes / *Tales from Topographic Oceans*	Nassau Coliseum – 2/14/1974
Black Sabbath / *Sabbath Bloody Sabbath* + Lynyrd Skynyrd	Nassau Colisexum – 2/25/1974
Deep Purple / *Burn*	Nassau Coliseum – 3/17/1974
Crosby, Stills, Nash & Young + The Beach Boys + Joni Mitchell	Roosevelt Raceway – 9/8/1974

1975

Led Zeppelin / *Physical Graffiti*	Nassau Coliseum – 2/13/1975
Led Zeppelin / *Physical Graffiti*	Nassau Coliseum – 2/14/1975
Jethro Tull / *War Child*	Nassau Coliseum – 3/3/1975
Jethro Tull / *War Child*	Nassau Coliseum – 3/4/1975
Rod Stewart & Faces / *Hits* + Peter Frampton	Nassau Coliseum – 10/12/1975
Black Sabbath / *Sabotage* + Aerosmith / *Toys in the Attic*	Madison Square Garden – 12/3/1975

1976

David Bowie / *Station to Station*	Nassau Coliseum – 3/23/1976
Robin Trower / *For Earth Below*	Madison Square Garden – 3/24/1976
Bad Company / *Run with the Pack* + Kansas	Madison Square Garden – 4/5/1976
Aerosmith / *Rocks*	Madison Square Garden – 5/10/1976
Yes / *Solo Albums*	Nassau Coliseum – 6/16/1976
Foreigner / *Foreigner*	OBI/Hampton Bays, NY – July 1976
Jethro Tull / *Too Old To Rock n Roll*	Shea Stadium – 7/23/1976

1977

Queen / *A Day at the Races* + Thin Lizzy	Nassau Coliseum – 2/6/1977
Boston / *Boston*	Nassau Coliseum – 2/10/1977
Eagles / *Hotel California* + Jimmy Buffet / *Changes in Attitudes, Changes in Latitudes*	Nassau Coliseum – 3/16/1977
Bad Company / *Burnin' Sky*	Nassau Coliseum – 6/28/1977
Yes / *Going for the One* + Donavan	Madison Square Garden – 8/7/1977
Peter Frampton / *I'm in You*	Madison Square Garden – 8/23/1977
Rod Stewart / *Footloose & Fancy Free*	Nassau Coliseum – 10/23/1977
Jethro Tull / *Songs from the Wood*	Nassau Coliseum – 11/20/1977
Kiss / *Alive II*	Madison Square Garden – 12/14/1977

1978

Eddie Money / *Eddie Money*	My Father's Place – 2/24/1978
Eric Clapton / *461 Ocean Boulevard*	Nassau Coliseum – 4/3/1978
Bruce Springsteen / *Darkness on the Edge of Town*	Nassau Coliseum – 6/3/1978
Neil Young / *Rust Never Sleeps*	Nassau Coliseum – 9/29/1978
Jethro Tull / *Heavy Horses* + Uriah Heep	Madison Square Garden – 10/11/1978
Aerosmith / *Live Bootleg* + Golden Earring + Heart	Nassau Coliseum – 11/12/1978

1979

The Police / *The Police*	My Father's Place – 3/29/1979
The New Barbarians / *Gimme Some Neck* (Ron Wood + Keith Richards)	Madison Square Garden – 5/7/1979

Yes / *Tormato*   Madison Square Garden –
                                             6/14/1979

Lou Reed / *The Bells*   My Father's Place – 7/10/1979

James Taylor / *Flag*   Nassau Coliseum – 7/21/1979

The Cars / *Candy-O*   Nassau Coliseum – 10/9/1979

Jethro Tull / *Stormwatch*   Nassau Coliseum – 10/22/1979

Grateful Dead / *Shakedown Street*   Nassau Coliseum – 11/1/1979

Fleetwood Mac / *Tusk*   Nassau Coliseum – 11/12/1979

1980

Pink Floyd / *The Wall*   Nassau Coliseum – 2/26/1980

Billy Joel / *Glass Houses*   Nassau Coliseum – 7/24/1980

Bruce Springsteen / *The River*   Nassau Coliseum – 12/28/1980

1981

The Clash / *Sandanista!*   Bond's NYC – June 1981

The Rolling Stones / *Tattoo You*
+ Tina Turner   Byrne Arena, NJ – 11/6/1981

ACDC / *For Those About to Rock*   Madison Square Garden –
                                             12/2/1981

1982

The Police / *Ghost in the Machine*
+ The Go-Gos   Nassau Coliseum – 1/19/1982

J. Geils Band / *Freeze Frame*
+ George Thorogood   Madison Square Garden –
                                             2/20/1982

Jethro Tull / *Broadsword &*
The Beast   Nassau Coliseum – 9/18/1982

The Who / *It's Hard*
+ The Clash + David Johansen   Shea Stadium – 10/12/1982

Billy Joel / *The Nylon Curtain*   Nassau Coliseum – 12/29/1982

1983

Neil Young / *Trans*	Nassau Coliseum – 2/23/1983
Aerosmith / *Rock in a Hard Place* + Zebra	Nassau Coliseum – 3/1/1983
Billy Squire / *Emotions in Motion* + Def Leppard / *Pyromania*	Nassau Coliseum – 5/23/1983
ZZ Top / *Eliminator* + Sammy Hagar	Nassau Coliseum – 7/20/1983
Robert Plant / *The Principle of Moments*	Madison Square Garden – 9/12/1983

1984

Ozzy Osbourne / *Bark at the Moon* + Mötley Crüe	Nassau Coliseum – 1/25/1984
Aerosmith / *Rock in a Hard Place*	The Ritz – 2/8/1984
Aerosmith / *Rock in a Hard Place*	Calderone Concert Hall – 2/11/1984

...and the list goes on and on...

28

Suggested Listening

THE LIST THAT FOLLOWS is not meant to be a mixtape, that meticulous curation of a cassette consisting of songs that you believed made you who you were and which would test the taste and authenticity of your latest love interest. No, my list is more of a memory reel, an inconsistent assembly of tunes that I think will add an audio accent to what you'll have read or be reading.

Some songs are personal favorites that I danced to in the wings. Some are reminders of meaningful events and the scenes that still play in my head. Some just seem to fit the action on the page. Some are well-worn hits, while others are deep cuts that only a fanatic or savant like me may be familiar with. All, though, are firmly ensconced in my heart and soul, evoking the same emotions now as they did way back when. I recommend finding live versions whenever possible to have the best listening experience. And listen to it loud, "Turn it up to eleven!" loud, as I expect I always will.

▶ CHAPTER 1: BACK ROW TO BACKSTAGE

Toys in the Attic	Aerosmith
Dream On	Aerosmith
Walkin' the Dog	Aerosmith

A few of the songs that sold me when Aerosmith opened for Black Sabbath at Madison Square Garden in '75. No big surprises here, though the Rufus Thomas cover may be a bit obscure for fans that didn't discover Aerosmith until their second coming a dozen years later.

▶ CHAPTER 2: I KNOW, IT'S ONLY ROCK & ROLL

Long Live Rock	The Who
Long Live Rock 'n Roll	Rainbow
I Love Rock and Roll	Joan Jett
It's Only Rock & Roll (But I Like It)	The Rolling Stones

Sorry to be so obvious, but it had to be done.

▶ CHAPTER 3: LEARNING TO LISTEN

Norwegian Wood	The Beatles
Fat Man	Jethro Tull
Brown Sugar	The Rolling Stones
Don't Be Denied	Neil Young

One from my sister, one from my brother, one from my best buddy, Louie, plus the one from Neil that would make me a lifelong fan.

▶ CHAPTER 4: FIRST LOVE

For Michael Collins, Jeffrey & Me	Jethro Tull
Passion Play	Jethro Tull
Only Solitaire	Jethro Tull
Cheerio	Jethro Tull

Ian Anderson is the master of the abbreviated ditty as well as the grand gesture. While "For Michael Collins…" may last a fairly standard 3:47, "Passion Play" is one long song, clocking in at 45:05. "Only Solitaire" lasts only 1:38, "Cheerio" just 1:09.

▶ CHAPTER 5: MAJORING IN THE MUSIC BUSINESS

Embryonic Journey	Jorma Kaukonen
One Bourbon, One Scotch, One Beer	George Thorogood & The Destroyers
The Devil Went Down to Georgia	The Charlie Daniels Band
Green Grass and High Tides	The Outlaws

Our college bookings were predominantly rootsy, made-in-America events.

▶ CHAPTER 6: FIRST HOUSE

Breakdown	Tom Petty
Surrender	Cheap Trick
The Wheel	The Jerry Garcia Band
You Can't Be Too Strong	Graham Parker & The Rumor
Oliver's Army	Elvis Costello & The Attractions

A few from my personal list of priceless performances at The Calderone Theatre.

▶ CHAPTER 7: DRIVING MR. PINK

In the Flesh?	Pink Floyd
Goodbye Blue Sky	Pink Floyd
Comfortably Numb	Pink Floyd
Outside the Wall	Pink Floyd

One from each dark side of *The Wall.*

▶ CHAPTER 8: A FALLEN IDOL

Back in the Saddle	Aerosmith
Mama Kin	Aerosmith
I Wanna Know Why	Aerosmith
Reefer Headed Woman	Aerosmith

These four songs, in this order, were as far as Steven Tyler got on the evening of his collapse in Portland, Maine.

▶ CHAPTER 9: UP-AND-COMERS...

Beat the Brat	Ramones
Dancing with Myself	Billy Idol
Brass in Pocket	Pretenders
I Will Follow	U2

Britain's second invasion of the U.S. alongside *their* American Idols, Ramones.

...HAS-BEENS...

Rock and Roll Hoochie Coo	Rick Derringer
Frankenstein	Edgar Winter
Born To Be Wild	Steppenwolf
Mississippi Queen	Mountain

Rick and Edgar had the same manager that kept them constantly working the club circuit to wring every dollar out of their singular hits and fading fame. John Kaye and Steppenwolf coined "heavy metal" in 1968 and didn't walk off stage for good until 2018. Leslie West continued to recycle Mountain's handful of hits, even from a wheelchair, until he passed away.

& NEVER WASSES

Sorry, I got nuthin'.

▶ CHAPTER 10: ON THE ROAD WITH A BAND ON THE ROCKS

Walkin' in the Sand	Aerosmith
Sweet Emotion	Aerosmith
Train Kept' a Rollin'	Aerosmith

On the Mystery Club Tour the set list never deviated, yet Tyler had to have the lyrics to "Walkin" taped to the floor.

▶ CHAPTER 11: A DAY IN THE LIFE

Lights	Journey
The Loadout	Jackson Brown
Turn the Page	Bob Segar

The audience's mid-show lighter display during this Journey fan favorite was the nirvana of the rock show experience. I never worked with either Jackson or Bob, but their odes to the road always leave a tear in my eye.

▶ CHAPTER 12: BUSTIN' BALLS ABOUT BROWN M&MS

And the Cradle Will Rock	Van Halen
Unchained	Van Halen
Little Guitars	Van Halen

One from each of my three tours of duty with the Van Halen Army.

▶ CHAPTER 13: FORGING A METAL MASTERPIECE

Hells Bells	AC/DC
Back in Black	AC/DC

The lead tracks from each side, but just listen to the entire friggin' album!

▶ CHAPTER 14: AIN'T NOTHING LIKE THE REAL THING

Starship Trooper	Yes
Video Killed the Radio Star	The Buggles
Tempus Fugit	Yes

Big hits from each of the ingredients along with the concoction that resulted. My Brit publisher tells me that a lot of European fans loved it, but the Yuggles lineup only lasted for one record.

▶ CHAPTER 15: RITCHIE'S REVOLVING DOOR

Smoke on the Water	Deep Purple Mark II with Ian Gillan
Burn	Deep Purple Mark III with David Coverdale
The Man on the Silver Mountain	Rainbow 1 with Ronnie James Dio
All Night Long	Rainbow 5 with Graham Bonnet
I Surrender	Rainbow 6 with Joe Lynn Turner
Under A Violet Moon	Blackmore's Night with Candace Night
Praetorius (Courante)	Blackmore's Night with only Ritchie

Six distinctly different lead singers backed by the virtuosity of a singular rock iconoclast. (NOTES: "Smoke on the Water" *must* be the live version found on *Made in Japan*, with the unedited sounds of Blackmore breaking a string. Also... I couldn't resist throwing in an instrumental composed by my late renaissance ancestor, Michael, a piece that Ritchie made his own.)

▶ CHAPTER 16: BREAKING CONTRACTS & PICKING UP THE PIECES

Livin' After Midnight   Judas Priest
White Room   Jack Bruce & Friends

These cuts will forever be reminders to me that a deal is always a deal, until one party decides that it's not. (NOTE: Cream's "White Room" was one of the tunes that Jack Bruce & Friends performed while touring with the Allmans to promote their own LP, and you'll likely find their version only on YouTube. Despite a star-studded line-up that included guitarist Clem Clemson, drummer Billy Cobham, and keyboardist David Sancious, nothing on their collaboration *I've Always Wanted to Do This* interested me enough to recommend it.)

▶ CHAPTER 17: A FEW NOTES ABOUT PIANOS

Southbound   The Allman Brothers Band
Jessica   The Allman Brothers Band

These two of the Allman Brothers Band's standards would never have sounded the same if the keys had been out of commission.

▶ CHAPTER 18: "JUST CALL ME DICK."

Sweet Jane   Lou Reed
Only Women Bleed   Alice Cooper
I Do the Rock   Tim Curry

The legendary twin-attack guitar performance that likely got Dick Wagner and Steve Hunter fired by Lou. Dick's one big hit with Alice. A production credit from Tim, but no songwriting royalties for Dick. (NOTE: "Sweet Jane" *must* be the complete live version found on Reed's *Rock and Roll Animal* LP.)

▶ CHAPTER 19: GETTING BY WITH A LITTLE HELP FROM OUR FRIEND

Flying High Again   Ozzy Osborne
Shout at the Devil   Motley Crue

A pair from the two metal maniacs' U.S. tour in early '84. I was in the pit in front of the stage-left stack. My ears still ring from time to time.

▶ CHAPTER 20: THE END OF THE ROAD

Draw the Line   Aerosmith
Cry Me a River   Aerosmith

Two fitting cuts to mark the close of the arc of my adventures with the Boston bad boys.

▶ CHAPTER 21: NURTURING NEW TALENT & HAWKING OLD TEES

Who's Behind the Door   Zebra
Don't Close Your Eyes   Kix
Everyone's A Star   TNT

The biggest hits from three journeyman bands that just couldn't sustain the juice they needed to finally break wide.

▶ CHAPTER 22: YOU CAN'T ALWAYS JUDGE A MAN BY HIS MASCARA

We're Not Gonna Take It	Twisted Sister
I Wanna Rock	Twisted Sister

The MTV anthems that launched the Long Island glam metal band to international success…and onto the PMRC's Most Wanted list.

▶ CHAPTER 23: HE'S ALWAYS JUST BILLY TO US

Scenes From An Italian Restaurant	Billy Joel
Only the Good Die Young	Billy Joel
The Stranger	Billy Joel

Deep dives into the Long Island middle-class, Catholic school repression, and getting in touch with your dark side, all from *The Stranger*, Billy's first perfect album.

▶ CHAPTER 24: A TALE OF TWO WOODSTOCKS

Woodstock	Joni Mitchell

The best retelling of the original Woodstock story, from an artist that wasn't even there.

▶ CHAPTER 25: TOSSING 'EM BACK WITH THE REAL CAPT'N JACK

Better Walk Before They Make Me Run	The New Barbarians: *Buried Alive: Live in Maryland*
Happy	The X-Pensive Winos: *Live at the Hollywood Palladium*
You Got the Silver	The Rolling Stones: *Shine A Light*

While all three of these Keith-sung songs are Rolling Stones LP standards, I've chosen live recordings for each, two performed with short-lived but beloved side-projects. Keith is best enjoyed warts and all.

▶ CHAPTER 26: BITS & PIECES

Land Of A Thousand Dances	Ted Nugent: *Intensities in Ten Cities*
Ain't Nothin' But A House Party	J. Geils Band: *Blow Your Face Out LIVE*

Just a couple more rousing live performances to sum it all up.

Happy Listening,
GDP

PHOTO & IMAGE CREDITS

I HAVE OBSESSED OVER the images that you see in this book. It was a must that every one of them be both authentic and relevant to the story.

I am a stickler for licensing and have attempted in every case to source the original photo, give it its due, and pay for the rights to reproduce it when necessary. When professional photographers were involved, I tracked them down and worked with them personally or with representatives or archivists to obtain the proper permissions. But then there are those for which I have exhausted my ability to ascertain who actually took them or where their true ownership lay.*

In regards to mementos, because I saved nothing, most of those shown in this book were lent to me out of friendship, courtesy or charity, and I shot photos of many myself. A few were located on eBay and other e-commerce sites. Some of those items I was able to purchase. Some had already been sold, but their images remained floating in cyberspace and I was lucky enough to grab them as they passed by.

If you are a professional photographer and see a photo that you believe is yours and can prove copyright ownership I will be more than happy to license it from you at the same rate as I have agreed to with others and give you all due credit in future printings. If you are an amateur, like me, I hope that you will grant me the proper permission to use your image out of kindness and kinship in your love for rock and roll.

CHAPTER 2: I KNOW, IT'S ONLY ROCK & ROLL

Stratocaster house key
© G.D. Praetorius

CHAPTER 3: LEARNING TO LISTEN

CSNY at Roosevelt Raceway aerial view
Photo by Unknown

CSNY at Roosevelt Raceway crowd scene
Courtesy of G.D. Praetorius
I purchased this photo print on eBay with someone's cataloguing on the
back attributing it to a photographer named Meurer. I've been unable
to uncover any more information. The shot was taken from the general
vicinity of where I squatted.

CHAPTER 4: FIRST LOVE

My Gemeinhardt flute
© G.D. Praetorius

Jethro Tull *Broadsword and the Beast* Backstage Pass
© G.D. Praetorius
One of several items I had to buy online almost 40 years after the fact
because I never kept any mementos on my own.

CHAPTER 5: MAJORING IN THE MUSIC BUSINESS

Hofstra Concerts program booklet
© G.D. Praetorius
Program designed by Bruce Colwin for Hofstra Concerts

Delta T band members
© Frank Bolz
Frank and I were Delta T's roadies. Here's to hangin' in the wagon with
three dollar six packs. R.I.P. to my best buddy, Tommy U.
The Outlaws
© G.D. Praetorius

Jorma Kaukonen backstage at Hofstra University
Photo by Unknown

CHAPTER 6: FIRST HOUSE

The Calderone Theatre orchestra seating
Reproduced by permission of Hofstra University's Special Collections

The Calderone Theatre under construction
Reproduced by permission of Hofstra University's Special Collections

Freefall Presentations/Cheap Trick newspaper ad

Jerry Garcia at The Calderone Concert Hall
Photo by Unknown, from Hofstra University's Special Collections

The Calderone marquee
Photo by Arthur Fields

CHAPTER 7: DRIVING MR. PINK

Pink Floyd / *The Wall* STAFF pass
© G.D. Praetorius, pass courtesy of Brian Schuman
Unlike me, Brian had the foresight to keep just about everything.

CHAPTER 8: A FALLEN IDOL

Aerosmith onstage in Portland, Maine
© Ron Pownall (More about Ron a little further on.)

CHAPTER 9: UP-AND-COMERS, HAS-BEENS & ALMOST-BUT-
NOT-QUITES

Duct tape
© G.D. Praetorius
Joey Ramone
Photo by Unknown

Hammerheads Ramones Ticket
© G.D. Praetorius

I saw this ticket to my first Ramones show for sale online and I bought
it. The company that printed this "hard" ticket and hundreds of
thousands like it was owned by a guy named John in Dix Hills, New

York. John ran his ticket factory out of his sprawling basement and at any given time he had tickets for dozens of events stacked side by side on folding tables that filled the room wall to wall. John also had numerous cats that hopped from table to table, constantly knocking over the pillars of tickets that had been meticulously sequentially stacked.

WLIR Presents backstage pass
Posted on YouTube along with complete audio of U2's performance at Malibu on 12/13/81

U2 in concert at Malibu Beach Club on 12/13/81
Photo by Unknown

CHAPTER 10: BABYSITTING A BAND ON THE ROCKS

Aerosmith Mystery Club Tour jacket
© G.D. Praetorius, jacket courtesy of Billy Colwin
Photo by Alexandra Hiner-Diana
I had one of these jackets, too, but I traded it to the Nassau Coliseum's Zamboni driver for an official New York Islanders hockey jersey. I think my wife gave the jersey away when I wasn't looking.

Aerosmith Mystery Club Tour logo wall
© G.D. Praetorius, created by Georgina Abella

CHAPTER 11: A DAY IN THE LIFE

Arena rock concert set-up
© Poll Sound Audio Production
4026 S. Main Street, Salt Lake City, UT 84107
P: (801) 261-2500

CHAPTER 12: BUSTIN' BALLS ABOUT BROWN M&MS

Van Halen 1982 concert contract rider cover letter and excerpt
It's kind of all over the Internet, so I just picked one. The brown M&M's thing actually began two tours before this contract, in 1980. They must have thought it such a hoot and a great band/brand hook that they kept it going. 1981's Coney Island Whitefish never reappeared in their rider a second time, at least as far as I am aware.

Hide Your Sheep artwork
A highlight from an "authentic" and "vintage" 1982 Van Halen
crew shirt

CHAPTER 13: FORGING A METAL MASTERPIECE

ACDC bell at John Taylor & Co. Bellfounders, Loughborough, Great Britain
Photo by Unknown

The Hell's Bell in its custom road case, December 4th, 1980
Photo by Unknown

CHAPTER 14: AIN'T NOTHIN' LIKE THE REAL THING

Oil painting of Jon Anderson
© Kevin Alun Parrish
Kevin has been a huge Yes fan since the early 1970s and he requested
that I tell you that he is also follower of Jon's *Philosophies*. Visit Kevin's
website to view his *Yes Art Page*, inspired by the band's music. At the
time of this writing his original oil painting of Jon Anderson was
available for sale.
+44 (0) 1926 332708 / *kevinparrish.co.uk* / *parrish@quicknetuk.com*

Steve Howe
© Bill O'Leary/Timeless Concert Images

CHAPTER 15: RITCHIE'S REVOLVING DOOR

Rainbow family tree
© G.D. Praetorius, created by Georgina Abella

Ritchie Blackmore's smashed Stratocaster
Photo by Unknown

Ritchie Blackmore at The Calderone Concert Hall
© Fin Costello/Getty Images

CHAPTER 16: BREAKING CONTRACTS & PICKING UP THE PIECES

Allman Brothers Band backstage pass
© G.D. Praetorius
I thought that I had bought this ABB pass from my show at Nassau Coliseum, but shortly after my purchase on the memorabilia site I was told that "the item you have ordered is not available at this time…" and my payment was refunded. I knew that it was authentic because of The hand-sharpied "JB." John Scher forced us to acknowledge that Jack Bruce was on the bill. That's my handwriting.

CHAPTER 17: A FEW NOTES ABOUT PIANOS

Steinway Model D serial number plate
Photo reproduced courtesy of Michelle's Piano Company
Michelle's Piano Company, 600 SE Stark Street, Portland OR 97214
Phone: (503) 295-1180 / Fax: (503)295-3015
michellespiano.com / lotof@michellespiano.com

CHAPTER 18: "JUST CALL ME DICK."

Richard Wagner, German operatic composer
Photo by Unknown
Once again, this is an image that is all over the internet with no definitive attribution. At best guess it was shot circa 1860-1875.

Richard Wagner, "The Maestro of Rock"
© Victory Tischler Blue

Dick Wagner performing with Lou Reed
From the private collection of Dick Wagner
Courtesy of Susan Michelson, Managing Director of the *Dick Wagner Remember the Children Memorial Fund*
The Fund creates and supports music therapy programs to bring the healing power of music to hospitalized children. Donate at *dwrtc.com*.

CHAPTER 19: GETTING BY WITH A LITTLE HELP FROM OUR FRIEND

Chemical equation
© G.D. Praetorius, illustrated by Georgina Abella

CHAPTER 20: THE END OF THE ROAD

Steven Tyler and Cyrinda Foxe
Photo by Unknown

Joe Baptista
Photo by Unknown
Some years ago I found this grainy image in an early 1970s Midwest newspaper profile written before Joe hooked up with Aerosmith. I remember having to shoot it from my laptop screen, using my iPhone.

CHAPTER 21: NURTURING NEW TALENT & HAWKING OLD TEES

T-shirt rack graphic
© G.D. Praetorius, created by Georgina Abella

CHAPTER 22: YOU CAN'T ALWAYS JUDGE A MAN BY HIS MASCARA

Dee Snider
© Andreas Rentsch
Andy's my brother-in-law, and as his gift to me for my 50th he shot the party like a wedding. Andy is actually an artist, and you can see his real work at *AndreasRentsch.com*.

CHAPTER 23: HE'S ALWAYS JUST BILLY TO US

Billy Joel equipment ticket
© G.D. Praetorius
At least my wife was wise enough to hold onto a little piece of rock history. Billy signed for the pick up on the other side.

Billy Joel "There is no stranger" plus autograph
© Brian Schuman
Another piece from Brian's hoard of mementos.
Billy Joel backstage at Nassau Coliseum in December, 1977
© Bobby Bank/Getty Images

Jonathan's Ristorante
© Jonathan's Ristorante, Huntington, New York

CHAPTER 24: A TALE OF TWO WOODSTOCKS

Peace sign lovers
Photo by Unknown, yet one more of those passing internet grabs that I
now can't trace back to where I found it.
Woodstock '94 Pepsi cans
Photo by Unknown

Woodstock memorial plaque
Photo by Unknown

CHAPTER 25: TOSSING 'EM BACK WITH THE REAL
CAPT'N JACK

Keith Richards illustration
© Rob van der Pol / AKA Robert Lee Jordan
I found my new Dutch friend online, quite by accident. This was his first
serious attempt at rock art after a very long hiatus. You can now view and
purchase his gallery-worthy work at www.RobertLeeJordan.com

Keith Richards on Parrot Cay
© Luis Sinco/Getty Images

CHAPTER 26: BITS & PIECES

Tommy Lee's MAYHEM tattoo
Photo by Unknown

CHAPTER 27: KEEPING SCORE

Tom Petty at The Calderone Concert Hall
© Ebet Roberts/Getty Images

Santana at The Calderone Concert Hall
© Christopher J. Davies/www.DaviesPhotos.com

The Calderone Concert Hall Crew
Photo by Arthur Fields

COLOR PAGES

Aerosmith rehearsal and performance in Binghamton, NY

- AE79-1600 (Steven Tyler & Jimmy Crespo rehearsal) © Ron Pownall
- AE80-0891 (Steven Tyler leaping onstage) © Ron Pownall
- AE79-4776 (Steven Tyler & Joey Kramer onstage) © Ron Pownall

Aerosmith performing in Portland, ME

- AE79-4663 (Tyler portrait) © Ron Pownall
- AE79-1300 (Tyler laying onstage) © Ron Pownall

A huge *Thank You!* to Ron for digging into his now almost 40-year-old archives to find this stuff. Ron has shot artists from Abba to Zappa, and you can view his gallery at *rockrollphoto.com*.

Pink Floyd's performances of The Wall at Nassau Coliseum, on Long Island

- Roger Waters © Ron Akiyama
- David Gilmore © Bill O'Leary/Timeless Concert Images
- Mother © Ron Akiyama
- The Band Waves Goodbye © Bill O'Leary/Timeless Concert Images

Van Halen performances and backstage parties in Detroit, MI

- The Westenberger Archives, 1974-2008. Autry Museum, Los Angeles; MSA.25.286.2 (David Lee Roth costume fitting)
- The Westenberger Archives, 1974-2008. Autry Museum, Los Angeles; MSA.25.286.3 (Eddie Van Halen backstage guitar room)
- The Westenberger Archives, 1974-2008. Autry Museum, Los Angeles; MSA.25.286.4 (Backstage birthday cake)
- The Westenberger Archives, 1974-2008. Autry Museum, Los Angeles; MSA.25.286.8 (Backstage cake fight)
- The Westenberger Archives, 1974-2008. Autry Museum, Los Angeles; MSA.25.286.5 (David Lee Roth's bodyguards)
- The Westenberger Archives, 1974-2008. Autry Museum, Los Angeles; MSA.25.286.2 (Hotel party)
- The Westenberger Archives, 1974-2008. Autry Museum, Los Angeles; MSA.25.286.7 (Backstage Samurai)
- The Westenberger Archives, 1974-2008. Autry Museum, Los Angeles; MSA.25.286.9 (David Lee Roth in cheekless Chaps)

Theo Westenberger was the photographer assigned by Life to shoot Van Halen with us in Detroit. Since Theo passed away her catalogue of images has been held in The Autry Museum's archives. After reading my Van Halen story Mallory Furnier slogged through hundreds of photos to find the images you see in this book, and Marilyn Van Winkle worked with me on the licensing.

ALBUM COVERS

All album images are used in the spirit of Fair Use, and I truly hope that all of them see a resurgence of sales. I personally own almost all of these records, having purchased a few two or even three times as audio formats evolved (LP, 8-Track and CD).

Aerosmith *Rocks*
© Columbia Records

The Beatles *Meet the Beatles*
© Capital Records

Jethro Tull *Aqualung*
© Chrysalis Records

Aerosmith *Night in the Ruts*
© Columbia Records

The Buggles *The Age of Plastic*
© Island Records

Aerosmith *Rock in a Hard Place*
© Columbia Records

Twisted Sister *Stay Hungry*
© Atlantic Records

Zebra *Zebra*
© Atlantic Records

Ted Nugent *Intensities in Ten Cities*
© Epic Records

ACKNOWLEDGEMENTS

THERE ARE HUNDREDS OF people that I should thank for helping to make this book happen, most of whom I think would classify themselves as unwilling participants, or at least unknowing. Space, or at least my budget, does not permit me to speak at length of every one, but each of the artists I met, their managers, tour managers, road managers and roadies left at least a little something behind with me. But more directly, there are those in my Dedications whose names you don't know as well as the others who also contributed greatly with their encouragement.

Michael Benson was a college friend and is an accomplished author, and upon reading an earlier, less-focused work of mine, he convinced me to expand my rock bits into a full-blown book. He has been an invaluable resource for advice and criticism, both of which I have been in dire need of.

Two other college buddies also deserve a shout-out: Larry Beck and Ed Behringer. They've taken the time to read my drafts, call me out and correct my memory (at least where they were concerned).

Then there are my Calderone brothers that were in the thick of it with me: Bruce Colwin, Ira Maltz, Joe Molinare, Frank Rubino, and of course Brian Schuman, who lent me of few of his personal recollections and mementos that were just too much fun to pass up. At the same time, I have to thank Mark Puma, who saw something in Pam and I that convinced him to put enormous trust and responsibility into the hands of two kids barely twenty years old. And I can't forget my first musical family, the boys of Delta T – Steve Beach, Paul D'Andrea, Eddie Hoffman, and Tom Uehlinger. "Smoke on the Water" forever.

Early on in this effort, I posted a work-in-progress version of "Bustin' My Balls..." on LinkedIn. I happened to come across a forum regarding management practices which featured an interview with David Lee Roth where he specifically addressed the very real myth of the brown M&Ms. David Lee confirmed my own thirty-year-plus suspicions that the whole mad exercise was actually a very serious test of professionalism, and I wanted to make a point to everyone posting negative comments that Van Halen should instead be celebrated as an MBA case study. Two people contacted me directly because of that post. One was a retired police lieutenant living in North Carolina. He wanted to know if it was true. I assured him that it was, and I never heard from him again. The other was Michael Allen, a VP at a Southern California digi-company with whom, over the past several years, I have developed a wonderful keypal connection. Michael was a huge supporter from that day on and he was the most passionate voice telling me that I could not only do this but that people like him would want to read it.

I can't forget the Greeks: Nicky C., Chris T. and George Lucas' doppelganger, John B., all of whom were kind enough to read my earlier attempts at authorship. From the very beginning, Nicky has been telling me that I should be writing full time to make my living. From your mouth to God's ears, Nicky, but I'm not sure that she is a big fan of either one of us.

Michael Benson also forwarded me a Craigslist ad posted by a producer seeking a writer to script his documentary-in-the-making focused on the ambition and grit of rock stars, particularly one Steven Tyler. I didn't end up writing the doc, but I became great friends with George Hudak, who at one point in his process filmed me in front of a green screen to tell some of my tales. His young crew seemed genuinely in awe of my racantouring and further validated my efforts.

George has consistently lent me his support along with a sympathetic ear.

And perhaps my biggest "Thank You!" goes out to my designer and compatriot in this new adventure, Ms. Georgina Abella. Georgina is an extraordinarily talented young woman who has visually transformed my reminiscences into a sensationally scenic ride. I look forward to whatever we have the opportunity to collaborate on next.

The Calderone Crew, circa 1979.

About the Author

G. D. PRAETORIUS IS A life-long rock music fanatic. From the moment as a six-year-old that he saw the Beatles on Ed Sullivan, he knew he had to be part of the action. After coming to grips with the fact that he had no musical talent of his own, he turned left and before long was involved in the production of almost 200 rock shows with some of the classic era's biggest stars. Even after leaving the business to pursue more conventional careers, Gregg continued to have rock encounters worth recounting.

On Track series

Barclay James Harvest – Keith and Monica Domone 978-1-78952-067-5
The Beatles – Andrew Wild 978-1-78952-009-5
The Beatles Solo 1969-1980 – Andrew Wild 978-1-78952-030-9
Blue Oyster Cult – Jacob Holm-Lupo 978-1-78952-007-1
Kate Bush – Bill Thomas 978-1-78952-097-2
The Clash – Nick Assirati 978-1-78952-077-4
Crosby, Stills and Nash – Andrew Wild 978-1-78952-039-2
Deep Purple and Rainbow 1968-79 – Steve Pilkington 978-1-78952-002-6
Dire Straits – Andrew Wild 978-1-78952-044-6
Dream Theater – Jordan Blum 978-1-78952-050-7
Emerson Lake and Palmer – Mike Goode 978-1-78952-000-2
Fairport Convention – Kevan Furbank 978-1-78952-051-4
Genesis – Stuart MacFarlane 978-1-78952-005-7
Gentle Giant – Gary Steel 978-1-78952-058-3
Hawkwind – Duncan Harris 978-1-78952-052-1
Iron Maiden – Steve Pilkington 978-1-78952-061-3
Jethro Tull – Jordan Blum 978-1-78952-016-3
Elton John in the 1970s – Peter Kearns 978-1-78952-034-7
Gong – Kevan Furbank 978-1-78952-082-8
Iron Maiden – Steve Pilkington 978-1-78952-061-3
Judas Priest – John Tucker 978-1-78952-018-7
Kansas – Kevin Cummings 978-1-78952-057-6
Aimee Mann – Jez Rowden 978-1-78952-036-1
Joni Mitchell – Peter Kearns 978-1-78952-081-1
The Moody Blues – Geoffrey Feakes 978-1-78952-042-2
Mike Oldfield – Ryan Yard 978-1-78952-060-6
Queen – Andrew Wild 978-1-78952-003-3
Renaissance – David Detmer 978-1-78952-062-0
The Rolling Stones 1963-80 – Steve Pilkington 978-1-78952-017-0
Steely Dan – Jez Rowden 978-1-78952-043-9
Thin Lizzy – Graeme Stroud 978-1-78952-064-4
Toto – Jacob Holm-Lupo 978-1-78952-019-4
U2 – Eoghan Lyng 978-1-78952-078-1
UFO – Richard James 978-1-78952-073-6
The Who – Geoffrey Feakes 978-1-78952-076-7
Roy Wood and the Move – James R Turner 978-1-78952-008-8
Van Der Graaf Generator – Dan Coffey 978-1-78952-031-6
Yes – Stephen Lambe 978-1-78952-001-9
Frank Zappa 1966 to 1979 – Eric Benac 978-1-78952-033-0
10CC – Peter Kearns 978-1-78952-054-5

Decades Series

Pink Floyd In The 1970s – Georg Purvis 978-1-78952-072-9
Marillion in the 1980s – Nathaniel Webb 978-1-78952-065-1

On Screen series

Carry On… – Stephen Lambe 978-1-78952-004-0
David Cronenberg – Patrick Chapman 978-1-78952-071-2
Doctor Who: The David Tennant Years – Jamie Hailstone
978-1-78952-066-8
Monty Python – Steve Pilkington 978-1-78952-047-7
Seinfeld Seasons 1 to 5 – Stephen Lambe 978-1-78952-012-5

Other Books

Derek Taylor: For Your Radioactive Children – Andrew Darlington
978-1-78952-
Jon Anderson and the Warriors - the road to Yes – David Watkinson
978-1-78952-059-0
Tommy Bolin: In and Out of Deep Purple – Laura Shenton
978-1-78952-070-5
Maximum Darkness – Deke Leonard 978-1-78952-048-4
Maybe I Should've Stayed In Bed – Deke Leonard 978-1-78952-053-8
The Twang Dynasty – Deke Leonard 978-1-78952-049-1

and many more to come!